Splitting the Day of the Lord

Splitting the Day of the Lord

The Cornerstone of Christian Theology

Wayne Brouwer

WIPF & STOCK · Eugene, Oregon

Wipf & Stock
An Imprint of Wipf and Stock Publishers
199 W. 8th Ave., Suite 3
Eugene, OR 97401

www.wipfandstock.com

PAPERBACK ISBN: 978-1-5326-5227-1
HARDCOVER ISBN: 978-1-5326-5228-8
EBOOK ISBN: 978-1-5326-5229-5

Manufactured in the U.S.A.

For Brenda,
who lives in hope of the Day of the Lord,
and for Ralph and Cheryl,
who bring good touches of the Day of the Lord.

Contents

Introduction

The "Day of the Lord" and the Recovery of Biblical Theology

"WHY DON'T YOU BELIEVE in Jesus?"

I cringed as my student challenged our classroom guest. He was the distinguished head of the regional Chabad House, a deeply devout and highly respected Jewish rabbi. Everything about him oozed spirituality, from his black suit with the fringes of his prayer shawl peeking from under the coat, to his Moses-like white beard, to the shofar he blew at the beginning of class, announcing Rosh Hashanah.

We had tried to prepare our young scholars in the art of asking good questions without embarrassing our visitor. While reading Chiam Potok's powerful novel *My Name is Asher Lev* for our first-year seminar on cultural diversity, we had arranged for the good rabbi to come. He knew Potok and had taught this book in other settings. As a representative of the conservative Jewish community, he understood well the world that Potok sought to portray.

Now my student wielded her weapon of words against the man, believing that she could demand that he recognize the superiority of her updated version of his ancient religion. The class tensed, knowing that worlds were colliding.

He sighed. Not in capitulation or exasperation, but almost in gentle pastoral resignation, knowing that his next comment could prick the bubble of her carefully constructed theological presuppositions.

"You trust the Bible, don't you?" he asked, not specifying which Testament. She nodded, as did most in the room. "You believe what the prophets said about Messiah, right?" More affirmations.

"Well," he went on, "when I read the prophets, they tell me that when Messiah comes, wars will end, and people will no longer get sick, and there will be no famine or earthquakes. Everyone will live in peace and prosper."

He paused.

"Is that true of our world?" he asked.

Another weighty pause.

"You ask me why I don't believe in Jesus," he went on. "I do believe in Jesus. I am quite sure that Jesus was a good Jewish man who did many fine things for those around him in his day. But if I read the scriptures, the same ones that you read, then it is impossible for me to think that Jesus was the Messiah. The Bible itself keeps me from believing that."

And he went on, soliciting other questions about Judaism and the practices of conservative believers in his world, and that of Potok and Asher Lev.

Is Jesus the Messiah?

My mind went on too. I could not help but admire the simple beauty of his logic and conclusions. My Christian teachings had always affirmed that Jesus is the Messiah, predicted by the Israelite prophets, and whose coming fulfilled Old Testament divine promises.

Yet, through the multiple layers of my theology, collaged together from thousands of sermons, millions of devotional readings, and the clear declarations of dozens of seminary courses, I had presumed, faithfully, that Jesus was the Messiah, the one who lived out the fullness of God's redemptive purposes proclaimed through Israel. But if I were to set aside all my preconceptions, ignore the many New Testament passages that I had memorized, and step away from my family and church community, with the testimonies and confessions about Jesus that colored the air when I was with them, I wondered whether I could possibly connect Jesus of Nazareth with the prophetic prognostications.

Yes, Jesus was miraculously born. But so were Isaac, Samson, and Samuel.

Yes, people testified that Jesus did miracles. But so did Moses, Joshua, Elijah, and Elisha.

Yes, Jesus self-identified as the "Son of Man," and messenger of God. But so did Ezekiel, Isaiah, Daniel, and a host of other prophets.

Yes, Jesus rose from the dead. But that is also what Jesus' disciples said about Moses and Elijah, who appeared and engaged them on the Mountain of Transfiguration.

What Jesus did not do was end war in our world, cure all diseases, wipe away famine or natural disasters, or bring the nations to judgment for their crimes and rebellions. While human cultures are ever-changing, one would be hard-pressed to say that life on planet Earth was significantly different after Jesus showed up than before he came.

Can we say with confidence that Jesus is the Messiah who ushered in the eternal righteous Kingdom of God, as foretold by divine revelation through Israel's prophets? The answer to this question is at the heart of Christian theology. The two other great religions that share monotheistic perspectives with Christianity, and which also rely on the same prophetic revelation that Christians affirm, each came to different conclusions about Jesus. Jews say that Jesus was certainly a good man, a captivating and dynamic first-century rabbi, who did a lot of good and helped many lean into God's ways, rather than ignoring or skirting them. Muslims agree with Jews, and say that Jesus was one of the three greatest prophets ever. In effect, they affirm the perspectives of the good rabbi in my classroom. Jesus is wonderful. We must learn from him. We must listen to him. But the world around us is the strongest testimony that he is neither divine nor the ultimate expression of God's final declarations. Jesus came and taught and healed and prophesied. But the world did not change. The eschaton did not come. The Kingdom of God is no nearer now than it was before.

Unless . . .

Splitting the "Day of the Lord"

Unless Jesus did something that no one saw coming. Unless Jesus refused to bring in the final expression of the Kingdom of God with a single, mighty THWACK that would have destroyed the bulk of people on Earth in the fiery vengeance of God's judgment. Unless Jesus split the "Day of the Lord" in two, initiating its blessings without completing them, absorbing the first blows of divine judgment into himself rather than having the rage of heaven sear like a weapon of destruction across Earth, and establishing a remnant troupe of witnesses to change the world for good before the Final Act threatens.

Could it be that the very evidence my rabbi friend put forward to prove that Jesus is not the Messiah, read in another light, might be the testimony that he is precisely the Messiah?! Parents know this. They go out for a night, and leave the teens at home. "We will return at eleven," they say. "Don't invite others over! No booze! And keep the house relatively neat. Otherwise, you know what's coming!"

They leave. The teens text friends. Social media spreads. A riotous party happens. Neighbors call the police. Destruction reigns. And the parents come home to chaos.

They will be true to their words of judgment, to be sure. But the full fury of that righteous punishing will likely be muted and deferred and partially absorbed in their own losses and pains. They will pay for the cleanup and repairs. They will bail out of jail their children, the ones they love so dearly, even through cries of frustration. They will set new standards, new limits. And that single moment of Judgment Day will be split and extended into a period of time in which parents act like parents rather than tyrant dictators who unleash the full arsenal in a single quick-reaction doomsday apocalypse.

So with the prophetic foretelling of the "Day of the Lord." It is clear from John's identification of Jesus,[1] Jesus' own words to his disciples,[2] and the reflections of the apostles on the meaning of Jesus' coming,[3] that all believed the "Day of the Lord" had arrived in the person of Jesus. Yet, like with Saul the persecutor of Jesus' followers[4] who became Paul the chief witness of Jesus,[5] this mutation of understanding about the Messiah was not easy to comprehend, or immediately apparent.[6]

The Cornerstone of Christian Theology

Still, this theological shift and new understanding of Jesus' coming is at the heart of Christian testimony. What makes Christianity distinct from Judaism is the belief that the Messiah and the "Day of the Lord" have come in the person of Jesus. What distinguishes Christianity from Islam is the same, along with the proviso that all necessary revelation was culminated in Jesus.

The concept of Christian biblical theology is rooted in this. Although biblical theology, the investigation of the scriptures that speak authoritatively into the faith community, is foundational for systematic theology, their relationship with one another has often been inverted since the struggles of the Trinitarian and Christological controversies of the second through fifth centuries. As the identity of Jesus and the trinitarian character of God was nuanced through the articulations of the ecumenical creeds, systematic

---

1. Matt 3:1–12; Mark 1:1–15; Luke 3:1–20.
2. Luke 4:16–30; Matt 4–8; Mark 2–3; Acts 1:1–11.
3. Gal 4:1–5; 1 Cor 15; 1 and 2 Peter; Heb 1–13.
4. Acts 9.
5. Eph 3.
6. Acts 1:6.

theology came to be viewed as the official voice of the church, with biblical theology useful only for finding texts to support its tenets.

This reduction of biblical theology's role in Christianity's public testimonies led to further shifts in the use and understanding of the Bible. First, the New Testament superseded the Old Testament in importance and significance. While the original Christians studied the Hebrew scriptures (or their Septuagint Greek translation) as they confirmed the preaching of the apostles, within a generation there were Christian communities, like the Marcionites and the Gnostics, which would simply erase the Jewish Bible from Christian consideration.

Second, even when the official position of Christian theology refused to eliminate the Torah, Prophets, and Writings from its scriptural canon, systematic theology often shifted the relationship between Old and New Testaments strongly in favor of the latter, and consciously against the former. The gospels and apostolic writings became the very word of God, while the Old Testament contained documents that espoused "law" which could only be overcome through Jesus, or "context" that informed Christians about the world into which Jesus came, or "prophesy" that had little meaning for Israel and would only become useful in confirming what Christian systematic theologians were saying about Jesus.

Third, as biblical theology split into "Old Testament Theology" and "New Testament Theology," the tools of higher criticism silenced the voice of God in the former and muted it in the latter. Any truth to be found in the Old Testament was either created by David's comrades as they tried to give a meaningful backstory which would buttress his tyrannical creation of a supposed nation of Israel, or it was whispered into life by the scribes and priests of the exile and its aftermath as they looked for justification for their existence following a trauma that nearly wiped out the community. Different interpretations of the supposed strands of religious development that produced an amalgamation of scriptures read the data one way or another. But on this they could all agree: there was no Exodus from Egypt, no great Sinai covenant, and no historic interruption of God into human history. Israelite religion was born out of human necessity, not divine initiative. As this perspective influenced New Testament theology, Jesus remained a great teacher and insightful prophet, but his message was limited because it was built upon the mythological understandings of an unsupported presumed Jewish identity.

The result has splintered Christian use of the Bible as its singular source of identity and a unified whole, and diminished any attempted design for a common and unique message. Now Christianity is about Jesus, apart from the Old Testament, except for quaint cultural practices that can be ferreted out by Jewish scholars. Jesus becomes a larger-than-life action figure whose teachings can be interpreted in almost any way, and whose impact is reduced to merely personal and exemplary iconism, rather than transformative and cosmological perspective-shaping.

Recovering the significance of the "Day of the Lord" in Jewish identity and biblical theology as a whole, along with the surprising reworking of it that lies at the heart of Jesus' mission, would re-energize both biblical theology as a discipline that supersedes limited focus on one Testament or the other. It would also center the elements investigated by both Old and New Testament theologies around an intrinsic normative marker highlighted in each.

Is Jesus the Messiah, foretold by Israel's prophets? The answer depends on how the Hebrew Bible "Day of the Lord" is understood, and whether Jesus is a failed apocalyptic Jewish rabbi or the genius heaven-sent Christ who split the anticipated divine interruption into our history in two, as an act of deep care and blessing for the human race.

1

Divine Intrusion

The Development of the
"Day of the Lord"

THIS APOCRYPHAL STORY RE-EMERGES every few years: a Children's Ministry leader has gathered the youngsters at the front of the congregational worship space, and is giving a talk to inform and inspire them. On this occasion, he has decided to play-act an animal's behaviors.

"Try to guess who I am," he tells the little ones. "I am small, I live in trees, and I gather nuts."

There are no takers. Not a hand is raised, nor any voice shouts out with pride of discovery. So, he tries again.

"I have a bushy tail, and sometimes my nose goes like this." In his best imitation, he mimics the twitching nostrils of a small rodent.

Tension mounts as none of these children, all above average, according to their parents, can solve such a complex riddle of identity. "Who am I?" he invites. "Come on," he chides. "You know this one!"

A hand shivers up tentatively. "Good, Sarah!" the leader affirms. "You got it! What's the answer?"

"I know the answer is supposed to be Jesus," says young Sarah timidly, "but it sounds like a squirrel to me . . . "

And the congregation laughs in delight.

Is the Bible All about Jesus?

"I know the answer is supposed to be Jesus." Little Sarah has learned her theology well. "Jesus is the answer," according to Christian psalms, hymns, and spiritual songs over the centuries, but to what question?

Certainly not when the issue at stake is, what is the main focus of the Christian Bible? Nothing in the first three-quarters of the Bible (the Old

Testament) specifically and directly references Jesus. In the New Testament quarter itself, the letter of James only references him once, rather obliquely.[1] Paul's short letter to Philemon contains ten nods to Jesus,[2] while Jude's longer epistle mentions him only six times.[3] Jesus is mostly missing from the central chapters of the book of Revelation,[4] and hardly mentioned in Paul's letter to Titus.[5]

Thus, about four-fifths of the Bible does not mention or focus on Jesus. True, the other one-fifth is almost entirely consumed with the person, teaching, and work of Jesus. Yet it is impossible to declare meaningfully that the Bible is all about Jesus.

Jesus himself makes that clear in a number of ways. First, each gospel writer positions Jesus' coming as a fulfillment of scriptural promise,[6] indicating that the redemptive work of God is a long process in which Jesus plays a limited and specific role. Second, Jesus' early testimony about himself, according to Matthew 5:17, is a culmination and fulfillment of the "Law" and the "Prophets," the two divisions which encompassed all that was considered to be "scripture" by the Jews in his time. Third, Jesus self-identifies

1. Jas 1:1—"James, a servant of God and of the Lord Jesus Christ . . . "

2. Phlm 1, 3, 5, 6, 8, 9, 16, 20, 23, 25.

3. Jude 1 (2X), 4, 17, 21, 25.

4. Only two references to "the anointed one" in Revelation 8–11.

5. Five references, in Titus 1:1, 1:3, 1:4, 2:13, and 3:6.

6. Mark's initiating description of Jesus' coming (Mark 1:1–13) is linked to a conflation of Yahweh's announcement through Malachi that the divine arrival will be preceded by "my messenger" (Mal 3:1) and Isaiah's forecast of the voice of this messenger declaring God's arrival (Isa 40:3). Mark uses these to identify John, the baptizer, as the messenger, insinuating that in the coming of Jesus, God is arriving among God's people. Matthew locks Jesus' birth into a genealogical matrix (Matthew 1:1–17) that ensures an understanding of Jesus as both part of divine redemptive history and also its culmination (the third grouping of fourteen generations requires Jesus to be both the thirteenth (human) participant and also the fourteenth (divine—"Christ") participant. Then Matthew goes on (Matt 1:18–7:29) to parallel the early life of Jesus with the early life of Israel—both miraculously born, both experiencing a ruler who tried to kill all of the boy babies, both emerging from Egypt, both spending forty days in the wilderness, both passing through the waters of the Jordan in order to be readied for their divine calling and ministry, both stopping at the mountain to receive (or declare) the very covenant of God. Luke places Jesus' birth in a Jewish historical and liturgical context (Luke 1), and has his mother (Luke 1:46–55) sing a song imitating Hannah's hymn of divine favor and salvation (1 Sam 2:1–10), while Zechariah lifts his voice in a connection between David's theocratic kingdom and that to be brought into being by the one his son will proclaim (Luke 1:68–79). John reaches all the way back to creation (Gen 1–2; John 1:1–18), tying Jesus' incarnation to a re-creation event that overcomes the effects of the fall into sin (Gen 3). John goes on with themes of darkness and light to indicate the manner in which Jesus functions as the recreating Light in a world where the original light of creation has gone out.

as the God of Israel, who has been at work for centuries seeking Israel's good and the salvation of the world.[7] Fourth, Jesus explained his entire life, identity, ministry, and even death and resurrection as the fulfillment and outcome of all that Jewish scripture has focused upon.[8]

In summary, however important Jesus is to Christian faith, Jesus' coming into our world as redeemer is not the beginning of the biblical story. Furthermore, whatever Jesus taught and did were both prefigured and rooted in a much longer arc of divine redemptive activity.

Israelite identity, inexorably tied to Hebrew scripture, explained the origin of this redemptive story as the liberating exodus from Egypt.[9] While the collection of sacred writings always begins with Genesis, the actual story of salvation found in the Bible, essential to why these scriptures exist in the first place, does not. Jews knew that the scriptures and their message started with the singular event of Israel's miraculous release from Egyptian slavery by the One who betrothed them to the divine self and mission through the Sinai covenant.[10]

True, for the Bible it would seem most obvious that its beginning is the opening chapters of Genesis. After all, Genesis is at the front of the book that we all have become familiar with it. Moreover, Genesis deals with origins, as its very name implies. In fact, Genesis ferrets out the original Big Bang beginning, when from nothing (or out of primeval chaos) God blasted the universe into existence. After that, Genesis goes on to describe beginnings of all other sorts—the origins of fauna and flora, the elemental steps of the human race, the critically disruptive entrance of evil, the formation of communities, nation states, cultures, and races, and

7. Cf. John 17, among many other passages.

8. Luke affirmed this in the last unique story about Jesus that he records (Luke 24:13–35). On Resurrection Sunday, two men traveling from Jerusalem to Emmaus found themselves suddenly in the company of a familiar stranger who explains to them from "Moses" and the "Prophets" that the life, ministry, death and resurrection of Jesus are a fulfillment of divine revelation within the context of the larger arc of redemptive history.

9. This redemptive event was repeatedly recited in the prologue of the Ten Commandments (Exod 20:2; Deut 5:6), declared to be a basis for Israel's ethical expressions (Deut 5:12–14), remembered in the annual community-origins celebration of the Passover (Exod 12; Num 9:1–5; Deut 16:1–8; Josh 5:10; 2 Kgs 23:21–23; 2 Chr 30:1–5; Ezra 6:19–21; Ezek 45:21–24), identified as the foundation of Israel's unique existence (Isa 43:1–13; Mic 6:4), and celebrated in Israel's worship (Pss 68, 78, 80).

10. The story of the Exodus became a type of parable, retold within the Israelite community in a variety of ways. Asaph put it into verse, painting world pictures about it in Ps 80. Isaiah picked the theme up as a song embodying Israel's unique history (Isa 5). Hosea heard the voice of Yahweh lamenting about the divine initiatives with Israel in this manner (Hos 11).

even the birth of the tribal grouping called Israel, which will dominate the rest of the Bible's pages.

But, as logicians caution, simply because pages currently are found in a certain order, this does not mean that the first ones we encounter necessarily came into being prior to those that follow. Did someone sit down one day and decide to write about the creation? Was the Bible initiated by an obscure scribe with too much time on his hands who was exploring the family tree, and then hit upon the idea of writing a best-seller about Abraham and Kin, only to be bested over the centuries by others who turned the tale into an endless serialization with subplots that finally destroyed the original narrative? Or were there ethicists in collegial dialogue who despaired of the condition of their societies and together formulated a new code of behavior, surrounding it with a mythical world to give it staying power?

The Exodus as a Starting Point

While speculations might swirl, the Bible's own pages are quite clear about its presumed beginnings. If by "Bible" we mean a book of writings that purport to have revelatory or religiously shaping significance (i.e., "scripture"), then we must ask where such writings first happened and under what conditions within the Bible's own literary self-understanding. With this in mind, it becomes apparent that we need to start by looking at the events reported to have taken place at Mount Sinai, in the middle of the book of Exodus.

Why? Because none of the stories reported in the Bible about events occurring prior to the Sinai event make mention of or imply the presence of a written source of revelation or inspiration. For instance, important as he was to biblical history, Adam had no "Bible." Nor did Noah, during all those years that he tried to hear a voice speaking of impending world destruction. Even Abraham, whose story is so central to the biblical record in both Testaments, was not guided by a collection of sacred writings to which he could turn for devotional reflection each morning.

In clear and unambiguous testimony, the Bible's own internal evidence expresses that the writing down of important ideas or history as a sourcebook of revelatory insight was begun when the Israelites encountered God in a unique way at Mount Sinai. It was there, according to the pages of Exodus, that God and Moses collaborated to create written documents which would travel with the community that eventually became the settled nation of Israel.

So, it is imperative to understand more clearly what was taking place at Mount Sinai. To do that, we need to know something of the broader history of the second millennium BC.

Suzerain-Vassal Covenant Documents

One of the dominant civilizations of the second millennium was the Hittite kingdom. Somewhat secluded in the mountainous plateaus of Anatolia (east-central Turkey today), the Hittites shaped a vast web of international relations which, at the height of their power in the fourteenth century BC, encompassed most of the ancient Near East.[11] While they were companions of other similar civilizations that shared commonalities of culture and conquests and cities, the Hittites linger in archaeological and historical studies for, among other things, their standardization of a written code used extensively in the normalization of international relations.[12] In order to establish appropriate structures that would spell out the Hittites' ongoing interactions with subjected peoples, a prescribed treaty form appears to have been widely used.[13] The parameters of the typical Hittite Suzerain-Vassal covenant included:[14]

- A **preamble** which declared the identity and power of the ruler responsible for establishing this relationship.

11. See Christopher Scarre and Brian M. Fagan, *Ancient Civilizations* (Upper Saddle River, NJ: Pearson, 2008); Marc Van De Mieroop, *A History of the Ancient Near East ca. 3000–323 BC*, 2nd Edition (Oxford: Blackwell, 2007). Also, Joshua J. Mark, "The Hittites." *Ancient History Encyclopedia*. Ancient History Encyclopedia, 28 Apr 2011. Web. 02 Oct 2017.

12. See Noel Weeks, *Admonition and Curse: The Ancient Near Eastern Treaty/Covenant Form as a Problem in Inter-Cultural Relationships* (London: T&T Clark, 2004).

13. See Klaus Baltzer, *The Covenant Formulary: In Old Testament, Jewish and Early Christian Writings*, translated by David E. Green (Philadelphia: Fortress, 1971); Joshua A. Berman, *Created Equal: How the Bible Broke with Ancient Political Thought* (Oxford: Oxford University, 2008), 28–49; Michael D. Coogan, *A Brief Introduction to the Old Testament* (Oxford: Oxford University Press, 2009).

14. George E. Mendenhall, "Covenant Forms in Israelite Tradition," *Biblical Archaeology* 17 (September 1954) 50–76; Gordon J. Wenham, *The Structure and Date of Deuteronomy: A Consideration of Aspects of the History of Deuteronomy Criticism and Re-examination of the Question of Structure and Date in the Light of that History and of the Near Eastern Treaties* (Ph.D. diss., University of London, 1969); Herbert B. Huffmon, "Covenant Lawsuit in Prophets," *Journal of Biblical Literature* 78 (December 1959): 295; Meredith G. Kline, *Treaty of the Great King: The Covenant Structure of Deuteronomy: Studies and Commentary* (Grand Rapids: Eerdmans, 1963); K. A. Kitchen, *Ancient Orient and Old Testament* (Chicago: InterVarsity, 1966), and *The Bible in Its World: The Bible and Archaeology Today* (Downers Grove, IL: InterVarsity, 1977), 79–85.

- A **historical prologue** outlining the events leading up to this relationship, so that it could be set into a particular context and shaped by a cultural or religious frame.

- **Stipulations** which specified the responsibilities and actions associated with the relationship.

- **Curses and blessings** that evoked the negative and positive outcomes if this covenant were either breached or embraced by the parties.

- **Witnesses** who were called to affirm the legitimacy of this covenant-making event, and who would then hold the parties accountable.

- **Document clauses** which described ratification ceremonies, specified future public recitations of the treaty, and noted the manner in which the copies of the covenant were to be kept.

What makes this bit of ancient historical trivia so intriguing for biblical scholars is the uncanny correspondence between the elements of this Hittite covenant code and the literature at the heart of Israel's encounter with God at Sinai.[15] Note the following:

- When God is first heard to speak from the rumbling mountain, the words are essentially the **preamble** of a Suzerain-Vassal covenant: "I am the Lord your God" (Exod 20:1).

- Immediately following is a brief **historical prologue** reminding the people of the events that precipitated this encounter: "who brought you out of the land of Egypt, out of the house of bondage" (Exod 20:2).

- Then comes a recitation of **stipulations** that will shape the ethics, morality, and lifestyle of the community (Exod 20:3–23:19).

- Following these are the **curses and blessings** (Exod 23:20–33) of a typical covenant document. What is unusual in this case is that the order is reversed so that the blessings precede the curses. This provides the same rigors of participatory onus, but gives it a freshness of grace and optimism that are often absent from the quick condemnation of the usual ordering.

- The **witnesses** are the Elders of the Israelite community (Exod 24:1–2), bringing authentication of this process and these documents into the human realm, when it was often spiritualized in other covenants by listing local gods as moderators of these events.

15. René Lopez, "Israelite Covenants in the Light of Ancient Near Eastern Covenants," *Calvin Theological Seminary Journal* 9 (Fall 2003) 97–102, and 10 (Spring 2004) 72–106.

- Finally, there is the **document clause** (Exod 24:3–18) that spells out the ratification ceremony. It will be followed by a further reflection on the repositories of the covenant document copies once the tabernacle has been built.

The striking resonance between the usual form of the Hittite Suzerain-Vassal covenant and the essential first speech of Yahweh to Israel at Mount Sinai makes it difficult not to assess the beginnings of conscious Israelite religion in terms other than that of a Suzerain (Yahweh) Vassal (Israel) covenant-making ceremony. Furthermore, this appears to elucidate the mode and function of the first biblical documents. They were not intended to be origin myths, ancestor hero stories, mere legal or ethical or civil codes, sermons, prophecies, or apocalyptic visions (though all of these would later accrete to the initial writings of the first community encounter with Yahweh); they were initially the written covenant documents formulating the relationship between a nation and the (divine) ruler who earned, in battle, the right to order her world.

This is why the word "covenant" becomes an essential term for all the rest of the literature that will be garnered into the collection eventually known as the Bible.[16] The Bible begins with a covenant-making ceremony that produces certain documents, and then continues to grow as further explications of that covenant relationship are generated. One can read theology or ethics or politics or history out of the Bible, but one cannot do so

---

16. The biblical words most often translated "covenant" are תִּירְב (*berith*) in the Old Testament (about 280 times) and διαθηκε (*diatheke*) found at least thirty-three times in the New Testament. The origin of the Hebrew word might be from a custom of eating together (see, for instance, Gen 26:30; 31:54), since it implies the act of cutting for sharing. This also seems to be at least one aspect of the fascinating account of Yahweh establishing a covenant with Abram in Gen 15, where animals are partitioned (Gen 15:18). Whatever the origins, the word itself came to mean a ritualized engagement of parties established by way of relational bonds connected to mutual actions of reciprocal obligation: when Abimelech and Isaac decided to settle their land dispute, for instance, they made a binding agreement (covenant) to live in peace, confirming it with an oath (Gen 26:26–31); similarly, Joshua and the Gibeonites bound themselves, by oath, to live in peace together (Josh 9:15), even though Yahweh had commanded Israel not to bind themselves to the people living in the land of Canaan (Deut 7:2; see also Judg 2:2); later, Solomon and Hiram made a binding agreement to live and work in peace together (1 Kgs 5:12). These are examples of what are often termed "Parity Agreements," since they are established between parities of equal social stature. The Hittite Suzerain-Vassal covenants, however, were viewed as prescribed relationships between socially unequal sets: a powerful (often conquering) king and the plebian mass of territorial or ethnic subjects. This is the nature of the Sinai Covenant in Exod 20–24, sealing a relationship between Yahweh and Israel that is inherently one-sided in both formation and execution. Israel (and with her, the New Testament church) is redeemed by the acts of salvation initiated by God, and lives in benevolent service to its champion and savior.

while ignoring the essential role of the Sinai covenant between Yahweh and Israel.[17] Even the idea of "kingdom," so prevalent and pervasive in the Bible, is predicated on the covenant, for it is by way of the covenant that Israel becomes the dominion of the great King. The Kingdom of God is the context for all that is portrayed in the Bible, but the covenant is the administrative document through which the Kingdom takes hold and adheres in the human societies, which form the front ranks of Yahweh's citizenry.

The Battle of the Superpowers

This perspective is further confirmed in the rest of the writings that surround Exodus 20–24. First, Exodus 1–19 forms an extended "historical prologue" to the Sinai covenant by declaring Israel's precarious situation in Egypt (chapter 1), the birth and training of the leader who would become Yahweh's agent for recovering Yahweh's enslaved people (chapter 2), the calling of this deliverer (chapters 3–4), and the battle of the superpowers (the Pharaoh and Yahweh) who each lay claim to Suzerain status over this Vassal nation (chapters 5–19). Second, Exodus 25–40 focuses on the creation of a suitable residence for Israel's Suzerain. Thus, the whole of Exodus may be quickly outlined as struggles (1–19), stipulations (20–24), and symbols (25–40) surrounding the Sinai covenant-making event. Each of these deserves further reflection.

The struggles of chapters 1–19 involve a number of things. At the start there is the nasty relationship that has developed between the Pharaoh of Egypt and the Israelites. An editorial note declares that "Joseph" has been forgotten, and this small reference forms the bridge that later draws Genesis into an even more broadly extended historical prologue to the Sinai covenant. We will find out, by reading backwards, that Joseph was the critical link between the Egyptians and this other ethnic community living within its borders. When the good that Joseph did for both races was forgotten, the dominant Egyptian culture attempted to dehumanize and then destroy these Israelite aliens.

The deadly solution proposed by the Pharaoh in dealing with the rising population of his slave community may sound harsh, but it was likely a very modest and welcomed political maneuver among his primary subjects.

17. See, for instance, Walter Eichrodt, *Theology of the Old Testament*, vol. 1, translated by J. A. Baker. OTL. Edited by G. Ernest Wright, et al. (Philadelphia: The Westminster Press, 1961); Meredith. J. Kline, *The Structure of Biblical Authority* and *The Treaty of a Great King* (Grand Rapids: Wm. B. Eerdmans Publishing Co., 1972); D. J. McCarthy, *Old Testament Covenant*, 2nd Edition (Hoboken, NJ: Blackwell Publishers, 1973).

Because there is virtually no rain in Egypt, with most of its territory lying in or on the edge of the great Saharan desert, the Nile is and was the critical source of water that sustained life throughout the region. The Nile "miraculously" ebbed and flowed annually, responding to the rains of central Africa, thousands of miles away. Far removed from Egypt's farmlands and cities, this process was attributed to the gods that nurtured Egyptian civilization. Thus, it was fitting for the people to pay homage to these gods, especially by giving appropriate sacrifices to the power of the Nile. In that manner, having the boy babies of the Hebrews tossed into the Nile's currents would not have been considered genocide, but instead it would be deemed a suitable civic and cultural responsibility. Such a practice provided the Nile god with respectably dear tribute, and at the same time allowed the bulk of the Egyptian population to save its own babies by substituting those of this surrogate vassal people living within their borders.

A Uniquely Qualified Leader

Moses' own name ties him to the royal family of Egypt and its influence,[18] and his training in the palace schools would provide him with skills that set him apart from the rest of the Israelites in preparation for his unique leadership responsibilities. Moses' time in the wilderness, on the other hand, made him familiar with Bedouin life, and similarly fortified his ability to stand at the head of a wandering community once Israel was released from slavery.

In Moses' unique encounter with God at Mt. Horeb (chapters 3–4), he experienced the power of the forgotten deity of Israel, and learned a name by which this divinity would soon become known again to the people. "Yahweh" (הוה‍י) is a variation on the Hebrew verb of existence, and that is why translators bring it into English with terms like "I am" or "I will be." Furthermore, through the voice from the burning bush, this God immediately connected the current events with a specific past through a historical recitation that would later be explicated at length in the extended Genesis

---

18. Note the frequent occurrence of the letters represented in English by MSS in the names of Pharaohs of the eighteenth through twentieth dynasties—*Thutmoses, Ramses*, etc. The "mss" portion of each name indicated being "drawn from" or "emerging from" the being identified at the beginning of each name. Thus, Thutmoses' name declared that he was drawn from (Moses) "Thut," the guardian of the high god in Egyptian religious understandings. Similarly, Ramses' name indicated that he was descended from (emerged out of) "Ra," the sun god. Since Moses carried the idea of emerging or being drawn from (the Nile), without any divinity designation, he was able to live among Egyptian royalty without having a named that committed him to Egyptian religious identity.

historical prologue to the Sinai covenant: Yahweh is the God of Abraham, Isaac, and Jacob. Because of the promises made to that family, Moses is now to become the agent through whom the Israelites will be returned to the land promised to their ancestors. Of course, this is what triggered the battle for control of the nation, and eventually set the stage for Yahweh to claim Suzerainty over Israel at Mount Sinai.

The conflict intensifies in Exodus 5:1–6:12 when Moses makes his first dramatic appearance back in Egypt. The Pharaoh's initial reaction is disdain; why should he listen to the apocalyptic ravings of a wilderness wild man, even if he seems unusually aware of Egyptian language and protocol?

At this point the famous plagues enter the story. While these miracles of divine judgment make for great Hollywood screenplay, the reason for this extended weird display of divine power is not always apparent to those of us who live in very different cultural contexts, especially when it is interspersed with notes that Pharaoh's heart was hardened, sometimes, in fact, seemingly as an act of Yahweh. Could not Yahweh have provided a less destructive and deadly exit strategy for Israel?

Yahweh vs. the Pharaoh

The plagues begin to make sense when they are viewed in reference to Egypt's climate and culture. After the initial sparring between Moses and the Pharaoh's sorcerers (Exod 7:10–13) with snakes to show magical skills, the stakes are raised far beyond human ability merely to manipulate the natural order. First the waters are turned to blood; then the marshes send out a massive, unwelcome pilgrimage of frogs; next the dust is beat into gnats, soon to be followed by even peskier flies; subsequently the livestock gets sick from the dust, and this illness then spreads to human life in the form of boils and open sores; penultimately the heavens send down mortar shells of hail, transport in a foreign army of locusts, and then withhold the light of the sun; finally, in an awful culmination, the firstborn humans and animals across Egypt die suddenly.

Strange. But not quite as much when seen in three successive groupings. Among the many deities worshipped in ancient Egypt, none superseded a triumvirate composed by the Nile, the good earth, and the heavens, which were the home of the sun.[19] So it was that the initial plagues of bloody

---

19. Cf., "Plagues of Egypt," in *New Bible Dictionary*, third edition, edited by I. Howard Marshall, A. R. Millard, J. I. Packer, and Donald J. Wiseman (Downers Grove, IL: InterVarsity Press, 1996). Also, commentary on Exodus 7 in *The Jewish Study Bible*, edited by Adele Berlin and Marc Zvi Brettler (Oxford: Oxford University Press, 2004).

water and frogs both turned the Nile against the Egyptians, and showed the dominance of Yahweh over this critical source of national life.

The ante was then upped when Yahweh took on the farmland of Egypt, one of the great breadbaskets of the world. Instead of producing crops, Moses showed, by way of plagues three through six, how Yahweh could cause these fertile alluvial plains to generate all manner of irritating and deadly pestilence, making it an enemy instead of a friend. Finally, in the third stage of plagues, the heavens themselves became menacing. Rather than providing the sheltering confidence of benign sameness, one day the heavens attacked with the hailstone mortar fire of an unseen enemy. Next these same heavens served as the highway of an invading army of locusts. Then old friend *Ra* (the sun), the crowning deity of Egyptian religion, simply vanished for three days. The gloom that terrified the Egyptians was no mere fear of darkness but rather the ominous trepidation that their primary deity had been bested by the God of the Israelites.

All of this culminated in the final foray of this cosmic battle, when the link of life between generations and human connectedness with ultimate reality was severed through the killing of Egypt's firstborn. The Egyptians believed that the firstborn carried the cultural significance of each family and species, so in a sudden and dramatic moment the very chain of life destroyed. Furthermore, since the Pharaohs themselves were presumed to be deity incarnate, descending directly from the sun by way of firstborn inheritance, cutting this link eviscerated the life-potency of the Egyptian civilization not only for the present but also for the future. It was a true cultural, religious, political and social knockout punch.

The plagues originally served not as gory illustration material for modern Sunday school papers, but rather as the divine initiatives in an escalating battle between Yahweh and the Pharaoh of Egypt over claims on the people of Israel. The plagues were a necessary prologue to the Sinai covenant because they displayed and substantiated the sovereignty of Yahweh as Suzerain not only over Israel but also over other contenders. Israel belongs to Yahweh both because of historic promises made to Abraham, and also by way of chivalrous combat in which Yahweh won back the prize of lover and human companion from the usurper who had stolen her away from the divine heart. Furthermore, Yahweh accomplished this act *without* the help of Israel's own resources (no armies, no resistance movements, no terrorist tactics, no great escape plans), and in a decisive manner that announced the limitations of the Egyptian religious and cultural resources.

For this reason, the final plague is paired with the institution of the Passover festival (Exod 12). The annual festival would become an ongoing reminder that Israel was bought back by way of a blood-price redemption, and that the nation owed its very existence to the love and fighting jealousy of its divine champion. In one momentous confrontation, Egypt lost its firstborn and its cultural heritage, while Israel became Yahweh's firstborn and rightful inheritance.

Covenant Marking

These things are further confirmed in the reiteration of the importance of circumcision (Exod 13:1–16). The rite of circumcision was practiced by most peoples of the ancient Near East,[20] but invariably as either a mark of elitism (only those of a particular class in the community were circumcised)[21] or as a rite of passage (boys or young men who did heroic deeds in battle or the hunt would be circumcised to show that they had become part of the adult warrior caste).[22] What is unique about the commands regarding circumcision for Israel is that it is egalitarian (all males are to be circumcised, and through them all females gain the right to be called the people of Yahweh), and that it is to be done typically on babies or young boys prior to any efforts on their part to perform deeds of valor. This transforms a regional practice that had been identified primarily as a badge of honor earned, into a mark of ownership given, as expressed in the patriarchal antecedent found in Genesis 17. It is through this lens that the New Testament practices of baptism must also be viewed; John's baptism (along with many purification rituals among, e.g., the Essenes and Pharisees) carried with it the flavor of a ritual of passage leading to earning the colors of heightened spiritual maturity, while the use of baptism in the church followed the ownership markings of Israel's practice of circumcision (see, for instance, Jesus' command regarding baptism in Matt 28:18–20 and Paul's connection of baptism and circumcision in Col 2:11–12).

20. As Herodotus traveled and received reports regarding the practices and lifestyles of many civilizations in his world, he stated that the Egyptians, Colchians, and Ethiopians, from very early times, were circumcised, and that he knew also of this practice among the Phoenicians and Syrians of Palestine (his term for the Jews) (*History*, II, 104).

21. E.g., the priests of Egypt; the Aztec and Celebes tribes. Cf. Hubert Howe Bancroft, *The Native Races* (San Francisco: History Company, 1886), 439-440.

22. James Frazer, *The Golden Bough: A Study in Magic and Religion* (Hertfordshire, England: Wordsworth Reference, 1993), 691–701; Andrea Wilcken, Thomas Keil, and Bruce Dick, "Traditional male circumcision in eastern and southern Africa: a systematic review of prevalence and complications," *Bulletin of the World Health Organization* 88: 907–914.

Related to this divinely initiated ownership theme is the miraculous deliverance of Israel through the Red Sea, coupled with the annihilation of the Egyptian army and its national military prowess in the same incidents. While Exodus 14 narrates the episode in the nail-biting urgency of a documentary, chapter 15 is given over largely to the ancient song of Moses, which unmistakably identifies the entire exodus event as divine combat against Pharaoh over the possession of Israel. Furthermore, the victory ballad also clearly anticipates the effect of this battle on the other Near Eastern nations, with the result that Yahweh is able to march the Israelites through many hostile territories, and eventually settle the nation in Canaan as an ongoing testimony to Yahweh's rightful prestige. So it is that the exodus itself is not the divine goal, but only the first stage toward something else.

A House for God

What this further divine intention might be is then illumined by the singular event that follows from the covenant-making ceremony of Exodus 20–24: the construction of the tabernacle. The narrative of Exodus 25–40 has three major sections. In chapters 25–31, preparations for the tabernacle are made and detailed plans are formulated. Then comes the intruding and jarring incident of the golden calf (chapters 32–34), in which not only Israel's loyalty to Yahweh but also Yahweh's loyalty to Israel are tested. Finally, the architectural initiatives of Exodus 25–31 are resumed in the actual construction of the tabernacle and its dedication (chapters 35–40), almost as if the dark blot of the interlude had never happened.

Why all of this emphasis on building the tent-like tabernacle? Why invest in a movable shrine rather than rally around some sacred hilltop (Mount Sinai, for instance)? The answer is intrinsically related to the covenant-making event itself. If Israel is now the (reclaimed) possession of Yahweh, then Yahweh must take up visible residence among the people.[23] The tabernacle is not a strange phenomenon of the natural order, like an unfailing spring or a volcanic vent or a residual meteor rock. Instead, it is the fabrication of a civilization that is intentionally on a journey, guided by an in-residence deity who travels with them. These people do not make pilgrimage to a shrine and then return to their homes; rather they move about in consort with the source of their identity actually residing within the center of their unwieldy sprawl.

---

23. See Exod 25:8—"have them make me a sanctuary, so that I may dwell among them."

Testimony of this is contained within the very architectural plans for the tabernacle. Although parts of the facility will be off limits to most of the people (and thereby somewhat mysteriously remote), the basic design is virtually identical to that of the typical Israelite portable residence and the living space that surrounds it. First, the cooking fire of any family unit was found in front of the tent. Second, there would be vessels for washing located near the door of the tent. Third, while many meals might be taken around the fire, some were more ordered and formal, and occurred in the initial spaces within the tent. These required atmospheric accoutrements like dishes, lamps for lighting, and the aromatic wafting of incense. Finally, the privacy of the intimate acts of marriage and family were reserved for the hidden recesses of the tent where visitors were not allowed.

This, then, became the plan for the tabernacle. Its courtyard was public space for meals with God and others of the community around the Altar of Burnt Offerings (see Lev 1–7). The Laver or Bronze Basin held waters for washing and bodily purification. In the closest part of the tabernacle itself was found the hospitality area where Yahweh figuratively dined more formally with guests at the table, in the soft ambience created by the lamp and altar of incense. To the rear of the tabernacle Yahweh reserved private space, yet had it fashioned with all of the symbolism of royalty. The Ark of the Covenant was essentially a portable throne upon which Yahweh was carried with the people, for its uppermost side was designated as the Mercy Seat. Furthermore, this throne was under the guard of two representative heavenly creatures simply called "cherubim." In a manner akin to the sentries posted at the Garden of Eden in Genesis 3, these beings stood watch to ensure that the holiness of the deity was protected.

Thus, the tabernacle existed uniquely in its world, representing the physical home of the community's deity as a residence within its own spatial and temporal context. Israel was not a people who needed to create representations of powers that it then idolized; instead, the very society in which it lived emanated from the identity of the chief citizen who lived at its heart.

Honeymoon Argument

It is in this context that the Golden Calf incident of Exodus 32–34 must be understood. Moses' delay on the mountain, talking with Yahweh on behalf of the people, bred frustration and anxiety within the community. So, they begged Aaron for symbols around which to rally, and what emerged was a bull calf made of gold. The Israelites were probably not seeking to worship something other than the God who brought them out of Egypt so recently;

rather they were trying to find a representation of that God within their cultural frame of reference, so that they could cajole (or manipulate) this deity into further meaningful actions, rather than wasting time in the seeming stall of their current lethargy. Since the bull calf was revered among the Egyptians for its ability to portray the liveliness of sentient power, it could well serve the Israelites in their quest to display national adolescent brash energy.

The problem for Yahweh, however, was twofold. First, the calf was an *Egyptian* symbol, and thus essentially blasphemous in light of Yahweh's recent decisive victory over all aspects of Egyptian power and civilization. Second, the calf reflected brute strength in the natural order, and of a kind that could be controlled by human will. A bull was meant to be yoked and harnessed and guided by whips and goads. True, it was more powerful than its human driver, but at the same time it became a tool in service to the human will. For Yahweh to be represented in this manner undermined the significance of the divine defeat of Egypt and its culture, and appeared to turn Yahweh into a mighty, albeit controllable, source of energy serving the Israelite will.

Under Moses' leadership, his own tribe, the Levites, rallied to avenge Yahweh's disgrace. Because of that action, they were appointed to the honored position of keepers of the House of God. Meanwhile, Yahweh himself wished to break covenant with Israel and instead start over with Moses' family; after all, Moses and Yahweh had become great partners and almost friends over the past few years, and especially through their time on the mountain. Moses argued against this divine turnabout, however, for two reasons. First, he reminded the Great One that Yahweh had sealed this Suzerain-Vassal covenant with Israel, and it could not so easily be discarded or broken. Yahweh had deliberately invested Yahweh's own destiny into this people, and while they might wrestle with the chafing fit of the new relationship, Yahweh no longer had a right to deny it. Second, Moses raised the card of shame. What would the nations say if Yahweh quit this project now? The peoples of the ancient Near East had begun to tremble because of Yahweh's decisive victory over Pharaoh; if the God of Israel was able so clearly and convincingly to topple the deities of Egypt and their power in both the natural and supernatural realms, what hope could there be for any other mere national interest or powers? But if Yahweh now suddenly left the Israelites to die in the wilderness, the nations around would see that this god was no more than a flash-bang, a one-hit-wonder, a dog with more bark than bite. Moses used Yahweh's own covenant to make the deity toe the line and get back into bed with Israel on this honeymoon night.

God's House among God's People

All of this is affirmed in various ways through the text of these chapters. For instance, prior to the construction of the tabernacle, Moses sought to commune with Yahweh not only on the mountain but also in a small structure called the "Tent of Meeting," which was located slightly outside the camp (Exod 33:7–11). Once the tabernacle had been built, however, this designation of the "Tent of Meeting" was transferred to that newer edifice (Exod 39:32–40:38). Furthermore, the term used to describe the grander "Tent of Meeting" is מִשְׁכָּן (*mishkan*), which means place of dwelling.[24] The same root is also found in the Hebrew term שָׁכֵן (*shakhen*), which communicates the idea of neighbor, or someone who chooses to pitch a tent next to one's own (so the significance of Yahweh moving into the neighborhood).[25] This gave rise, in Talmudic literature, to the cognate שכינה (*shekinah*), a term used to describe the ("presence") cloud of glory that settled on the tabernacle as its divine occupant moved in.[26]

Similarly, Moses was to chisel out two tablets of stone (Exod 34:1, 4) on which Yahweh would inscribe the summary of the covenant stipulations (Exod 34:27), which were identified as the Ten Commandments (Exod 34:28). Most of our representations of the Ten Commandments today picture them as too large to fit on one stone surface, so two tablets are needed to contain all the words. Furthermore, since the first four commandments seem to focus on our relationship with God while the last six have the human social arena in purview, the Ten Commandments are typically arranged on the two stone tablets to reflect this division. Such is not the intention of the ancient text, however. There were always two copies made of a Suzerain-Vassal covenant: one to remain with the subjected people in their homeland and the other to take up residence in the distant palace library of the king. What is unique about Israel's situation is that the two copies of the covenant were to be kept in the very same place—within the Ark of the Covenant. While we might miss the significance of this because of our lack

---

24. E.g., Num 24:5; Ps 132:5.

25. Cf., Exod 24:16; 25:8; 29:45-46; 40:35; Lev 16:16; Num 5:3; 9:17; 9:18; 9:22; 10:12; 14:30; 23:9; 24:2; 35:34; Deut 12:5; 12:11; 14:23; 16:2; 16:6; 16:11; 26:2; 33:12; 33:16; 33:20; 33:28.

26. Cf. *Talmud*, Tractate Shabbat 30b. Note also The *Asader Bishvachin* song, written in Aramaic by the Jewish mystic Isaac Luria (1534–1572), and sung at the evening meal of *Shabbat*: "Let us invite the *Shechinah* with a newly-laid table and with a well-lit menorah that casts light on all heads. Three preceding days to the right, three succeeding days to the left, and amid them the Sabbath bride with adornments she goes, vessels and robes . . . May the *Shechinah* become a crown through the six loaves on each side through the doubled-six may our table be bound with the profound Temple services."

of sensitivity to the ancient customs, the impact on the Israelites would be nothing short of astounding: the king was planning to live in the same place as the people! Both copies of the covenant could be kept in the same receptacle (which also functioned as the king's throne) because Israel's monarch was not a distant absentee landlord. As went the fortunes of Israel, so went the identity of Yahweh, for Yahweh covenantally committed the divine mission to the fate of this nation.[27]

This is why the tabernacle was more than a religious shrine for Israel. It was different than a mere ceremonial place for offerings. It was, in fact, the home of Yahweh at the center of the Israelite community. When the sun settled behind the horizon and the cooking fires were banked to save wood as the people traveled through the wilderness, one tent continued to have a light on all night. In the heart of the camp the lamp glowed in the fellowship hall of the tabernacle; Yahweh kept vigil while the community slept. In the morning and evening, a meal could be taken with Yahweh (the sacrifices, burnt so that Yahweh might consume the divine portion by way of inhaling the smoke), and constantly the feasting room was made ready for the King to meet with his subjects.

What happened at Mount Sinai? God formally claimed Israel as partner in whatever the divine mission was for planet Earth. Israel, in turn, owned Yahweh as divine King and Suzerain. In effect, Yahweh and Israel were married, and their starter home was built at the center of the camp.[28]

The Beginning of the Bible

Thus, the literature of the Bible began as the documents of a divinely initiated covenant-making ceremony, using the formulae of the common Hittite Suzerain-Vassal treaty to shape its words.[29] Added to this, almost immediately, were the plans for the divine residence within the community, and

27. Meredith Kline, "Two Tables of the Covenant," *Westminster Theological Journal* 22 (1960) 133–46.

28. This is the reason why the Exodus/Sinai event is tied so closely to the themes of judgment and the emergence of a new order for a new age throughout the Bible. It is, in effect, the original "Day of the Lord." Note, for instance, the manner in which this is celebrated in the earliest Hebrew poem, found in Exod 15:1–18. This theme is carried forward in the searing prophetic indictment of Obad (note, especially, verse 15), the reflective-anticipatory images in the rhetoric of Joel 1:15 and 2:31, and in the conflations that both remember and project in Isa 2:11, 13:6, Jer 46:10, Amos 5:20, Zeph 1:7–18, Ezek 13:5, 30:3, and Mal 4:1.

29. See Meredith Kline, *The Structure of Biblical Authority* (Grand Rapids: Eerdmans, 1972).

an extended covenant prologue which rehearsed the very recent context in which Yahweh had battled the Pharaoh of Egypt for the right to dance with Israel. So it is, that in its literary origins, at least as portrayed in the text of the Bible itself, the purpose of scripture is to identify the parameters of the covenantal partnership between God and the people who share God's life and mission. It exudes ethical pronouncements not because it is a book of morality, but because it functions as the shaper of a culture where Yahweh has chosen to move into the neighborhood and breathe through Israel an ethos of witness in a world that was no longer consciously aware of its Creator or of its own truest character.

So, if the Bible begins at Mount Sinai, as the initial documents of the covenant between Yahweh and Israel, what is the purpose of Genesis? In order to answer that question, we must first probe carefully the literary development of the text of the Bible's sequentially first book.

It is fairly obvious, when reading Genesis in a single sitting, that there is a marked shift in the text between chapters 11 and 12. The first eleven chapters of Genesis are further removed from our day-to-day experiences, having more of a mythological character to them, somewhat similar to the cosmological origins stories found in many ancient societies. At the same time, although chapters 12–50 seem to enter our historical arena more fully, because of their attention to extended descriptions of the daily lives and interactions of people we might know, they still feel something like the ancestor hero stories that are told in nearly every community as means to define social or ethnic identity.

Competing Worldviews

The "mythical" qualities of Genesis 1–11 ought not to be interpreted as synonymous with either "untrue" or "non-historical." Myths are stories that summarize worldviews in elided prose, giving snapshots of the value systems that drive a culture, or providing hooks on which to hang the unspoken but ubiquitous understanding of a social group's values and self-perception. This is why the stories told by way of myths may sometimes appear to be cartoonlike fairy tales, or at other times they may be a selection of emblematic events from the actual unfolding of a community's early history. In fact, many times they appear to be a combination of both. Myths, by their very nature, are not scientific descriptions or journalistic documentaries, and should not be read in that manner. Myths serve, instead, to carry the fundamental values and worldview understandings of a culture in a manageable, memorable collection of tales.

It is in this way that Genesis functions as an extended historical prologue to the Sinai covenant. The stories of Genesis answer a number of important questions that arise simply because Israel has been shaken loose from four hundred years of enslaved slumber, and is now being reshaped as the marriage partner of God in a divine mission that has not yet been fully clarified. Genesis gives the context to the Suzerain-Vassal treaty formed in Exodus 20–24. It takes important moments from both Israel's distant and recent past, and uses these as the shepherding banks by which direct the flow of the people's river of identity into their new and uncertain future.

Because there is no authorial self-disclosure within the pages of Genesis, we are left to speculate about its specific origins. An interesting and important clue emerges from the text itself when the Hebrew nomenclature for God is analyzed. Most often, especially beginning with the stories of Abram in Gen 12, "Yahweh" (יהוה) is used to name the divinity. According to the book of Exodus, this name emerged in Israel through the deity's self-disclosure to Moses in the encounter between them at Mt. Horeb (Exodus 3). This would indicate that whoever wrote Genesis, and whenever the writing happened, this book was created no earlier than the lifetime of Moses, and functions within the scope of the covenant-making events of Exodus. Thus, if one is to listen to the internal testimony of the literature of the Bible, Genesis must be understood to function as a companion volume to the covenant documents of Israel's national identity formation at Mount Sinai. Therefore, Genesis must be read not as a volume preexisting in a disconnected primeval world, but rather as the interpretation of events leading up to the engagement of Yahweh and Israel at Sinai in the Suzerain-Vassal covenant established there. Genesis is the extended historical prologue of the Sinai covenant.

Viewed this way, the message of Genesis is readily accessible. To begin with, the cosmological origins myths of chapters 1–11 are apologetic devices that announce a very different worldview than that available among and within the cultures which surrounded Israel. The two dominant cosmogonies in the ancient Near East were established by the civilizations of Mesopotamia (filtered largely through Babylonian recitations) and Egypt. Cosmogonic myths describe the origins of the world as we know it, providing a paradigm by which to analyze and interpret contemporary events.

While this may raise eyebrows in a modern world shaped significantly by monotheistic views and theologies, such an understanding of the world was resoundingly different from and overtly challenging to the Egyptian origins myths. Distilled from the various records that are available to us,[30]

---

30. See, for instance, David Adams Leeming, *Creation Myths of the World* (Santa

the generalized creation story of ancient Egypt goes roughly like this. *Nun* was the chaos power pervading the primeval waters. *Atum* was the creative force which lived on *Benben*, a pyramidical hill rising out of the primeval waters. *Atum* split to form the elemental gods *Shu* (air) and *Tefnut* (moisture). *Tefnut* bore two children: *Geb* (god of earth) and *Nut* (goddess of the skies). These, in turn gave birth to lesser gods who differentiated among themselves and came to rule various dimensions of the world as we now know it. Humanity was a final and unplanned outcome, with these newly produced weaklings useful only to do the work that the gods no longer wished to do, and to feed the gods by way of burning animal flesh as a means to transform the physical food into a form—vaporous smoke—that was accessible to the gods.

Similar, and yet uniquely nuanced, are the cosmogonies of ancient Mesopotamia.[31] The name *Mesopotamia* literally means "between the waters." It denotes that region of the Near East encompassed by the combined watersheds of the Tigris and Euphrates rivers. Early civilizations here, enveloped by a somewhat different climatic environment than that found in Egypt, reflected this uniqueness in their origin myths. *Apsu* was the chaos power resident in the primeval waters. *Tiamat* was the bitter sea within the primeval waters upon which earth floated. *Lhamu* and *Lahamu* were gods of silt (at the edges of earth) created from the interaction of the primeval waters and the bitter seas. The horizons, *Anshar* and *Kishar*, were separated from one another by the birth of their child *Anu* (sky). *Anu* engendered *Ea-Nudimmud*, the god of earth and wisdom. All of these gods were filled with pent-up energy and this caused them to fight constantly. Since they existed within the belly of *Tiamat*, *Apsu* got indigestion and made plans to destroy all his restless and noisy children (i.e., the rest of the gods). In order to survive, *Ea* cast a spell which put *Apsu* to sleep. Then *Ea* killed *Apsu*, but his remains formed new gods, all of which were now in bitter struggle with each other and with their older relatives. Among the gods, *Marduk* rose as champion, quelling the fights and resurrecting order. To celebrate his success, *Marduk* created Babylon, which thus became the center of the universe and the source of all human civilization. These late-on-the-scene beings were created from the spilled blood of the gods, and they were deliberately fashioned as slaves who would do the work that the gods no longer wished to do.

Barbara, CA: ABC-CLIO, 2010); George Hart, *Egyptian Myths* (Austin, TX: University of Texas, 2004).

31. Cf., *Myths from Mesopotamia: Creation, The Flood, Gilgamesh, and Others*, edited by Stephanie Dalley (Oxford: Oxford University Press, 2000).

A Different Understanding

When placed alongside these other cosmogonic myths, the Genesis creation story is very spare and poetically balanced. In brief testimony it declares that God existed before the world that is apprehended by our senses was brought into being. It also asserts that creation happened by way of divine speech rather than through the sexual interaction of deities, or as the animation of guts and gore left over and emerging out of their conflicts. Moreover, creation was an intentional act that took place by way of orderly progression:

- Day 1: Arenas for Light and Darkness
- Day 2: Arenas for Sky and Sea
- Day 3: Arenas for Earth's dominant surfaces
- Day 4: Inhabitants of Light and Darkness
- Day 5: Inhabitants of Sky and Sea
- Day 6: Inhabitants of Earth

In the balanced rhythm of poetic prose, the Genesis creation story shows how divine planning and purpose brought the world into being specifically as a home for humanity. These creatures are not the byproduct of restless fighting among the gods. Nor are they a slave race produced in order to give the gods more leisure. In fact, according to the Genesis account, human beings are the only creatures made in the image of God, thus sharing the best of divine qualities.

It is obvious from the careful structuring of the Genesis creation account that it is neither a journalistic description of sequential events, nor the scientific report of an unfolding lab experiment. "Light" is the first "creation," cutting through and overturning the power of darkness and chaos which otherwise precluded meaningful existence. Yet the sources of light that actually make illumination happen in our world do not begin to exist until the fourth "day" of creation. What is going on? Why are things about creation expressed in this manner?

The answer seems to be a combination of contrast and organization. All other ancient stories of cosmological beginnings also start with chaos, but none of them ever fully emerges from it. Elements of random functionality may present themselves at times in or out from chaos, but behind and above and around such moments of meaningful structure the cosmos remains a chaotic entity. In some civilizations competing forces within chaos (such as *yin* and *yang*) may balance one another enough to provide temporary stability and even creative energy. Yet they remain the restless tentacles of chaos which pervades everything.

The Genesis cosmological myth sees the world very differently. Before existence and chaos, there is/was God. Existence itself is not the roiling of quasi-independent powers, but the expression of thoughtful divine intent. The manner in which things came into being had purpose and organizational structuring from the start.

If, as the literature itself requires, the creation stories of Genesis 1–2 are part of a lengthy historical prologue to the meeting of Yahweh and Israel at Mount Sinai, these cosmogonic myths are not to be read as the end product of scientific or historical analysis. They are designed to place Israel in an entirely different worldview context than that which shaped their neighbors. Humanity's place in this natural realm is one of intimacy with God, rather than fear and slavery. The human race exists in harmony with nature, not as its bitter opponent or only a helpless minor element. Women and men together share creative responsibility with God over animals and plants.

Moreover, there is no hint of evil or sin in the creation stories themselves. In fact, the recurring refrain is that God saw the coming-into-being of each successive wave of creation and declared it to be good. There is no eternal dualism of opposing forces that in their conflict engendered the world as we know it. Nor is the creative energy of human life itself derived from inherent and coequal powers of good and evil which, in their chasing of one another, produce the changes necessary to drive the system. Instead, evil appears only after a fully developed created realm is complete, and then enters as a usurping power that seeks to draw away the reflected creativity of the human race into alliance with forces which deny the Creator's values and goals. Evil and sin are essentially linked to human perspectives that are in competition with the one declared true and genuine by the creation stories themselves.

Recovery Attempts

In Genesis 3–11, following the devastating effects of evil which leach their way through the world, there appear to be two divine attempts to recover the pristine qualities of the original creation. First, after the initial humans step out of the worldview of the Creator and enter the perspectives of the tempter, the Creator displays graciousness in delaying the sentence of death upon them, and also by way of providing promises that this conflict need not end their existence. Instead, the human creatures are driven out of the Garden of Eden, in what seems to be a divine desire to pull them to their senses through the restlessness of homelessness. They become exiles, and their descendants, in order to compensate, build cities as an apparent attempt to regain civility. All these efforts fail, however, and the cancer of disobedience explodes in acts of killing and violence.

Then comes the second recovery effort. Just as his name seems to imply, Noah is heralded as one who will bring "comfort" from the afflictions of both sin and the curses of God that accompany it (Gen 5:29). What takes place, however, is the famous flood story (Gen 6–9) in which God designs a massive "do-over." The natural realm is destroyed, except for a floating biological bank called the ark. Noah and his family are spared the ravages of a massive flood intended to wipe out the terrestrial dimensions of the universe created in Genesis 1. All that survive are the few humans and the species restorers that have been kept safe in the big boat.

In God's instructions to Noah following the flood (Gen 9:1–7), there are clear echoes of the divine mandate given to Adam and Eve in the Garden of Eden (Gen 1:28–30). In other words, the tale of the flood is as much a story of re-creation as it is of judgment and destruction. A new element is added, however, one which would be vital for Israel to understand as it stood before God at Mount Sinai. After the words of blessing by which Noah and his family are given earth again as their home, there are words of self-reflection by the Creator (Gen 9:8–17). For the first time, chronologically speaking, the idea of a "covenant" enters the biblical record. Interestingly here, though, it is shaped in the manner of a Babylonian Royal Grant rather than a Hittite Suzerain-Vassal treaty.

The Babylonian Royal Grant was a formula by which kings could record their acts of beneficence.[32] Unlike the Suzerain-Vassal covenant, it did not bind the receiver of the gift into some form of specific responsive obedience. Instead, it assured the one who had received the gift that this was intended by the king, and could not be revoked by others. Sometimes, in fact, a maledictory oath accompanied the donation, assuring the recipient that the burden of following through on the gift remained the responsibility of the giver. The maledictory oath was a promise, made at the expense of personal well-being, that the king would guarantee the gift.

This is clearly expressed in the divine promise of protection and continuation of earth's natural order in Genesis 9:8–17. There will never again be a catastrophic destruction on the scale of the great flood just finished, nor will any other initiative be launched either by the Creator or by any other threatening power to attempt the annihilation of life on planet Earth.

---

32. J. A. Brinkman, "Babylonian Royal Land Grants, Memorials of Financial Interest, and Invocation of the Divine," *Journal of the Economic and Social History of the Orient* 49 (2006) 1–47.

A sign accompanied this assertion, but not as a reminder to humanity. Instead, God declared that the bow in the heavens will frequently appear as a recurring memory jogger *for the deity*. There is no word for "rainbow" in the Hebrew language; the term used in this divine speech is simply "bow," like the weapon a hunter brought into the forest after his prey or an archer stretched with arrows on the field of battle. Understood as it was initially intended, the "bow" thus takes on sinister significance. Whenever God viewed the bow, it was curved with tension, ready to release its projectile. Toward heaven. The implication would be clear to the ancient Israelites. God was taking a self-maledictory oath as part of this Royal Grant to spare creation; in it the deity professed self-annihilation if no other solution was found to bring safety and everlasting continuity to the natural order, including the human race. This, in anticipation, heightened the significance of the role of the divine mediator both in its Israelite context and beyond.

In the end, neither remedy intended to countermand the intrusion of evil into the world order, which had been created "good," had any lasting merit. On the one hand, Eden's exiles fabricated cities where, rather than finding a return to the garden, they compounded the menace and suffering of sin. Similarly with the other initiative: the re-creation attempted through Noah failed, as the stories immediately following show. Noah's son Ham ridiculed his drunken father, resulting in a sharp curse placed upon his descendants (Gen 9:20–25). Then the entire human community gathered itself into a monolithic empire that threatened to become self-sufficient (Gen 11:1–9). Suddenly evil resided not only in specific individuals who did bad things, but took on a corporate face. As God challenged this power play the story turned in a new and decisive direction.

Three Story Cycles

If Genesis 1–11 is analogous to the cosmogonic myths that informed the societies among which young Israel was wrestling for a place, the rest of the book has a character not unlike that of the ancestor hero stories which also shaped other national cultures. Once again, comparing the tales of Abraham, Isaac, Jacob and Joseph to the mythology of neighboring civilizations does not imply that these biblical tales are false or untrue. Rather, it is helpful to see the manner in which the literature functions in defining the identity of the emerging culture; ancestor hero stories provide a genre of comparison. In other words, the narratives of the patriarchs are not merely documentary history through which Israel could fashion a set of lively bedtime stories. Instead, the very heart of Israel's identity was shaped as the nation reflected on certain aspects of the lives of its forebears. For this reason, there is no complete history of Abraham, or entire biography of Isaac, or fully developed life of Jacob. Indeed, one would be hard pressed to formulate these from the limited amount of historical information given about each.

Instead, the purpose of these stories, particularly since they appear to emerge from the Sinai covenant-making events of Exodus, is to provide a basis for Israel to understand who she is as a nation. This becomes more apparent when the essential focus of each major story cycle is probed.

Although later references to Israel's ancestral parentage would emerge as the standardized phrase "Abraham, Isaac and Jacob," in reality the second part of Genesis contains three major story cycles in which Isaac is only a footnote to those of Abraham and Jacob, and Joseph is added as a key player in the larger drama. In rough overview, Genesis 12–50 may be outlined in this manner:

- Abraham story cycle (chapters 12–25)
- Jacob story cycle (chapters 26–36)
- Joseph story cycle (chapters 37–50)

Each of these story cycles adds a unique element to Israel's self-identity when read backwards from the covenant-making ceremony at Mount Sinai. In this way they form, with Genesis 1–11, a deliberate extended historical prologue to the Suzerain-Vassal treaty by staging that event over against the prevailing worldviews of the day, and within a certain missional context that illumines the purpose of Israel's existence and the reason why Yahweh takes such interest in this tiny nation.

The Abraham Story Cycle

Abram is an Aramean from the heart of Mesopotamia, whose father Terah begins a journey westward which Abram continues upon his father's death. Whatever Terah's reasons might have been for moving from the old family village—restlessness, treasure-seeking, displacement, wanderlust—Genesis 12 informs us that Abram's continuation of the trek was motivated by a divine call to seek a land which would become his by providential appointment. This is the first of four similar divine declarations that occur in quick succession in chapters 12, 13, 15, and 17. Such repetition cues us to the importance of these theophanies, but it ought to also cause us to look more closely at the forms in which the promises to Abram are made.

In brief, Abram's first three encounters with God are shaped literarily as Royal Grants. Only in Genesis 17 does the language of the dialogue change, and elements are added to give it the flavor of a Suzerain-Vassal covenant. This is very significant. When Abram receives Royal Grant promises of land or a son, he seems to treat these divine offerings with a mixture of indifference and skepticism. He immediately leaves the land of promise in Genesis 12, and connives with his wife Sarai and her handmaid Hagar to obtain an heir in Genesis 16. Even in the stories of Genesis 13–14, where Abram sticks with the land and fights others to regain his nephew Lot from them after local skirmishes and kidnappings, Abram turns his thankfulness toward a local expression of religious devotion through the mystical figure of Melchizedek (Gen 14:18–20). Only when God changes the language of covenant discourse, bringing *Abram* into the partnership of a Suzerain-Vassal bond, does *Abraham* enter fidelity and commitment to this new world and new purpose and new journey.

For Israel, standing at Mount Sinai in the context of a Suzerain-Vassal covenant-making ceremony, the implications would be striking. First of all, the nation would see itself as the unique and miraculously born child fulfilling a divine promise. Israel could not exist were it not for God's unusual efforts at getting Abram and Sarai pregnant in a way that was humanly impossible. Second, the people were the descendants of a man on a divine pilgrimage. Not only was Abram *en route* to a land of promise, but he was also the instrument of God for the blessing of all the nations of the earth. In other words, Israel was born with a mandate, and it was globally encompassing. Third, while these tribes had recently emerged from Egypt as a despised social underclass of disenfranchised slaves, they were actually landowners. Canaan was theirs for the taking because they already owned it! They would not enter the land by stealth, but through the front door; they would claim the land, not by surreptitious means or mere battlefield bloodshed, but as rightful owners going home. This would greatly affect their common psyche: they were the long-lost heirs of a kingdom, returning to claim their royal privilege and possessions. Fourth, there was a selection in the process of creating their identity. They were children of Abraham, but so were a number of area tribes and nations descending from Ishmael. What made them special was the uniqueness of their lineage through Isaac, the miraculously born child of Abram and Sarai's old age. Israel had international kinship relations, but she also retained a unique identity fostered by the divine distinctions between branches of the family. Fifth, in the progression of the dialogue between Yahweh and Abram, there was a call to participation in the mission of God. As the story of Abram unfolded, it was clear that his commitment to God's plans was minimal at best until the change from Royal Grants (Gen 12; 13; 15) to the Suzerain-Vassal covenant of chapter 17. Each time Abram was given a gift, he seemingly threw it away, tried to take it by force, or manipulated his circumstances so that he controlled his destiny; only when God took formal ownership of both Abram and the situation through the Suzerain-Vassal Covenant of Genesis 17 was there a marked change in Abram's participation in the divine initiative. The renaming of Abram and Sarai to Abraham and Sarah were only partly significant for the meaning of the names; mostly they were a deliberate and public declaration that God owned them. To name meant to have power over, just as was the case when a divine word created the elements of the universe in Genesis 1, and when Adam named the animals in Genesis 2. Furthermore, in the call to circumcise all the males of the family, God transformed a widely used social rite of passage symbol into a visible mark of belonging now no longer tied to personal achievements like battlefield wins or hunting success, but merely to the gracious goodness of God, and participation in the divine mission.

But what was that divine mission? Only when Israel heard the rest of the covenant prologue, and then followed Moses to the promised land, would it become clear. Still, in recalling the tale of father Abraham in this manner, Genesis places before Israel at Sinai a very important element of its profound identity: we came into this world miraculously as a result of a divine initiative to bless all the nations of the earth; therefore, we are a unique people with the powerful backing of the Creator, and participating in a mission that is still in progress.

The Jacob Story Cycle

Only a few details of Isaac's life are told on the pages of Genesis, and they occur in the transitional paragraphs from the Abraham story cycle (Gen 12–25) to the Jacob story cycle (Gen 26–37). Isaac is to have a wife from within Terah's larger family back in the old country, and this is accomplished through clear divine intervention and leading (chapter 24). To Isaac and Rebecca are born twins who are opposites in character, and always in competition with one another (chapter 25). Rather than emerging with an identity of his own, Isaac seems doomed to repeat his father's mistakes (chapter 26).

After those few notes, Jacob takes center stage. He is a conniver from birth (Gen 25:21–34), favored by his mother (Gen 25:28; 27:1–28:9), cheats his family (father Isaac—27:1–39; brother Esau—25:29–34, 27:1–39; uncle Laban—30:25–43; daughter Dinah—34:1–31), works for his uncle Laban to earn wives Leah and Rachel (Gen 29:15–30) and cattle (Gen 30:25–43), is cheated by his uncle (Gen 29:25–27), afraid of his brother (Gen 32:3–21), a cowardly wrestler with God (Gen 32:22–32), and finally receives the covenant blessing and mandate (Gen 35:1–15).

While all of these stories are fascinating in themselves, there are two significant themes that emerge as dominant. First, in the character of Jacob, the nation of Israel will always find itself reflected. After all, it is Jacob who bequeaths his special covenant name "Israel" to the community formed by his descendants. Hearing about Jacob and his exploits would be like reading a secret diary mapping Israel's psychological profile. Even before leaving Egypt, the people were wrangling with Moses about burdens and responsibilities, seeking ways to shift workloads and blames elsewhere. Once the wilderness trek began, a variety of conniving subterfuges showed up, including complaints about who really had a right to lead. The spirit of Jacob remained with his namesakes.

Second, the meaning of the name "Israel" and the circumstances surrounding it became a defining moment in Israel's theology. Rarely does the text of Genesis crack open to reveal an origin outside of its narrative timeline, but as the tale of Jacob's night-long wrestling match concludes, there is indeed a note that identifies the organized nation of Israel as the audience reviewing these matters (Gen 32:32). The story itself is more sordid than it appears at first glance. Jacob and his amassed company are heading back home to Canaan. Jacob hopes that his brother Esau has miraculously had a bout of amnesia and is excited to welcome him with no dark thoughts about Jacob's nasty subterfuge a few decades earlier. But Esau has a good memory, and the report quickly arrives that the maligned brother is racing toward Jacob's retinue at the center of an aggressive army seeking revenge.

Always the manipulator, Jacob strategizes ways to save his skin. First, he splits the caravan in two, hoping Esau will target the wrong camp. Then large gifts are sent ahead in the expectation that Esau will be slowed by the herds offered, and his men distracted by the feasts of fresh roasted meat from the animals they are given. Perhaps a little drunkenness might accompany the barbecue rituals, and because of these subterfuges, Jacob's groups will be able to slip past in the night.

But Jacob knows the depth of his guilt, and his manic attempts at self-preservation continue. He sends his wives and children and remaining possessions across the Jabok River while he remains behind. This is a sinister and cowardly move, for it exposes Jacob's family to the possible onslaught of Esau's army without the moderate natural moat of the river to make their position more defensible. Meantime, Jacob himself would be sitting in the protection of the rearward hills, and will have the advantage of hearing the screams of his children and wives while they are slaughtered as a warning order to escape, even if they do not. Jacob is always the conniver, and a master of self-preservation.

Yet it is here, in the quarters where he had taken such pains to make himself safe, that he becomes most vulnerable. "A man wrestled with him till daybreak" (Gen 32:24). We know even less about this figure than the little that Jacob seems to know. Nevertheless, both he and we are to infer that this was a divine engagement, and that God would not allow Jacob's hiding to keep him aloof from the court of heaven or a confrontation with himself and the tests of righteousness. At the same time, there is a graciousness in the story that reminds us that the divine messenger does not overpower or overwhelm Jacob, but continues to grapple with him, and even provides a blessing he does not deserve. This, then, is the meaning of "Israel"—one who wrestles with God.

Looking back at Jacob, Israel at Mount Sinai would see herself. She carried the conniving DNA of her forebear in her social makeup. But here at Mount Sinai she also carried his divinely appointed name. In the Suzerain-Vassal covenant Yahweh formulated with her, the wrestling continued. Yahweh and Israel were bound in an embrace that would change them both.

The Joseph Story Cycle

Although Abraham hears a disembodied voice and Jacob has a vision of heaven one night at Bethel, it is Joseph whose Genesis record is entirely shaped by dreams. He enters the narrative as a self-absorbed, privileged son, who foolishly antagonizes his family by reporting nighttime revelations that he is the most important among them, destined to become their lord and master (Gen 37:2–11). His arrogance precipitates a plot among his siblings to get rid of him (Gen 37:12–35), and this brings him to Egypt as a slave (Gen 37:36; 38:1–6). Now the dreaming takes center stage again as Joseph is unjustly thrown in prison (Gen 39:7–23) where he meets two men from the Pharaoh's court who are awaiting adjudication on treason charges (Gen 40:1–4). They each have dreams (Gen 40:5–8), which Joseph is able to interpret (Gen 40:9–19) in a way entirely consistent with the events that follow (Gen 40:20–22).

Joseph's unique skills come to the attention of the Pharaoh two years later, when the ruler's nighttime reveries plague him like a nightmare, and Joseph is brought in to make sense of it all (Gen 40:23–41:36). This earns Joseph a spot as co-regent of Egypt (Gen 41:37–57), and it is from this position that he becomes savior of his family during the ensuing famine (Gen 42–46). Joseph's tale ends with his sons Manasseh and Ephraim gaining equal status with Jacob's other sons in the inheritance distributions (Gen 48–49), and Joseph burying his father with honors in Canaan (Gen 50:1–14) while keeping alive the dream of having the whole family return there one day when the current crisis had passed (Gen 50:15–26).

In its focus on dreams, the Joseph story cycle that concludes Genesis deals with two issues. First, it answers the question of how this nation of Israel, springing from such illustrious stock, become an enslaved people in land not their own. Second, it creates a vision for the way in which the future is brighter than the past: along with their forebear Joseph, they need only take hold of the dream of God for them.

The Meta-Narrative of Genesis

When viewed through its obvious literary development, the book of Genesis is reasonably perceived as an extended historical prologue to the Sinai covenant. It provides the information necessary for Israel to understand why Yahweh is establishing this treaty with this particular people and what will be the outcome of it. In its pages are described the divine explanations about the character of reality, including creation's original goodness and the devastating effects of sin. Genesis informs Israel of God's long-standing plan to reassert divine connections with all the races of humanity, and that this is now to be done through a particular community shaped by way of the Sinai Suzerain-Vassal covenant. Furthermore, Genesis describes Israel's unique, miraculous origins, and spells out something of its edgy character. Finally, it explains the more recent history that tells why Israel was in Egypt rather than in Canaan, where it belonged.

In effect, the literary design of Genesis, in its largest arcs, has this shape:

- **1–11 Origins Story Cycle**

  - What is the nature of reality?

  - It is divinely good, but thoroughly contaminated by evil.

- **12–25 Abraham Story Cycle**

  - Who are we as a unique people?

  - We are miraculously born to be God's witness to the nations.

- **26–36 Jacob Story Cycle**

  - What is our character as a people?

- We are deceitful connivers who nevertheless wrestle with God, and God with us.

- 37–50 Joseph Story Cycle

  - How did we get to Egypt?

    By dreaming our own dreams

  - How did we get out of Egypt?

    By dreaming the dreams of God

Genesis, then, cannot be separated from Exodus, because it is first of all addressed to the nation of Israel standing at Mount Sinai, gaining its new identity through the Suzerain-Vassal covenant being made there. Furthermore, Genesis is not an independent text of either mere ancestor stories or chronologies of creation and national origins. Because it is literature that illumines the Sinai covenant, it only gives information relative to that event. Chapters 1–2 are not so much about the documentation of timelines and details in the divine creative activity, as they are a clearly articulated worldview against the current understandings of humanity and the natural realm found in neighboring nations. The Sinai covenant only makes sense if there is a sovereign creator who still has a stake in human society. Furthermore, although sin and evil are part of the pervasive common earthbound experience, these are not coequal or coeternal with God, good, or the way things are supposed to be. Finally, Israel's unique patrimony contains a story that separates this nation from the rest of humanity, not in anthropological superiority, but in mission and mandate.

The four worldview questions addressed on the pages of Genesis linger throughout history as critical issues of human life and society. As Modernism swept the sacral world out of the heavens, Postmodernism continues to look for meaning somewhere in the clouds of dust below. The four questions of Genesis serve as a link between the biblical record and current quests for meaning.

What is the nature of the universe in which we are living? Is it a random collection of happenstance occurrences that is at best the provenance of chaotic fate, and at worst weighted against us by vindictive unseen powers? Or is it the product of a loving, intelligent, and personal deity who is still seeking restoration and renewal with the human race after our centuries of bratty willfulness that have nearly annihilated civilization?

What is the unique purpose and meaning of the "church" or the "people of God? Does religion (or at least Christianity) make one deluded and irrelevant? Is there meaning that goes beyond repetitive ritual to be found in becoming part of a religious movement? Why is "mission" so important to the church and what is the truest nature of that mission? Are we still on the journey of Abraham, and what is the blessing we are holding out to the nations of this world?

Who are we in our core beings? Just because we were born and raised in the church, does that mean we are more noble, more pious, more godly, or more deserving than others who did not have the same heritage? What does it mean to be a scrapping human being? Who are we fighting for, even in our "religious wars?" What happens to us when God comes down to wrestle with us? Who is winning? Who is losing? And what does the wrestling itself mean for how we understand our nature and our place in life?

How did we get to Egypt? How did we get to Chicago, to New York, to Johannesburg, to Moscow, to Des Moines, to Mexico City, to Kyoto, to La Paz, to Padunkaville? What are the dreams we are chasing in our mad pursuit of self? In what prisons do we find ourselves the morning after we've seen our names in bright lights? Is there another dream to see, a vision to grasp, a world still waiting to be born that gives us a context in which to live and move and breathe and grow again? How are we going to get out of Egypt? When will we begin to dream the dream of God?

The Morally Weighted Genealogies of Genesis

This grand perspective of Genesis is confirmed by another literary overlay that subtly weaves together all of the smaller sections of Genesis. A recurring textual device in the book is the phrase "These are the generations of . . . " (2:4; 5:1; 6:9; 10:1; 11:10; 11:27; 25:12; 25:19; 36:1; 37:2). When surveying the book through this grid, several ideas emerge. First, the initial story of the creation (Gen 1:1–2:3) does not begin with this phrase, and therefore stands apart from the rest of the sections that follow. Second, these subsequent ten sections, which each begin with the phrase, appear to be morally weighted, so that the dominant evaluation in each is either positive or negative with respect to responsive obedience or disobedience to God. Third, there is a progression to the series which highlights the unique character and role of the group that will ultimately emerge as the nation of Israel.

The outcome is an unfolding explanation of human history which moves from original perfection (the creation story of Gen 1:1–2:3), through the corrupting influence of individual expressions of sin and rebellion (the "generations" of "heaven and earth" and "Adam"),[33] into a divine response

33. Gen 2:4–5:32.

that targets an individual for salvation (the "generation" of "Noah");[34] this is followed by a communal rebellion (the "generation" of the "Sons of Noah"),[35] precipitating a divine counteraction which produces a community designed for obedient witness (the "generations" of "Shem" and "Terah").[36] Along the way this family experiences separations tracking the line of the missional community (the "generations" of "Isaac" and "Jacob") in distinction from others (the "generations" of "Ishmael" and "Esau").

By the time Genesis ends, Israel at Mount Sinai is placed into an interpreted natural order shaped by a particular worldview, has been informed about its unique calling and character, and understands the reason for Yahweh's recent political battle and victory over the Pharaoh of Egypt in order to reclaim Israel as a redemptive community of witness. In response to the failed attempts at winning back humanity by way of the homeless restlessness of Adam and Eve and their early decedents just outside the Garden of Eden, and again through the re-creative efforts to restart the human race through Noah following the purging flood, Israel now can see its place as a nation with a peculiar identity that is intended to become a city on the hill, providing a divinely inspired lifestyle and religion in contrast to those which are more or less the products of human invention gone bad.

The hope for a global return of humanity to its Creator looms large in the excitement of the Exodus and the establishment of Israel as a witnessing community on the world stage of Canaan. But this "Day of the Lord" fizzles precipitously over time. As the strength of the theocratic kingdom wanes, Israel's prophets look for a new divine intrusion, and talk of the "Day of the Lord" becomes emblematic.

34. Gen 6–9.

35. Gen 10–11.

36. Gen 12–50.

2

Eschatological Expectation

"Day of the Lord" as Prophetic
Warning and Hope

ALTHOUGH THE STORY OF Israel's origins and unique deliverance continues almost without disruption into the book of Joshua, the literary character changes dramatically. Instead of focusing primarily on what Yahweh has done and is doing to stake a missional claim in the ancient Near East, the vantage point shifts to terrestrial action. True, it is still Yahweh who serves as Israel's commander in chief, but the emphasis is refocused toward how the army itself is faring on the battlefield.

The book of Joshua is clearly all about the land of Canaan. The Israelites presume to own it, even though they have never lived there. Yahweh declares it to be their homeland, even though, in order for this to become a reality, bloody battles will ensue, and current settled communities will have to be displaced or destroyed. The promises made to Abraham (Gen 12; 13; 17), owned by Jacob (Gen 28; 35; 50), and claimed by Joseph (Gen 50) serve as the theological justification for taking by force what, from a human point of view, belongs to other people. This is the critical issue that must be faced when reading Joshua. Either Canaan, as a specific piece of territory, has a deeply religious significance, which is used by Yahweh and Israel in a certain way for ends that are meant to bless the surrounding nations, or it is a scandalous record of cruelty done by nasty people who wash their defiled consciences in a horrible pious testimony, "The Deity made me do it!" Only if the Pentateuch is indeed a revelation of God with a missional intent that is to be accomplished through the nation of Israel, does this sordid chapter in Israelite and human history make sense. Even facing this matter head on does not make the conquest of Canaan easily palatable. No serious student of the Bible ought to dance lightly through these pages and make facile judgments. Either Yahweh is engaged in a crucial galactic civil war battle to wrestle humanity back to its creational senses, and Israel is to play a part in that decisive conflict, or the religions of Judaism, Christianity, and Islam are built upon a scandalous foundation of inflated, self-important delusion. The book of Joshua forces us to face the desperation of biblical religion: Is this simply another moralistic ethic among the do-gooder philosophies of the nations, or is there a unique and all-encompassing polarizing choice engendered by this worldview that demands allegiance or condemnation?

In answering this dilemma, what is at stake is an understanding of the unique location and purpose of a small piece of real estate. There are four major literary sections to the book of Joshua, and each is focused on "the Land":

Penetrating the Land (chapters 1–5)

Purging the Land (chapters 6–12)

Possessing the Land (chapters 13–21)

Promising the Land (chapters 22–24)

The identity of Israel will become inextricably connected to this land. Canaan, as a divinely designated homeland, is ineradicably intertwined with Hebrew theology. The location becomes essential to Israelite self-perception, so it is very important to ask why: Why this land, and not some other, better paradise? Why this piece of property, rather than an uninhabited region of northern Europe, or a tropical island in the South Pacific? What is so terribly important about this land, that it has become a constant source of theological embarrassment to generations of biblical scholars and the enemies of Judaism and Christianity?

Penetrating the Land (Joshua 1–5)

The restless energy at the close of Joshua 1 is almost palpable. After forty years of promises and delays, the final fight for the homeland is on! So, the story of the spies in Joshua 2 seems at first chronologically misplaced. After all, in Joshua 1:11, the command to cross the Jordan River begins a three-day countdown, while the full scope of the action described in Joshua 2 could not possibly fit into that time frame. It is precisely in this seeming anomaly that the clear intentionality of the literature of Joshua is seen. There is more than meets the eye initially in both the development and placement of chapter 2.

This story of the spies sent to Jericho is told chiastically. "Chiasm" is the name given to reflexive enveloping repetitions that are frequently found in Hebrew poetry and storytelling. Whereas Western linear thought tends to flow either inductively (with the information proffered building toward a concluding climax), or deductively (with a thesis declared at the beginning, followed by supporting evidence and implications), chiasm flows out from a normative center. The name "chiasm" is derived from the Greek letter *chi*, the form of which is sometimes used to describe the literary movement of the lines or themes in chiastic section.[1]

While we are not accustomed to hearing or reading literature that is shaped in this manner, the ancient Hebrews had both an eye and an ear for it, as is evident in the wide use of chiasm throughout the Old Testament. Here in Joshua 2, the impact of chiastic literary flow would be immediately apparent. For our untrained senses, a diagram will help us see what was obvious then:

Spies commissioned (2:1)

  Officers of the king [of Jericho] address Rahab (2:2–3)

    Rahab saves the spies (2:4–7)

      Rahab declares Yahweh's victory (2:8–10)

        Rahab's great testimony (2:11): "Yahweh your God is God in heaven above and on the earth below."

      Rahab declares Yahweh's victory (2:11–13)

    Rahab saves the spies (2:14–16)

  Officers of the King [of Heaven and Earth] address Rahab (2:17–21)

Spies debriefed (2:22–24)

---

1. Chiasm is the name given to a reflexive mirror parallelism in Hebrew poetry and storytelling:

Idea A

  Idea B

    Idea C

  Idea B1

Idea A1

The main idea or implications are declared at the center of the passage ("C"). When diagrammed, the Greek letter *chi* (χ) is often used to show the movement of the ideas; hence "chiasm."

Idea A   *Idea B*

      χ *Idea C*

Idea B1   *Idea A1*

When read or heard in this manner, the literary purpose of the story becomes much more obvious, and the placement crucial. Although the events that are reported may have happened a week or two prior to the actual crossing of the Jordan River, the meaning of the spies' encounter in Jericho is of paramount significance to those who are suddenly stepping into the churning waters, fearing both its tumult and the turmoil that waits on the other side. Rahab is a representative of the people of Canaan, and as such she gives a testimony that would bolster Israel's challenged nerve. She declares that the peoples of Canaan already know the power and domination of Yahweh, Israel's God. This is a particularly striking statement coming from Rahab, whose occupation of prostitution may well tie her to the religious shrines of Jericho and its official priesthood.[2] Whatever her station in that city's society, she gives an unequivocal report, as a member of the enemy community, that Yahweh has already crossed into the land and possessed it. All Israel has to do is follow Yahweh.

Rahab's testimony is a reminder that Yahweh is not merely a tribal god owned by Israel. Instead, Yahweh is the Supreme Divinity over both territory and lesser gods. Every nation ought to bow to Yahweh, as Rahab has already begun to do. Israel need only go into the land to perform the mopping-up operations, for the decisive battle has already been won. Whatever "Day of the Lord" is taking place, it is not at the initiation of Israel, but part of the divine intrusion into human history for the sake of restoring the creational designs.

This message is confirmed in several ways in the next three chapters. First, the crossing of the wild waters of the Jordan River is told in a way reminiscent of Israel's movement through the Red Sea a generation earlier (Exod 14). Both situations required a divine act to overcome a natural barrier. The single significant difference between the former story and this one is that then, Moses was the vehicle for dispensing the power of Yahweh as he stood with arm and staff outstretched over the Red Sea, and now it is the

---

2. Herodotus writes pointedly about such practices in *The Histories* 1.199: "The foulest Babylonian custom is that which compels every woman of the land to sit in the temple of Aphrodite and have intercourse with some stranger at least once in her life. . . . most sit down in the sacred plot of Aphrodite, with crowns of cord on their heads; there is a great multitude of women coming and going; passages marked by line run every way through the crowd, by which the men pass and make their choice. Once a woman has taken her place there, she does not go away to her home before some stranger has cast money into her lap, and had intercourse with her outside the temple . . . It does not matter what sum the money is; the woman will never refuse, for that would be a sin, the money being by this act made sacred. So she follows the first man who casts it and rejects no one." See also James Frazer, *The Golden Bow*, chapter 31; Fernando Henriques, *Prostitution and Society: A Study* (London: MacGibbon & Kee, 1962), I,1.

visible portable throne of Yahweh (the Ark of the Covenant) which moves ahead of the people to stem the flow. In both instances, it was the power of Yahweh that parted the waters; now there is the added luxury of having that royal action expressed in a more direct manifestation of Yahweh's local movements through the furnishings of the house of the Deity resident among the people.

Second, a memorial is created out of twelve stones gathered from the riverbed. These stones would be rounded and smooth from years of polishing as the currents pushed and tumbled them along the riverbed. Therefore, they would look strikingly different from the rocks that littered the torrent's banks and formed the cliffs at its edges. The Israelites were supposed to take family outings to this site in the subsequent years and have picnics next to the pile. The unusual monument was to be used as a teaching tool, reminding the next generations what Yahweh had done to create their unique identity and settle them in this land.

Third, the report of this miraculous act of crossing the Jordan River at flood stage zipped along the gossip channels of the nations and tribes living in Canaan, until a great fear of Israel and her God enveloped all of them. This is the only reason why Joshua can then command what has to be either the greatest act of leadership lunacy in the history of warfare, or its ultimate act of confidence and faith: On the west bank of the Jordan, standing on enemy territory, in full sight of the great sentinel city of Jericho, Joshua orders all Israel's males to be circumcised. Such an act would effectively render the entire army of Israel helpless for about a week. Only if there was absolute certainty that Yahweh was, in fact, in control of this land already, as Rahab had testified, would this debilitating decision make sense. In the days ahead, as the Israelites were going to go into battle stripped down and naked, their circumcision might be the only armor they would wear. It would remind them of the promises of their covenant Suzerain, and serve as identifying markings for their fellow comrades on the battlefield, where all men would otherwise look alike.

Fourth, the Israelites cross the Jordan River at exactly the same time of the year as when the nation, a generation before, left Egypt (Josh 5:10). This "coincidence" effectively ties together the exodus from Egypt and the entrance into the promised land, as if no time at all had elapsed between the two. In effect, the waywardness of the wilderness generation is dismissed from the history books like it never happened. This seems to be the implication of the note in Joshua 5:9: *Then Yahweh said to Joshua, "Today I have rolled away the reproach of Egypt from you."*

Fifth, the miraculous food (*manna*), divinely dispensed during the wilderness wanderings, suddenly ceases (Josh 5:11–12). Now that the

Israelites are "home," they have a right to eat from the food provided by the divine inheritance.

Sixth, there is the strange and powerful story of Joshua and his midnight restlessness that causes him to wander sleepless on the plains of Jericho, the night before the confrontation with the residents of Canaan is to take place (Josh 5:13–15). Out of the black night suddenly looms a mighty warrior who blocks Joshua's path. Reaching for his sword, Joshua demands to know which side this brute soldier is on: "Are you for us or them?" The stranger's response seems odd at first: "Neither!" (In Hebrew, it is actually simply the strong word "No!") Yet when he introduces himself, it all makes sense. He is, he declares, the "commander of the army of Yahweh." This information puts everything else into perspective. Joshua may be called and commissioned by Yahweh to serve a mighty leadership purpose, but he is not the field operations commander. Yahweh has deployed several regiments to fight the war ahead, and Israel, under Joshua's leadership, is only one of those divisions. Even Joshua must respond to a general with more stars, as the theater of operations erupts. Thus, it is clear that Yahweh is the great Suzerain, not just over Israel, but throughout the universe; Israel's part in the battle is only a single facet of a larger engagement God is waging in the cosmic civil war, where only one Creator-Divinity can ultimately be sovereign.

This reminder, at the start of the conquest of Canaan, recapitulates the message of both Genesis and Exodus, that the world has lost its bearings and has come under the sway of evil forces. The mission of God is the game plan outlined in the Bible—to reclaim the territory and beings created good at the beginning of time, but to do so in a way that enlists a human community shaped by the covenant in the enterprise, and maintains general human freedom of choice when calling all back to the Creator. The "Day of the Lord" is underway.

Purging the Land (Joshua 6–12)

The conquest of Jericho seems very odd when first read. Why would Yahweh order that a huge contingent of Israelites march around the city day after day, led by armed warriors and priests blowing trumpets, and followed by another weapons-ready contingent? And why would Yahweh wish, in this strange foray, to have the Ark of the Covenant lifted to shoulder height, bobbing around at the center of the swarm that circles the city? Furthermore, why should the walls of Jericho fall of their own accord in this encounter, rather than be left to the usual siege tactics that will be employed by the Israelite army throughout the rest of the conquest battles?

There are several unique things about Jericho and its situation that called for unusual action in bringing it down. First, this is the initial battle on the soil of Canaan itself. For that reason, it is likely that Yahweh wanted to make perfectly clear to both Israel and the nations of the region that this was a divine engagement. Israel needed to experience the power of a conquest that was not pinned on its ability to produce, by way of military strength, and the other city-states and nations of Canaan had to learn quick fear of the God who energized this invading horde. Both were accomplished through the unusual battle tactics at Jericho reiterating that this is not the "Day of Israel;" it is the "Day of the Lord!"

In this regard, it is helpful to visualize the manner in which the citizens of Jericho would have observed the week-long march of the Israelite armies. In effect, it would look like a mighty flood rippling and flowing around the city, with all the individual marchers disappearing into a kind of tidal wave. Meanwhile, the Ark of the Covenant would appear to be floating on top of this undulating "liquid," at its very center. The correspondence between the name for Noah's boat in Genesis 6–9 and that given to the portable throne of Yahweh in this era can hardly be a coincidence. What the people of Jericho were to imagine was a fright similar to that experienced by the ancient civilizations when the waters of judgment roiled about them, and the ark floated above them in anticipation of the next stage in human civilization. Indeed, it is the tumult of Yahweh's judgment against this land that will wipe the slate clean and start a new human community where the old one disappeared. As Noah and his family rode the ark in safety above God's judgment on the nations of earth, so now Joshua and Israel are in the care of the ark, as a new tide of divine condemnation sweeps through.

Second, the site of Jericho was no accident. There were several major trade routes crossing the ancient Near East, and Jericho sat on the gateway to Canaan from what was called "the King's Highway."[3] This dominant artery of commerce, communication, and conquest ran from Damascus to Egypt just east of the Jordan River. One of the reasons for Jericho's wealth and strength was that it controlled access to any trade entering the land from the east. In other words, Jericho formed the door and welcome mat into Canaan. If Israel was to give the land a new identity, the old door and welcome mat had to be thrown out. This appears to be the significance of the

---

3. This highway is referred to twice in the narrative marking Israel's journey toward Canaan (Num 20:17; 21:22). It is one branch of the ancient international trade route that came to be known later as the *Via Maris*, based upon a reference in Isa 9:1 that Yahweh "will make glorious the way of the sea . . . "

curse against Jericho in Joshua 6:26. Since it had been established by peoples oblivious to the Great Creator, and dedicated to lesser gods and purposes than the true grand design of the original creation, it must now make way for Yahweh's redemptive intents. All would be welcome in the new Zion to be established by God through Israel. But woe to any who wished for the old ways and the old gods and the darkness of a world where the Creator was neither acknowledged nor wanted.

Once Jericho was out of the way, the Israelites headed straight for the mountains of Ebal and Gerizim in order to renew the Sinai covenant, as Moses had commanded.[4] The next town on that route was a much smaller city than Jericho, a place called Ai. Scouts reported to Joshua that a quick campaign with fewer soldiers was all that was necessary because of its limited size and fortifications. But Israel's strength to act as Yahweh's champion had been compromised, because Achan had prevented the total destruction of Jericho.

This transgression and its severe consequences are not the norm for divine punishment in the rest of the Old Testament. The incident seems to function as a warning sign for those witnessing it, so that they would understand the seriousness of what was taking place, and not seek quickly to deviate from the divine mission in order to pick up personal gain. A similar anecdote is recorded in Acts 5 at the very beginning of the New Testament Church's existence. There, Ananias and Sapphira used the concept of total devotion of goods as a means to gain public recognition, while hiding contrary deeds that would benefit their own economic station. In both instances, death is the divine judgment, and a great fear or awe consumes each community.

When Achan's sin and the city of Ai have both been dispatched, the Suzerain-Vassal covenant formulated at Mt. Sinai is renewed. The mountains of Gerizim and Ebal were roughly in the center of Canaan, and stood closely enough to one another that it was indeed possible to shout back and forth between them, as the recitation of covenant curses and blessings required.

As soon as the renewal ceremony was accomplished, the story of Canaan's conquest was quickly told in three literary sections. First, the Gibeonites, terrified by the unstoppable onslaught of the Israelites, deviously made an alliance with Joshua and the people, pretending to be from far away (Josh 9). The neighbors of the Gibeonites were incensed at their defection to these intruders, and mounted a battle against them. Since the Gibeonites were now allied with Israel, Joshua was required to go to their aid, and this became the excuse for the southern military campaign,

4. Deut 27; see Josh 8:30–35.

which netted Israel more than half of Canaan by the time the fighting ceased (Josh 10). In quick response, the city-states of northern Canaan banded together to keep Israel out. The strategy failed, however, and soon the entirety of the land belonged to Israel (Josh 11).

All of these wars make for great military reading, but they also raise a huge theological question. Why was Israel sent into battle to destroy cities and civilizations, old men and young babies, and cultures and economies? There is no easy way to respond, or to find quick harmony with the near-pacifist perspectives of the New Testament. Several ideas enter the conversation, however, and while these are not fully satisfying, they are helpful in refocusing the questions. First, although there is an ongoing covenant relationship between Yahweh and a human society throughout the Bible, the nation of Israel in the Old Testament is formed as a political entity, in contrast to the other countries and communities of the ancient world, while the Church of the New Testament is commissioned to be a pervasive influence within other societies, without becoming a political state in its own right. This means that there are aspects of Israel's existence that cannot be equated with the lifestyle promulgated for the early church, and vice versa. While the church is not to engage in slaughter and bloodshed, the nation of Israel was required to establish boundaries and control over civilian populations. In this respect, there is a close correspondence between the "Just War" theories explored by theologians of the New Testament Church and the manner in which Israel would promote and defend her statehood existence. While the mission of Yahweh through Israel demanded a particular covenant lifestyle, just as it does in the New Testament era of the church, the actual formation of the national territorial existence required other means, including war and international diplomacy, to establish and maintain it.

Second, there are several hints that at least a portion of the warfare commanded in the settling of Canaan was understood to be merely a restoration of the rightful claims of Abraham's descendants to the land. After all, they had buried their honored ancestors in these hills, and had never sold off rights to the land owned by their forefathers. In effect, some say, Israel held a type of manifest destiny, which required them to reassert ownership entitlement over the squatters who came later and dwelt surreptitiously in *their* land. This was a nasty and bloody business that could not be easily accomplished through neighborliness or negotiation (although, as the story of the Gibeonites affirms, it was sometimes possible).

Third, there is a hint that the conquest of Canaan was, in part, a judgment against the wickedness of the peoples living there. While the social conditions that prevailed among the tribes and clans of ancient Canaan are beyond a complete ethical assessment, the manner in which Yahweh commands the razing of Jericho in dramatic parallel with the flood of Noah's time seems to indicate that the conquest was, at least in part, a declaration of judgment against the Canaanites.

Fourth, it is clear that the skirmishes of battle were one way of revealing Yahweh's strength to those who opposed Israel's existence. Just as the plagues in Egypt unquestionably declared the astounding and unparalleled military capabilities of Israel's God, so in these subsequent battles a clear message was sent that "our God is bigger than your god." The miracles that accompanied Israel's battleground activities would provide incontrovertible evidence of Yahweh's power for those who observed. Hopefully, these peoples would give up their smaller deities and find new camaraderie with Israel and her God. In this way, the blessing for all nations, promised to and through Israel's founding patriarch, Abram (Gen 12), would come to pass, and the missional intent of the Creator to regather the crown of creation into new fellowship would be accomplished.

Fifth, there may well have been a need for Israel to experience a fairly sterile environment in its formative years, in order for it to become the community of covenant witness that Yahweh intended. This seems to be confirmed when Israel's failure to completely destroy other civilizations within its borders is declared, in Judges 2, to be sinful, and in violation of Yahweh's intentions. Earlier encounters with other nations, like that with the Moabites in Numbers 25, had proved how quickly the Israelites could be led away from their unique covenant commitments to Yahweh. If this young nation was to get started as a community of witness, it would need some time to grow in independence from other national and religious influences.

All of these reasons do not fully satisfy a Christian reading of the bellicose events in Israel's early existence, especially when considering that along with Judaism, it emerges from the same religious tradition and divine initiatives. These suggestions do, however, provide a basis upon which to understand the uniqueness of Israel's situation, particularly when the political theocracy, national geography, and religious mission get inextricably intertwined for Israel in a way that is not experienced by the Church of the New Testament. It also explains why the prophetic anticipations of the "Day of the Lord" involve massive battlefield campaigns, and why these become metaphorical images in Christian apocalyptic literature.[5]

---

5. See Rev 18–19.

Possessing the Land (Joshua 13–21)

Although Israel was in control of Canaan after the battle against the northern coalition, there remained pockets of resistance and competing claims for specific territories within its borders (Josh 13). Part of the reason for the allocations of boundaries for the tribes of Israel was to manage the final push for total dominance over residual alien clans. The general distribution is outlined over several chapters (Josh 14–19). Then provision is made for six "cities of refuge" (Josh 20), which would support a judicial system that provided a fair hearing for all who had been involved in major civil tragedies or crimes. Along with that, the Levites, who were not allotted a specific tribal territory, were given residences in a number of towns (Josh 21). This allowed the Levites to share in the economic fortunes of the nation, and also dispersed these families, who were very closely connected with the religious rituals and ceremonies, throughout the land, providing a kind of visible leavening to influence the people to stay true to Yahweh.

Why was it necessary for the Israelites to become landowners rather than Bedouins like their ancient ancestors? Partly, it seems to be a reflection on their changing role from slavery in Egypt. After all, when Moses restated the Ten Commandments in Deut 5, he tied together release from slavery and respect for other peoples as the basis for the Sabbath command. But the laws given about restoring family property after seven years and again in the Year of Jubilee (Lev 25) seem to indicate a deeper connection between land ownership and religious identity. If Israel were to serve as the new community of witness to the Creator's desire for re-engaging the nations of the world, it would need a stable platform. Tying Israel's future existence to this spot of territory ensured that it would always be visible amid the massive movements and migrations of the three general areas of human population at that time. There was no other location on the five dominant ancient trade routes that provided such concentrated and central merging of traffic.[6]

Promising the Land (Joshua 22–24)

Three incidents round out the literature of this book, each of which addresses some dimension of the future of the land and Israel's place in it. First, there is the story of the tension produced when the warriors from

6. Cf., Xinru Liu, *The Silk Roads: A Brief History with Documents* (Boston: Bedford/ St. Martin's, 2012); Jules Toutain, *The Economic Life of the Ancient World* (New York: Alfred A Knopf, 1930); Morris Silver, *Prophets and Markets: The Political Economy of Ancient Israel* (Springer, the Netherlands: Kluwer-Nijhoff Publishing, 1983), especially chapter 4, "Transport: Routes, Costs and Monopoly Power," 41–56.

the trans-Jordan tribes return home. While the early intent of taking and settling Canaan seems to have been limited to the area between the Jordan River and the Mediterranean Sea,[7] several tribes found the lands just east of the Jordan to be to their liking. They requested the right to settle in this territory that had previously belonged to the Ammonites and Moabites. Moses gave them permission, with the stipulation that their soldiers must first accompany the rest of the tribes in the looming conquest of Canaan proper. This they agreed to do.

Now, in Joshua 23, these warriors go back to their settlements east of the Jordan. As they forded the river, they built a huge altar and ignited a great blaze on it. Neighboring Israelite tribes grew suspicious, thinking that these trans-Jordan relatives were already bowing to other gods. In the ensuing conversations, all fears were quelled, and Joshua heard their testimony that they were not seeking a shrine for worship other than the tabernacle. Instead, they only wanted to set up a monument that would help them remember their ties with the rest of the tribes. In this way, a pledge was made for national unity, which transcended tribal identities.

Second, as he grew old and neared death, Joshua called together the elders who had shaped community life for the Israelites at his side (Josh 23). He took them on a verbal tour of their remembered history, and called from them a pledge to keep their villages and cities true to the identity promulgated in the Sinai covenant.

Third, in a final covenant renewal ceremony, Joshua gathered the whole nation together shortly before he died (Josh 24). Once again, he reminded them *who* they were and *whose* they were. The Israelites did not exist as an independent tribe negotiating its own way among the other nations of the ancient Near East. Nor were they free agents, determining their religious allegiance by taking offers from the open market. They were the people of Yahweh, the nation of the Sinai covenant, the human agency of God's mission to recover a relationship with the residents of planet Earth, as communicated to Abraham many centuries before.

The concluding appendix to the book (Josh 24:28–33) lists three graves: those of Joshua, Joseph, and Eleazer. Each is uniquely significant. Graves are a symbol of settlement and homeland. Abraham and his wives were buried in this land, as were Isaac and his wives. When Jacob died in Egypt, his family made sure to bring his body back to Canaan to bury it here. Now the generations are passing again, and upon their deaths, Joshua the leader, Joseph the ancestor, and Eleazer the religious head are all buried in this land. It is a fitting reminder that the land has finally

---

7. Cf. Num 32.

achieved its intended rest, and its rightful owners can rest here as well. They are truly home.

The Importance of This Land

It is in this light that the location of the promised land must be considered. Why was Canaan the land promised to Abraham? Why did Israel wrestle these acres away from other clans in order to establish its own settlements?

Without question, there are many geographical areas of the world that would have appeared to be far more desirable. Mesopotamia, with its well-watered valleys surrounding the Tigris and Euphrates rivers, had a much better agricultural base than did Canaan. Egypt experienced both a more stable climate and a more secluded location. Anatolia was better suited to permanent settlement, because of its mountain-ringed highlands, than was the open strip of countryside between the Jordan River and the Mediterranean Sea. In fact, Canaan was largely a rock pile, very indefensible, lacking any natural harbor for trade, and geographically splintered, so that it would be very difficult to forge a national identity across high mountainous ridges and deep separating valleys.

What made this piece of property so valuable, at least in Yahweh's eyes? In the words of every real estate salesman: location, location, location. Canaan was the unparalleled single piece of territory in the ancient world that connected the various civilizations with each other. It was the bridge between Africa and Asia. It was the rest stop on the trade routes from what would become Europe to both the Orient and Egypt. It served as the primary highway for marshaling troops in the military campaigns of its world, and formed a key segment in every major communication line or caravan trek.

Canaan was precisely the one spot in the world of that day where the nation of Israel could not be hidden from other tribes, countries, and clans and peoples. In other words, the promised land was, for Israel, not a secluded sanctuary or retreat where the pastoral scenes of Eden could be replayed, but rather the busiest street in town. Here, Israel was placed as the divine billboard, calling all nations back to a relationship with the Creator. Here, Israel's unique community character and moral ethos were on display to attract other civilizations to inquire and seek after the God of this people.

The choice of Canaan as the promised land was no accident, when seen in the larger perspectives of the Sinai covenant and its missional foregrounding provided by the book of Genesis. If the Creator was going to find a way back into the hearts of the races of humans who had long ago forgotten their Maker, it would require the formation of a community shaped by the Sinai covenant, and then displayed in the most prominent location possible in the world of the day: Canaan. In this sense, the mission of God was not first built out of Jesus and the New Testament Church, but was resident in the religion of the Bible from its very beginning. This is why Jesus would say that his disciples were to be like a city set on a hill,[8] for that is exactly what his ancient kin, the Israelites, were intended to be.

Leadership Odyssey

If the book of Joshua outlined the possession of Canaan by Israel (entering into its covenant mission as community of witness to the world), Judges next showed how the nation nearly lost its place and identity through covenant disobedience.[9] But it is in 1 and 2 Samuel that the journey of restoration takes place, ushering in a quickly shifting locus of leadership.

---

8. Matt 5:13–16.

9. In the book of Joshua, a clearly appointed and prepared leader brings Israel into its "rest," as provided by the unique location and provisions of the Promised Land, so that she can live out her covenant destiny as the divine missional community of witness to the nations of the world. In the book of Judges, however, Israel becomes alienated from her "rest" through covenant breaking, and nearly loses her place in the land because of failure to possess what has been given. The people of God are seemingly about to forfeit their honored relationship with Yahweh and the missional identity it brings. But there is light on the horizon. "In the days when the Judges ruled" (Ruth 1:1), another story was developing. During the time of the Judges, unsettled by a nasty famine, Elimelech removes his family from the hill country of Judah to find food and work. They settle in Moab long enough for the two sons to marry. Then, in short order, all the men of the family die, and Naomi is left a widow. Destitute, Naomi can only think of returning to Bethlehem, where she might find old friends who could give her a few handouts until she dies. Her daughters-in-law try to travel along, but Naomi resists their pity. She has nothing to offer them, not even future sons, if the unlikely should happen and she would marry again. Ruth, however, is stubborn, and doggedly determined to accompany Naomi, in order to share the burden of her desperate situation. On arriving in Bethlehem, Naomi is barely recognized, but warmly welcomed. She tells her woeful story and claims a new name, "Mara" (which means "bitter"), as an indication of her sorry state. Ruth joins the other poor people who glean the barley fields for leftover corner patches, fallen stalks, and loose kernels after the reapers have taken in the bulk of the crop (see Lev 19:9 and 23:22 about reaping and gleaning practices). She catches the eye of Boaz, a wealthy landowner of some of the fields where she labors. He gets friendly, and Naomi sees a good prospect looming on the horizon. She urges Ruth to return Boaz's kind intentions, and before long, the gentleman makes public his courtship intentions. Quickly, he cuts through community red tape, and the two are wed. Already on their honeymoon, a child is conceived, and when little Obed is born, Naomi claims him as a sign of Yahweh's renewed blessing on her life. Of course, everybody lives happily ever after, and the closing credits show that this is the origin of the

There are a number of key issues which emerge through the first half of 1 Samuel, as this new figure takes center stage. For one thing, the covenant theocracy with Yahweh as Israel's unseen King begins to seem inadequate to the people. This is so for at least two reasons: On the one hand, Yahweh's voice is hard to hear,[10] unlike the days of Moses and Joshua, when it was quickly apparent what God desired or decreed. On the other hand, the urgent military threats from neighboring nations seem to demand a readily visible and immediate leadership that is not dependent on lengthy rituals of ceremony and sacrifice before Yahweh might or might not put in an appearance. Precisely because of these concerns, Samuel stands as the transition figure between the judges (who gave quick military leadership and then faded away without establishing ongoing royal courts or dynasties) and the monarchy, as it will emerge in part through Saul and to its full extent by way of David and his family. Samuel, as his name indicates, was a new communication link between the people and their God, and also a mighty general in battle. But his appearance on the scene was too brief to nurture public confidence in long-range national stability without a clearly identified temporal rule and an expectation of solid succession plans.

The clues to Samuel's special gifts and leadership role are scattered throughout the initial seven chapters of 1 Samuel. First, there seem to be injustice and lack of divine blessing in the land. Elkanah's first wife, Hannah, is barren, a typical sign of divine displeasure or even curse. His second wife, Peninnah, bears a number of children, but acts rudely toward Hannah about their contrasting situations. In short, the good wife is punished, and the bad wife is blessed. Things are definitely wrong in this upside-down world!

Second, the official representative for Yahweh, a priest named Eli ("My God"), neither recognizes true need and absolute devotion in Hannah's silent praying, nor is able to intercede on her behalf with Yahweh. At first, he rudely accosts Hannah, calling her a drunkard. Then, when she pours out her deep frustrations, all he can do is wish her well. He does not

---

great family of David, who later restores glory and honor to Israel. The book of Ruth is much more than a good love story; it is a tale of covenant-breaking, judgment, faithfulness, and restoration. Both Ruth and Boaz lay their own selves on the line to meet the needs of Naomi's destitution. They embody the Sinai Covenant. Those who live in this way enter the true *shalom* (rest) that Yahweh intended for Israel. More than that, they bring others (Naomi/the nation of Israel) with them. Leave the land, the Covenant, the mission of Yahweh, as Elimelech did, and you only find death and destitution. Return home, and even the nations (cf. Ruth) are blessed, just as Yahweh promised Abram back in Gen 12. It is for this purpose that Israel exists, and why she is to live in Canaan, the platform from which the whole redemptive drama of Yahweh will be visible to the nations, and draw them also into covenant blessing.

10. See 1 Sam 3:1.

have Yahweh's ear, and Yahweh's voice does not speak through him, even though he is a priest.

Third, Eli's sons, who are priests in their own right, are wicked men. They fail to mediate between Israel and Yahweh. They rob the people to feed their own gluttony. They mishandle the sacrifices, although the rituals are clearly spelled out. They have sexual relations with women at the tabernacle, just like the priest and prostitutes at the fertility shrines of other nations and gods. They fail to heed their father's admonitions. And then, to top it off, they presume leadership of the armies of Israel, and brazenly take the Ark of the Covenant into battle as a weapon of war!

Fourth, the writer uses one telling event during Samuel's childhood as the defining image of both the times and the man. "In those days the word of the Lord was rare," he tells us (1 Sam 3:1). Then, simply, the story of Samuel hearing his name called in the night is told. Samuel does not know who is calling him, and at first, Eli does not either. But soon it becomes apparent to the older man that, while he has neither the ear nor the voice of Yahweh, this young child certainly does. The nation quickly learns the same, as the writer notes in his closing comments on this episode: "The Lord was with Samuel as he grew up, and he let none of his words fall to the ground. And all Israel from Dan to Beersheba recognized that Samuel was attested as a prophet of the Lord. The Lord continue to appear at Shiloh, and there he revealed himself to Samuel through his word. And Samuel's word came to all Israel" (1 Sam 3:19–4:1)

Fifth, in battles against the neighboring Philistines, the Israelites are impotent. Not only do they lose the war, but the throne of their God—the Ark of the Covenant—is captured by the enemy through the foolishness of Eli's sons. Still, Yahweh personally battles the Philistines and their god Dagon, until the Philistines recognize defeat and send the ark home. In the end, it is Samuel alone (1 Sam 7) who can reconcile Israel back to Yahweh, and turn the page on this horrible chapter, with a clear divine deliverance from the Philistines.

When the Israelites finally grow bold enough to demand a human king, Samuel is the one who must mediate between Yahweh and the people until each party understands the consequences. Then, Samuel anoints both of the first kings of Israel, the obvious leader who turns out bad, and the overlooked runt who turns out great.

Saul's Flawed Reign

Saul is also a transitional figure. He expresses both what the monarchy can be and what it should not be. In this sense, he is flawed and expendable. David, on the other hand, becomes the paradigmatic king against whom all other rulers will be assessed. This is why an everlasting covenant (royal grant) places his family on the throne forever (2 Sam 7). Throughout the Old Testament, this covenant is a source of hope for Israel (and later Judah), particularly during times of foreign oppression and alien occupation of the land. With the dawning of the New Testament era, the promised Davidic kingship feeds apocalyptic fervor and shapes messianic prophecy. When Yahweh fulfills the promises made to Israel, according to all religious and national expectations, it will take place through a descendant of this royal family.

The public transition from Saul's rule to that of David's actually begins on a battlefield, with the famous narrative of the shepherd boy who brought down the giant, Goliath. The story of David and Goliath stands in the ongoing tradition of tales that informed ancient Israel of its identity within its world. The younger son (Isaac, Jacob, Joseph) is preferred over the older brother (Ishmael, Esau, the sons of Leah) as the carrier of covenant promise, blessing, and initiative. The weaker (enslaved Israel, wandering Israel, Israel at Jericho, Israel among the powerful city-states of Canaan) proves to be the stronger in international clashes (over Egypt, Amalek, Moab, Ammon, Jericho, etc.). Even in the fairly recent (within David's context) remembered history, Samson became the agent of Israelite deliverance from the Philistines after he had been weakened through divine penalties on his corrupted Nazirite vows.

Now the morality play is acted out once more, with timid Israel no match for the Philistine mean machine. The Philistines controlled metallurgy in the whole region (see 1 Sam 13:19–21), dramatically unbalancing the stockpiles and effectiveness of weapons between the competitors. Israel was out of the Philistines' league entirely, a weakling child being bullied on the wrestling floor of the WWF, a primitive nation bringing crude sticks against armor-clad swordsmen.

Moreover, the early campaign promises of King Saul have evaporated. In recent times, he had become less than a caricature of his old self. No longer the tall warrior heading a battle charge, he slumps now in his tent with no inspirational retort to Goliath's taunts. Israel's army was demoralized and insulted; Israel's God had become a joke among the priests of Dagon.

Into the tale skips a young lad. His parents couldn't remember him on the day of Samuel's subversive visit to Bethlehem to crown a replacement king (1 Sam 16). Even now, after all of the secretive hoopla that identified him as future custodian of the realm, he remains only an overlooked messenger boy, bringing cheese sandwiches to his soldier brothers who are supposed to be the real men of the story.

David is a character of less-than-refined politeness. He hears Goliath's mighty screams, blaspheming Yahweh and shattering Israelite confidence. Rather than query diplomatically into what strategy might be developing as the generals huddle around Saul, David boldly asks about the rewards for the expected Israelite champion who must necessarily silence this audacity.

While David's brothers try to quiet his insolence, word reaches Saul that a newcomer is willing to take on the giant. The king is ever so ready to throw this young one to the enemy lion, for at least such action will detract attention from his own inaction. When David loses the contest (as obviously he will), Saul can shake his head at the tragedy, protest his own innocence in the matter, and use the boy's mangled body to rally indignation into a popular uprising. David is a key player in Saul's next move.

Even the enemy knows the obvious outcome to this silliness. Philistine soldiers who stand like a picket fence on the southern rim of the Elah valley laugh in derision at the comedy about to be played out. Goliath, their champion, is almost tenderhearted in his good-natured joshing with David, hoping to keep the wee one from obvious harm.

But the miracles of God's designs continue to shape history against its own flow. David's shepherding skills, honed through years of isolated vigilance, provide the underdog with guerilla tactics that reduce the favored combatant's skills to ineffective preponderance. Goliath falls, both the Philistines and the Israelites gasp, David claims the toys of the vanquished, and all craziness breaks loose. Where one minute there had been the interminable stalemate on the western front, now a torrent of repressed anger erupts from the Israelite camp, and quite literally the fear of God disrupts Philistine discipline into save-your-own-skin rabbit runs.

But what is the point? With regard to the development of the David arc in the annals of Samuel, this is the crucial corner at which David becomes king. From this moment forward, David is on the rise, and Saul is a lame-duck, brooding has-been. The message of this tale, at least in part, is to show the heart-commitment of David, from his earliest public disclosures, as a true through-and-through worshipper of Yahweh. David's first thought, when reaching the stalemated battleground camp, is that Yahweh's honor is being besmirched, and there is no one in Israel who ought to ignore this or let it slide. David is not concerned with winning or losing battles; he is completely sold on rallying to God's cause. Moreover, this is the whole reason for Israel's existence, according to David. In the end, David becomes king—not because he is so clever or capable—rather, he is raised to leadership precisely because he knows that he is not in charge. The true king in Israel is Yahweh. This is a lesson that Saul never fully learned.

Saul is savvy enough to recognize David's trajectory, and the fact that Yahweh is with him. So, Saul competes with both, seeking to destroy David, and trying to usurp Yahweh's place as Israel's rightful king. He fails miserably in both attempts. When Saul brings David into the royal palace to claim David's reputation and prowess as his own, David's goodness steals the hearts of Saul's son, Jonathan, and daughter, Michal (1 Sam 18). When Israel's armies continue their winning streak against the Philistines, all praise shifts from Saul to David. When Saul tries to kill David, David not only escapes numerous times, but actually turns the tables and refuses to harm Saul twice when the opportunities present themselves. When Saul tries to marginalize David, David builds a new community of misfits and cast-offs who will eventually become the leadership team in his new administration. And when Saul finds himself spiritually bereft, he turns to witchcraft rather than Yahweh, and finds himself rejected by both.

One of the last stories in the transitional narrative of Saul's downward spiral is that of David defeating and destroying the Amalekites (1 Sam 30), the nasty enemies of Israel whom Saul had earlier spared (1 Sam 15). Saul failed, David succeeded. Saul's big-bang beginning whimpers into a battlefield suicide. David's obscure origins rise quickly into shining salvation for Israel, clearly tied to complete devotion to Yahweh, the nation's true and only Sovereign.

David's Bold Leadership Moves

It is for this reason that David ties his reign to the restoration of the centrality of Yahweh and the visible indications provided by the tabernacle and the Ark of the Covenant (2 Sam 5–6). David is playing the political game with rules not appreciated by everyone, even in his own society. Within remembered history, the nation had emerged from its own "Dark Ages." Grandparents (and even some parents) could remember well the times during the Judges. Israel was, at best, a loose confederation of bickering tribes, each handicapped by inconsequential leadership. Now and again internal threats or neighboring nations would stir the political blood long enough for a savior to be identified (and sometimes martyred). These "judges" brought a bit of regional stability, but national unity and direction were more distant than the patchwork of a gaudy quilt.

More recently, David's predecessor, a Benjamite named Saul, rose to prominence and had welded the squabbling communities into a bit of an imperial hegemony. "Israel" now begins to take precedence over the clannish tribal names, especially in the face of Amalek and Philistine aggressions. But Saul's star has fallen by the time his body collapses in battle. The confederation is compromised, and not everybody wants young David to be on the throne; many even regret the establishment of a royal chair in the first place.

As David consolidates his rule, he makes a singular move on the national chessboard, which defines the character of his administration. In a stroke of genius which arose from the unswerving commitments of his heart, David brings the Ark of the Covenant up to Jerusalem from its forgotten and tattered site at Shiloh. Prophets and press would quickly point out to the people the remarkable history of this portable throne of the Creator, who had become Israel's chief resident at Mount Sinai. David's design was to restore national unity, but clearly mark it as solidarity under Yahweh, rather than under himself.

Who could deny that Israel's glory days were those of Moses and Joshua, when Yahweh was openly proclaimed as national King, and the Ark of the Covenant paraded through the deserts of the Sinai and the battlegrounds of Canaan as the visible symbol of the unconquerable power of the great God, who had claimed Israel as a divine possession? This is the theological and historical background that David claims as he brings the ark up to Jerusalem. Rather than quibble about whether he is a suitable replacement on a weak and challenged throne, David portrays himself as the servant of the One who rules beyond question among the tribes. Even if the religion of Yahweh has fallen onto hard times, it carries the great myth by which every Israelite stands tall and proud.

The brief setback in David's plans (2 Sam 6:1–1), when proper protocol for transporting the ark is not followed, only serves to reinforce all of these themes. At first, David tries to haul the ark up the rugged paths to his new and somewhat inaccessible capital city as if it is a piece of furniture. A little object lesson from Yahweh is enough to put the fear of God in everyone. After a decent period of mourning and waiting, David's tactic changes. He is no longer the new potentate, waiting for the moving company to finish furnishing his royal quarters. Instead, he becomes a shepherd boy again, dancing in humility around the throne of his Master, carried in solemn procession by its bearers through the countryside until it can take a commanding position over all from the heights of the Judaean mountains.

Of course, this disturbs some who think David's character is maligned in the process, and the dignity of his office quashed. Michal, in particular, spits on his exuberance (2 Sam 6:20–23). She is, after all, King Saul's daughter, and she knows how regents ought to conduct themselves in aristocratic separation from the hoi polloi. David, her husband, has displayed himself like a cheap commoner, a public entertainer.

But Michal does not understand. Her husband is not like her father. For David, at least at this stage of his life (and throughout his reign, according to his deepest desires), the ultimate goal is not to be king, but rather to be first minister to Emperor Yahweh. In this, David's politics are of a completely different strain than that of his predecessor. Saul played the politics of man quite well. David plays the politics of heaven superbly.

David's Demise

The demise of David's reign is tied to a fascinating story that seems to be constantly repeated in political annals: an extramarital affair. Why would David do such a thing? Not just the romantic encounter itself, but the deliberately planned murder (engaging some of his trusted subordinates as willing or unwilling accomplices), the massive deceptions, the elaborate cover-ups, and even the personal delusions that kept him from seeing his own guilt.

Part of the answer has to be found in the very first verse of 2 Samuel 11: "In the spring, at the time when kings go off to war, David sent Joab out with the king's men and the whole Israelite army . . . But David stayed in Jerusalem." This hints at several things. First, the time of the year lent itself to surging hormones and amorous thoughts. After the months of terrestrial hibernation, the world around David was beginning to bloom, the days were getting warmer (Jerusalem sometimes gets snow in winter), both animals and plants were exercising their mating rituals, and along with them the human crowd in the palace and the capital city were showing signs of frisky behavior. There is good reason to celebrate Valentine's Day in the spring, and David himself was a muscular male whose own body welcomed the virus of libido.

Second, David's life was a runaway success. His early contestants to the throne of Israel had all been killed, defeated, or swept aside. David was at the top of the corporate ladder, with no immediate challengers in sight. His kingdom was consolidated, his enemies vanquished, his market share a supreme monopoly, his income substantial and rising, his palatial mansion finished, and his goals achieved. David was at the place in his career where "can't" and "defeat" were no longer part of the vocabulary. What he wanted, he got. What he desired, he took. What he planned happened. No questions asked. Winning a new territory or another heart were essentially the same: Get the idea and make it so.

Third, David had begun to isolate himself from the masses. He had the disease of wealthy insulation, where immediate consequences of actions cannot, and need not, be felt. The armies went off to war, but David stayed in Jerusalem. The workers buzzed about in their daily rituals, but he sat on the roof of his palace and surveyed the scene. Regular folks had to labor for a wage, but there was no schedule David had to keep. He could sleep or sneak or sulk or skulk or sidle or stroll at will. Adultery was at one time mainly the prerogative of the rich, simply because only they had the time and means. Mass transportation, suburban domestic isolation, and a culture of leisure dispense it liberally to all classes of society. But David lived in one of those eras when "fooling around" was a natural correlation to being rich and powerful.

These things come through in Nathan's ingenious invective against his friend and lord. Telling a story of the difference in lifestyle between the uncaring and presumptive rich man and the tenderhearted poor fellow aggravated David, as it should have. But his self-deception was so great that he did not see himself in the mirror until Nathan bashed it against his psyche.

The outcome of David's devious treachery would be family squabbles and the disruption of the monarchy for the rest of David's life. David and Bathsheba's first child would die, followed by the tragic demise of several other children. David himself would limp from the throne in his old age, barely keeping the restive kingdom alive.

With the establishment of the monarchy, the history of Israel angles in a new and decisive direction. From this time forward, the national identity will be bound up, once again, in a regenerating cycle of point-person human leaders, who will coalesce the religious, moral, and political vision of the nation. While Solomon will take that mandate to the expansive heights expected by Yahweh in the world-changing mission imparted originally to Abraham, the journey of jubilation will soon turn into a trail of tears, as subsequent kings mostly make mockery of the whole business. Only when David's last kingly scion, Jesus of Nazareth, appears, will the divine mission and the royal line converge again in a new and unprecedented way.

Yahweh Wins! Israel under Solomon

First and Second Kings are a literary continuation of 1 and 2 Samuel. The current divisions are based upon the length of a text that could be written on a single roll of parchment. Because of this, the whole of "Kings" was subdivided into four manageable sections.

A huge focus of 1 Kings is on Solomon and the building of the temple. It is clear from various notes and references that the temple was to be considered the palace of Israel's true king, Yahweh. For one thing, the temple was located at the top of the slope on which Jerusalem was built, geographically elevated above Solomon's own lavish residence. Topography was important for the kings of nations and city-states in the ancient Near East; like children pushing and shoving in playground games, there could only be one positional "king of the hill."

More significant is the prayer of Solomon at the dedication of the temple in 1 Kings 8. Although Solomon is clearly in charge of the political realm he inherited from his father, his address to Yahweh leaves no one guessing as to who is really the supreme ruler of the land and its people. In this, scriptural theology from Genesis through the time of the monarchy is consistent: Yahweh is the Creator of all, and has entered into a special relationship with Israel, in order that this community might be a witness of the divine presence and favor from its strategic position on the bridge-land between the nations.

Quite remarkable is the note in 2 Chronicles 3:1 that the location of the temple is not only at the top of Jerusalem, the capital city, but also on the site where Abraham had been willing to sacrifice Isaac, the miraculous child born of divine promise to him and Sarah (2 Chr 3:1). Here, several strands of the great mission of Yahweh come together. First, by way of a Suzerain-Vassal covenant, Yahweh had claimed Abraham and his family as divine partners in the great redemption plan for the whole of the human race, and sealed the deal through Isaac ("Laughter"), who brought pleasure to his parents and hope for the world. On this very site, Abraham's faith and commitments were affirmed, Isaac was spared to carry on the promise and mission, and the hint of a substitutionary solution for meeting the needs of the human race was put in motion. Little did Abraham realize that two thousand years later, on this very spot, his later, greater son, the One who was more fully the Son of Man and the Son of God than any knew at the time, would become that substitutionary sacrifice. In Jesus, Abraham's prophetic words to his son Isaac ("God himself will provide the lamb for the burnt offering, my son." Gen 22:8) would actually be witnessed on this same spot as the mission of God culminated in the coming of Jesus, and then shifted its focus to the international witness of the church.

Second, because this was also the place where old King David pleaded for mercy after he had sinned in the pride of counting to see how great his military might really was (2 Sam 24, 1 Chr 21), the site had intercessory significance. Here, the power of heaven was checked by a human plea for divine mercy. Here, Yahweh remembered and recommitted himself to the joint relationship of the Sinai covenant. Here, an altar was erected for the burnt offering that knit eternity to time in communion and cooperation. Thus, for the Altar of Burnt Offering to be built in the grand and permanent temple that would replace the tattered and traveling tabernacle on this piece of real estate was extremely symbolic. It was right for the Ark of the Covenant, topped by the Mercy Seat of Yahweh's throne, to be situated in the royal palace of the temple ("My house . . . ") exactly where mercy had stalled judgment, and grace had shone so brightly.

In this manner, the great *Shekinah* glory light of Yahweh's presence fills the new temple and spills through the streets of Jerusalem, gushing and tumbling out through all of Israel to impact and change a darkened world that has forgotten its Creator. This is later pictured clearly by Isaiah and Micah, among others of the prophets:

> *In the last days the mountain of the Lord's temple will be established as chief among the mountains;*
>
> *It will be raised above the hills, and all nations will stream to it.*
>
> *Many peoples will come and say, "Come, let us go up to the mountain of the Lord,*
>
> *to the house of the God of Jacob.*
>
> *He will teach us his ways, so that we may walk in his paths."*
>
> *The law will go out from Zion, the word of the Lord from Jerusalem.*
>
> *He will judge between the nations and will settle disputes for many peoples.*
>
> *They will beat their swords into plowshares and their spears into pruning hooks.*
>
> *Nation will not take up sword against nation, nor will they train for war anymore.*
>
> *Come, O house of Jacob, let us walk in the light of the Lord.*
> (Isa 2:2–5; Mic 4:1–5)

For forty years, Solomon built the nation into an international superpower that could not be ignored anywhere in the ancient Near East. It is clear from the trade and commerce mentioned during Solomon's reign that people on three continents—Africa, Asia, and Europe—not only knew about Israel, but wanted to enter into her sphere of influence. This was the outcome envisioned by Yahweh a thousand years earlier when conversing with Abram about the divine intention to bless all the nations of the earth through his descendants.

Fractured and Disintegrating

The temple itself stood as a visible reminder of how the nation of Israel became great. For that reason, the story of Jeroboam takes on special significance. Jeroboam was obviously a gifted man. He was chosen by Solomon to head the national building projects (1 Kgs 11:28), then recognized as a political threat by the king (1 Kgs 11:40), and eventually identified as the spokesperson for the general population after Solomon died (1 Kgs 12:2). When Rehoboam, Solomon's spoiled brat of a son, publicly flouted his disdain of both the people and leadership wisdom, Jeroboam was poised to wrest away a portion of the kingdom.

One of the first things Jeroboam did was to consolidate his territory by fortifying its borders. But then he also built new cultic shrines for worship at both the northern (Dan) and southern (Bethel) limits of his realm. As the text indicates (1 Kgs 12:25–33), it is not likely that Jeroboam intended to change the religion of his portion of the nation of Israel; at the same time, he needed to replace the grand Temple of Jerusalem with other centers for worship so that his subjects would not be tempted to realign with Rehoboam, as might happen if they continued to journey to Jerusalem for sacrifices and festivals.

Thus, the grand kingdom of David and Solomon became divided, and its theological mission compromised. Yet, the perspective of Kings is that the northern tribes (now "Israel") and the southern portion (now "Judah") were never truly separated. Throughout the rest of these narratives, the political fortunes of both territories were equally considered. Furthermore, the kings of both realms were similarly judged by the prophetic author as either following in the ways of David and Solomon (and so seeking to fulfill the destiny intended by Yahweh), or compounding the covenant-breaking of those who caused the nation to stray from its divine calling and mission. This is most obvious in the harsh assessments given at the time of the northern kingdom's destruction by the Assyrians (2 Kgs 17).

While the rulers of the divided kingdom are mostly (in the north) and often (in the south) forgetting and being contrary to the ways and wishes of Israel's true monarch, Yahweh, there comes a new development in the idea of who is in charge as God's anointed and appointed. Note, as 1 and 2 Kings unfold, the emerging and changing role of the public "prophets."

Moses and Joshua each had a unique and ongoing relational interchange with Yahweh, which made their leadership positions virtually unassailable (cf. Num 12; 16–17). After the nation was settled in Canaan, such clear, regular and unequivocal communication with Yahweh appears to have been muted. During the times of Eli, we are told, "the word of the Lord was rare; there were not many visions" (1 Sam 3:1). That is why, when Yahweh began speaking directly with Samuel, the Israelites were ready to follow him (1 Sam 3:19–21). This seems to be the beginning of a national recognition of the status of prophets as part of the necessary social fabric.

When Samuel's leadership was challenged because the people wanted a king (1 Sam 8), it caused the first subtle separation of church and state. Samuel was a priest by adoption, and worked within the parameters of the cultic shrine. But the kings were clearly outside of the Levitical priesthood or its extended family. Prophets at first began to bridge the connection, and then later sparred with the kings as the sovereignty role of Yahweh was increasingly forgotten.

This tension is clearly seen in the dominant stories of Elijah and Elisha, who battled with the rulers of the northern kingdom in 1 Kings 17–2 Kings 8. Elijah was given the weapons of the curses of the Sinai covenant to bring Ahab and Jezebel to their knees (1 Kgs 17:1). He wielded divine power in public displays of combat (1 Kgs 18). He was authorized to determine and appoint the leaders of nations (1 Kgs 19). And when Ahab and Jezebel presumed that they could displace God-fearing Israelites from their divinely determined inheritance in the land (1 Kgs 21), Elijah confronted the pair with stern prophecies that they instead would be removed. In this iconic showdown, it became clear that point leadership for the covenant community had shifted once again. The golden chain of Yahweh's key appointees now looked like this:

- **Moses**—Original leader, mediator of Sinai covenant

- **Joshua**—Moses's clear successor, conquest and settlement leader

- **Elders**—Heads of clans who had served under Joshua

- **Judges**—Unique and divinely appointed deliverers in Israel's dark period

- **Kings**—Monarchs who were to serve as visible regents on behalf of Yahweh

- **Prophets**—Divinely appointed spokespersons communicating covenant values in changing times

Throughout the rest of the Old Testament history of Israel, the prophets would take on a changing and growing role as the legitimate and authorized spokespersons for Yahweh and the Sinai covenant. Most of their speeches are not new revelations, but rather interpretations of the covenant stipulations for current situations. Ultimately, the prophets became the interpreters of Israel's history, and their writings were collected as a unique section of Hebrew scripture.

While the Israelites were able to live in somewhat sheltered isolation during their early years in Canaan, Solomon's reign vaulted them into the political fray of new and increasingly powerful emerging nations. The Philistine threat, which had seemed so overwhelming during the days of Samuel and Saul, evaporated as an insignificant petty turf war before the successive onslaughts of first the Assyrians, and then the Babylonians. The expansive interests of these early superpowers were inseparably intertwined with the lives and preoccupations of four centuries of Israel's kings and prophets.

To the south of Israel lay Egypt, the oldest continuous civilization in the ancient Near East. Because of the Nile's regular seasonal rises and falls, Egypt had a stable economy and a constant supply of food. Other nations (especially in Mesopotamia), whose agricultural fortunes were more tied to cycles of rain and drought, coveted Egypt's treasury of staples, and knew that control of these resources would enhance their abilities to supply their armies. So, first Assyria, and then Babylon sought to make Egypt a subservient province. Of course, on the way, they needed to deal with the old—but still significant—kingdom made great by Solomon.

Israel among the Nations

The written messages of the prophets make it clear that there were a number of challenges and options for the people of Yahweh. First, it was understood that these invaders were the scourge of God in response to the covenant unfaithfulness of the Israelites. Yahweh's people ought not to miss the point that they were no pawns caught on the scrimmage line of an international football game. As Yahweh proved to Hezekiah during the days of Isaiah and the Assyrian threat, no military incursion was either outside of Yahweh's intended influence or superior to Yahweh's mighty control. Things happened by divine plan, not whimsical fate, and the sooner the people learned this lesson, the more quickly they would return to covenant fidelity with their true Sovereign.

Second, international political alliances would not save the people; only Yahweh could do that. Many in Judah were tempted to connect with

Egypt, hoping that its stable greatness would shield the tiny hill country from either Assyria or Babylon. Israel, on the other hand, was forever forming pacts with Syria (either willingly or under coercion) against Assyria, and wanted to take Judah into that coalition in order to strengthen it. Meanwhile, King Ahaz of Judah did an end run around Israel and Syria, appealing directly to Assyria for help. A generation later, King Hezekiah would do something of the same, this time cozying up to Babylonian ambassadors as a secret weapon against Assyrian assault. On each occasion, the prophets delivered a word from Yahweh, reminding the people that Israel was supposed to be a light to the nations, and not a mere ally among them. Moreover, Yahweh was not a small territorial god thumped about on the chessboard of international politics; Yahweh was the Master of nations, and the people must respect their Sovereign as such.

Third, the changing lead nations in this multinational strife shaped the history of bifurcated Israel in quite astounding ways. The northern kingdom was destroyed by Assyria in 722 BC. (2 Kgs 17). The Assyrians were fierce in battle and politics, and dispersed any local survivors of conquest in a grand Near Eastern mixing bowl of population displacement. For that reason, the remnants of the old kingdom of Jeroboam and Ahab became lost among the other peoples of the Assyrian empire, and eventually merged with the Arabic civilizations that would follow centuries later. By the narrowest of margins, the southern kingdom of Judah escaped this fate (2 Kgs 18–19), only to be struck down by Babylonia just over a century later (2 Kgs 24–25). The Babylonians considered themselves much more civilized than the Assyrians, however, and employed both provincial politics and deportation as tools of conquest. First, the Babylonians would try to amalgamate a newly overrun people into the burgeoning Babylonian empire by retraining leaders to become loyal to their new overlord (so the stories of Daniel and Ezekiel, who were taken to Babylon to be trained, with the goal of ultimately being sent back as ambassadors of their new master). If that did not work, the Babylonians destroyed the centers of political and religious life, and resettled a captured community near the city of Babylon as a way of forming a new mosaic of cultures. This was done to Judah, and it saved the tiny nation from extinction. Finally, the Persians, who conquered Babylon, built an even larger empire by restoring displaced peoples to their homelands, placing them in this way in the debt of Susa. That is how the "Jews" (i.e., the people of Judah) eventually returned from Babylonian captivity to make a new start.

The grand divine missional experiment of ancient Israel is judged at the close of Kings to be a failure. Israel was created by Yahweh to bring blessing to the nations of the world. That blessing would flow through these people who were intentionally situated on the crossroads of the nations as actors on the stage of life, revealing the character of human existence, as recovered and restored in fellowship with its Creator by way of the Sinai Suzerain-Vassal covenant. Unfortunately, like Samson, the Israelites ultimately became more enamored with the lifestyle and values of their neighbors than they did in giving witness to the unique treasure of religious insight they had received. During the sixth and fifth centuries BC, just at the time that Israel was losing its faith and covenant distinctiveness, seven of the world's other great religions were being formed.[11] One cannot help but wonder what our world would have looked like if these international seekers of transcendent meaning had found Yahweh through the witness of Israel.

The Rise of Israel's Prophets

Israel's prophets often appear, at first glance, to be strange creatures. A number of them harangue with incessant tirades (e.g., Amos), making us uncomfortable to spend too much time with such grumpy old men. Some are constant political gadflies (e.g., Jeremiah), always taking positions opposite of those in power. Others veer off into strange visions that are worlds removed from our everyday life (e.g., Zechariah), chafing readers with their oddness. There are even a few who have very compromised personal lives (e.g., Hosea), leading us to suspect more than a little psychologizing in their soap opera-ish theology.

Still, there is an inherent consistency of message and focus among all of these diverse religious ruminations and rantings. First of all, the prophetic sermons are invariably rooted in the web of relationships created by the Sinai covenant. Israel belongs to Yahweh, and her lifestyle must be shaped by the stipulations of that Suzerain-Vassal treaty. Obedience to Yahweh triggers the blessings of the Sinai covenant, while disobedience is the first reason for Israel's experiences of its curses: drought, war, famine, enemy

---

11. It is interesting to note the beginnings of these religious expressions, precisely during the time of Israel's demise:

604 Lao Tzu born (*Taoism*)

599 Mahariva born (*Jainism*)

590–550 *Upanishads* written (*Hinduism*)

565 Zarathustra born (*Zoroastrianism*)

563 Siddhartha born (*Buddhism*)

551 Confucius born (*Confucianism*)

470 Socrates born (*Greek Philosophies*)

occupation, destruction of cities and fields, deportation, etc. For this reason, the prophetic writings are laced with moral diatribes that carry a strong emphasis on social ethics.

This is not to say that Israel was held to a different behavioral standard than would otherwise be expected among the nations of the earth. Rather, through Israel's lifestyle, there was supposed to flow a witness toward its neighbors, revealing the unique splendor of its God. By looking at the people of Yahweh, living in Canaan, other tribes and nations were intended to gain a sense of the true character of life when it was experienced in harmony with the forgotten Creator of all. For this reason, the public actions of Israel were crucial to its covenant existence.

Second, the function and message of prophecy were very political. Since Yahweh alone was Israel's sovereign, for the nation to come under the domination of other political powers was always seen as a divine scourge which resulted from the application of the covenant curses due to Israel's disobedience. How Israel handled its international relations showed plainly whether she trusted Yahweh, or if she had otherwise become enamored with power and politics rooted in lesser gods. Constantly the prophets asked whether Israel was Yahweh's witnessing people, or if she was merely another nation with no particular mission or divine purpose. Israel's self-understanding was thus always very religious, and at the same time invariably political.

It is in this light that the typical prophetic litany against the nations surrounding Israel must be read. These other social and political entities were assessed for public moral behavior by Yahweh alongside Israel because Yahweh was the creator of all, and continued to be Lord of the nations. All countries are chided for their own internal social sins as well as for their inappropriate aggressions toward one another, including and especially for their treatment of Israel. While they may be used by Yahweh as a temporary tool of recompense and restoration, punishing Israel according to the covenant curses, they might never presume to hold dominance over either Israel or her God. This typical hubris of nations was regularly condemned as idolatrous by the prophets, and any society afflicted by it would receive divine retribution in its own turn.

Third, as the epochs of Israel's political fortunes unfolded, the message of the prophets became increasingly apocalyptic. There was a growing sense that because things had not gone the way they should have, producing heartfelt and ongoing national repentance and covenant restoration, Yahweh will have to intervene directly again, in a manner similar to that which happened during the time of Moses. When Yahweh interrupts human history the next time, however, along with judgments on the wickedness of the nations of the world, Israel will also fall heavily under divine punishment. But because Yahweh is on a mission to restore the fallen world, this next major divine intervention will be paired with a focus on establishing a new world order as well, even while the old is falling away under the conflagration. In this coming messianic age, everything in both society and the natural realm will finally function in the manner the Creator had intended in the beginning. Furthermore, because Yahweh is faithful to promises made, Israel will not be forgotten, and a remnant of God's servant-nation will be at the center of all this renewal and restoration and great joy.

This increasingly forward-looking thrust of prophecy leads some to think of it as primarily foretelling, a kind of crystal ball gaze into the future. In reality, however, the nature of prophecy in ancient Israel is more forthtelling: declaring again the meaning of the ancient Sinai covenant, explaining the mission of Yahweh (and thus Israel also) as witness to the world, and describing the implications of the morality envisioned by the Suzerain-Vassal treaty stipulations. Included in this forth-telling is the anticipation of how things will look when everything is renewed. This becomes the basis for the "new covenant" of Jeremiah and Ezekiel. This forms the background to the prophecies about the "new heavens and new earth" in Isaiah. This shapes the contours of the messianic age described by Isaiah, Ezekiel, Joel, Micah, and Zechariah.

The growing clarity of the prophetic message is best seen when these divinely called and authorized covenant spokespersons are reviewed in historical sequence. While not all aspects of each prophetic experience is fully known, a great amount can be learned from the information provided within most of the prophecies. The biblical prophets can be grouped in eras spanning about a century each.

Tenth–Ninth Century Prophetic Beginnings: Royal Advisers

The earliest prophets had several things in common. First, they were closely attached to the royal dynasties and functioned significantly as political, moral, and religious advisers. Second, few of their words were written down for posterity. Third, they seem to have had close connections vocationally with either the extended royal household or the priestly families that cared for the tabernacle and later the temple. Samuel was the archetype of these prophets, according to 1 Samuel 3, and appears to have given name and status to the role of prophecy in the nation as a whole (see 1 Sam 9).

Others in this group include **Nathan**, who had direct and easy access to King David (2 Sam 7; 12); **Ahijah**, who seems to have been significantly responsible for the partition of the nation of Israel after the death of King Solomon (1 Kgs 11:29–39), and later spoke a strong word of judgment against the king he had ensconced (1 Kgs 14); and the nameless prophets of 1 Kgs 13 who talk with the kings and advise them. Each played a direct role in the political life of the nation, but did so as an acknowledged representative for Israel's true king, Yahweh. For them, there was no distinction between the religious and political dimensions of society.

Eighth-Century Prophets: Loyal Opposition

Things appear to have changed significantly for prophets in the eighth century. While **Isaiah** was expressing the passion and purposes of Yahweh with lyric eloquence in the south, prophecy took on a decidedly angry character in the north. The powerful team of **Elijah** and **Elisha** railed against the royal pair of Ahab and Jezebel (1 Kgs 17–2 Kgs 9) for their anti-Yahweh religious stance and their anti–Sinai covenant betrayal of people like Naboth (1 Kgs 21). **Micaiah** joined their entourage for one brief incident (1 Kgs 22), lending credence to their pronouncements of judgment, even while having direct access to the royal council room.

The most enduring voices from this era belong, however, to those members of "the Twelve" Minor Prophets whose words were recorded in blunt detail. **Amos** left his large estate near Tekoa in Judah to travel northward into the territory of its sibling rival Israel around the year 760 BC. He explored the expansive prevalence of social sins in that realm which, he made clear, would soon result in divine judgment upon these people. According to Amos:

- There was a growing economic gap between very rich and very poor, accentuated by the callousness of the wealthy (6:4–6).

- Public worship had become repetitions of superficial liturgical acts (4:4–5; 5:21–23).

- The rich were stealing the lands of the poor through criminal lending practices, coupled with repossessions when impossible borrowing terms caused inevitable loan repayment defaults (2:6; 8:4; 8:6).

- Law courts were routinely denying justice to the helpless, simply because they could not pay bribes and had no social standing (2:7; 5:10; 5:12).

- In the marketplace, the poor were constantly cheated (8:5).

- Throughout the nation there was overt conspicuous consumption (4:1).

- Added to these were blatant debauchery and other forms of immoral lifestyle (6:5–6).

All in all, the word from Yahweh through Amos was dark, gloomy, and pointedly judgmental. Because of his pithy precision, coupled with verbal economy, Amos has become the model of street-corner prophets who rail against their societies in epigrammatic diatribes.

The same message was communicated in a very different tone and manner by **Hosea**, a contemporary of Amos. Hosea also spoke in the northern kingdom of Israel, but probably as a resident of that community. His oral and written communications are dated to the years 750–723 BC. because of the rulers identified within the prophecy's pages.

Hosea had a very bad marriage. His wife, Gomer, was a prostitute before they wed, and bore at least two sons during their time together. It is uncertain, though, whether these children were biologically related to Hosea, since Gomer was not one to stay in her marriage bed at night. Her escapades and his faithful pleadings, which sound more like a soap opera than a biblical drama, became the analogy for Yahweh's relationship with Israel. Through the voice of Hosea, Yahweh poignantly reviewed the past, detailing the amazing story of love that had brought young Israel into a very privileged and powerful position among the nations of the world. But this rehearsal grew bitter as both Hosea and Yahweh mourned their scorned loves, and wept for their respective wives who were each destroying themselves and their families.

Although more polished and less dramatic, the message of another contemporary was much the same. **Micah** orated his prophecies over a period of about five decades, from 740–690 BC. He began this ministry in the north, but after Israel was destroyed by the Assyrians in 722 BC, headed south and used the terrifying international political threat as a warning to Judah. God is faithful, Micah intoned, but Israel (and also Judah) has been unfaithful to the Sinai covenant. Therefore, judgment is surely coming. Indeed, precisely during Micah's prophecies it arrived in vengeful force against the northern kingdom, wiping it out of existence.

A truly strange incident was also unfolding on another front, during the years of these prophets. **Jonah** was commissioned by Yahweh to travel all the way to Nineveh, capital of the dreaded Assyrians, and speak a message of divine judgment against this aggressive civilization. One might think that any loyal Israelite would gladly rise to such a task. After all, Assyria was the great political enemy of the day, constantly threatening life in Canaan.

Jonah, however, was wise enough to understand the heart of Yahweh. It was not God's desire to destroy the Assyrians, he knew, but rather to bring them, along with all the other nations of the world, into a larger family of peoples who were returning to their Creator in worship and submission and the recovery of full human joy.

So Jonah tried to evade his task by getting as far away from Nineveh as possible. In the famous story told in Jonah 1–2, Yahweh pursues Jonah on the high seas, causes a storm that nearly swamps his ship, and preserves the prophet from suicide-by-drowning in the belly of a large fish. Yet when Jonah finally resumes his unwelcome mission to Nineveh, his suspicions come true, as the people of that great city actually repent for a time. God's promised judgment is put on hold, and Jonah cries like a spoiled brat.

The meaning of the tale is clear, however, and genuinely prophetic: although the Creator's world has turned against its maker, Yahweh has prepared Israel as a special missionary people; through it, as promised to Abram in Genesis 12, all the nations of the earth will be blessed. The tiny book of Jonah is one of the greatest affirmations of the missional nature of the redemptive covenant established by Yahweh with Israel at Mount Sinai.

Seventh-Century Prophets: Doomsayers

By the time the seventh century BC rolled around, the prophets were rarely welcome in the royal palaces, even though all that was left of once proud and expansive Israel was the tiny mountainous territory of Judah. During the 600s, although Assyria kept threatening Jerusalem, it was increasingly occupied in defending itself against its rebellious eastern province of Babylon. During these years, while **Jeremiah** developed his gloomy diatribes in the heart of the capital city, several among "the Twelve" also made brief statements about coming judgment. **Zephaniah** (630–610 BC) provided a few paragraphs against Judah and the nations that surrounded it (chapters 1–2), couching the imminent intervention of Yahweh in the increasingly common term, "the Day of the Lord." In a final, somewhat more lengthy chapter, Zephaniah turned his attention toward restoration and renewal, pointing to a future time when the fortunes of Yahweh's people would be made full once again.

Also, for just a brief moment (probably around 615 BC), **Nahum** renewed the mission of Jonah against Nineveh and the Assyrians. This time, however, there was no outcome of repentance and restoration. Instead, the short-lived turnabout that had followed Jonah's challenge evaporated entirely, and Nahum declared irreversible divine judgment against this fierce kingdom, which had wreaked so much havoc on its neighbors in the Fertile Crescent. Yahweh's word through Nahum would come true a few years later when the Assyrians were trounced by the Babylonians, first in the destruction of the capital city of Nineveh (612 BC), then at their secondary administrative center Harran (610 BC), and decisively in the battle of Carchemish (605 BC), where even the allied armies of Egypt proved insufficient to turn the Chaldean tide.

Finally, during this era also came the disconcerting dialogue between Habakkuk and Yahweh. Formulated around the year 600 BC, just as Babylon was rapidly overwhelming the whimpering remnants of the old Assyrian regime, Habakkuk asked Yahweh a series of questions which were answered in ways that almost brought more pain than the situations they were supposed to resolve. If summarized, the conversation would sound something like this:

> Habakkuk: "Why do you ignore the social evils that plague our land (Judah)?" (1:1–4)
>
> Yahweh: "I'm working on it. Very soon now I will bring punishment through my dreaded scourge, the growing Babylonian conquest machine that is rolling through the area." (1:5–11)
>
> Habakkuk: "O God, no! You can't do that! They are even worse than the most evil among us! How can you talk about balancing the scales of justice with such an unfair sentence?!" (1:12–2:1)
>
> Yahweh: "I understand your frustration. That's why I'm giving you a message for all to hear. The sins of my people are terrible, and require drastic measures. For this reason I am bringing the Babylonians against them. But the Babylonians, too, are my people, and will come under my judgment for the wickedness they perform. In the end, all will bow to me, as is appropriate when nations come to know that I am the only true God." (2:2–20)

At this point Habakkuk breaks into a song of confidence and trust (chapter 3) that rivals anything found in the Psalms. Habakkuk charts the terrifying movements of Yahweh on earth, bringing death and destruction as the divine judgments swirl. But in the end, Habakkuk raises a marvelous testimony of faith:

> Though the fig tree does not bud and there are no grapes on the vines, though the olive crop fails and the fields produce no food, though there are no sheep in the pen and no cattle in the stalls, yet I will rejoice in the Lord, I will be joyful in God my Savior.

The Sovereign Lord is my strength; he makes my feet like the feet of a deer, he enables me to go on the heights (Habakkuk 3:17–19).

Sixth-Century (Exilic) Prophets: Messianic Optimists

The prophets of the sixth century BC were mostly engulfed by the occupation of Judah and its quick demise (Jerusalem was destroyed in 586 BC), along with the subsequent Babylonian exile in which the bulk of the remaining population was deported. During these years, as we saw in the prophecies of **Ezekiel** and **Daniel**, the center of action shifted from Jerusalem to Babylon. There was only one tiny prophetic reflection from back in the homeland. **Obadiah**, whose name means "Servant of Yahweh," tossed off a brief but strident condemnation of Edom. This nation, which emerged from the same family as Israel by way of Jacob's fraternal twin Esau, had played gadfly to Yahweh's covenant nation for many centuries. Now, through the prophet's voice, Yahweh berated it for pride and willful cunning that leveraged Judah's demise for its own gain. When the Babylonians marshaled the deportees out of Jerusalem in 586 BC, the looters of Edom raided and scavenged that troubled city. Moreover, as the stragglers were being shepherded down the road to exile, sharpshooters among Edom's bowmen sat on the hillsides and picked them off in an unholy target practice. For these reasons, according to Obadiah, divine judgment was soon to destroy Edom's red rock strongholds.

While Obadiah's vision is too short to encompass the many dimensions of messianic optimism found in other prophets of his age, there is contained within it a firm confidence that Yahweh is still active among the nations. Once again, the "Day of the Lord" (verses 15–21) emerges as the catchall phrase for Yahweh's looming intervention that will redress injustice with divine punishment, and will usher in the renewed covenant order, spreading out from its epicenter in Jerusalem to the ends of the earth.

Fifth-Century (Post-Exilic) Prophets: Cheerleaders and Apocalyptic Moralists

Four among "the Twelve" remained after the first five centuries of Israelite prophecy were swallowed up into the Babylonian exile. Haggai and Zechariah appeared on the scene at exactly the same time (summer and fall of 520 BC); the former issued four brief messages from Yahweh on three separate days that year, while the latter continued to have visions for another two calendar cycles. Malachi showed up a generation or two later, and Joel's prophecy marks the conclusion of Old Testament revelations some time after.

Haggai was a cheerleader. He returned from Babylon to Palestine with the first wave of freed exiles under the leadership of Zerubbabel in 536 BC. Although it took a while for the community to get its bearings, eventually there was a push to sift among the stones still left at the site of Solomon's temple, and rebuild a house for Yahweh there. In 520 BC, Haggai urged the workers on with divine encouragement. No obstacle could stand in the way of this central task, neither disobedient lifestyles (1:2–11), fainthearted leadership (1:12–14), poverty (2:1–9), ritual defilement (2:10–19), or the rattling sabers of bellicose nations (2:20–23). Under Haggai's promptings and Zerubbabel's governing, the temple was rebuilt in the next four years. By 516 BC it stood again, only a mean miniature compared to the glorious structure created generations before by Solomon, in his seven-year building project. Nevertheless, with Haggai's oratorical help, Yahweh's house was reborn.

The visions of **Zechariah** began in exactly the same year as Haggai's brief prophecies (520 BC). But Zechariah's temperament was more like a combination of Jeremiah and Ezekiel; his graphic descriptions of Yahweh's revelations involved strange creatures and heavenly scenes and amazingly cartoonish episodes in which Yahweh's kingdom was confirmed as chief among the nations. Because of a change in literary style after chapter 8, Zechariah 9–14 is sometimes viewed as emerging from a second voice.

While Haggai's messages were quick, pointed, and easily understood in their references to the work of the day, Zechariah's allegorical pronouncements seem only obliquely connected to his contemporary setting. They pick up on the problems experienced by the post-exilic community, but then shimmer off into grand apocalyptic visions with no fixed chronology or tidy resolutions. Still, Zechariah's lofty homilies served well to remind the tiny and lackluster community that these people remained essential to Yahweh's original missionary purpose for Israel. Thus, the Sinai covenant and its stipulations continued to be Israel's greatest treasure, and the source of its public identity (see Zechariah 8:18–23).

About sixty years after Haggai's and Zechariah's brief prophetic careers, **Malachi** came on the scene. His name meant "My Messenger," and may well have been a nickname either given to him by Yahweh or assumed by the man himself in the course of his activities as spokesperson for God. As was true in Habakkuk's situation, Malachi's prophetic utterances take on the form of a dialogue. Here, however, the parties in conversation are not the prophet and Yahweh, but rather Yahweh and the people. Yahweh instigates the interlocutions, interrupting daily life around Jerusalem with a series of searing questions:

"Why have you people turned away from me?" (1:2–14)

"Why have you priests failed to honor me?" (2:1–9)

"Why do you divorce your wives?" (2:10–16)

"Why do you think I'm not coming back to my Temple?" (2:17–3:5)

"Why have you withheld tithes and offerings?" (3:6–15)

These issues match the problems Ezra and Nehemiah struggled with, and affirm Malachi's dates as contemporary with those leaders. Even the covenant renewal ceremony of Nehemiah 8–10 may have been the occasion for the brief note in Malachi 3:16, which tells of a scroll of testimony being penned by repentant Jews who wished to repossess their identity as the community of Yahweh.

It is likely that the short prophecy of Joel was written after Malachi's days, but the position of Malachi at the end of "the Twelve" is perfectly understandable. For Jews it closed off the post-exilic rebuilding of the temple. Now the community waited with eager anticipation for Yahweh to return again in the Shekinah glory cloud that first descended Mount Sinai into the tabernacle, and later came to dwell in Solomon's temple. Malachi's final vocalization of Yahweh's speech promised a speedy arrival of the divine presence.

For Christians of the New Testament age, Malachi's prophecy was viewed directly in connection with the gospels. The messianic church community quickly interpreted Jesus as the embodiment of Yahweh's returning glory. In fact, the gospel according to Matthew, which stands at the head of the New Testament, makes a very deliberate effort to choreograph the travels of Jesus in such a way that his arrival at the temple on the week of the final Passover is understood as the return of divine glory to the house of Yahweh, which has been left in the hands of clueless caretakers (see Matt 21).

The prophecy of **Joel**, although traditionally assigned a location near the beginning of the collection of "the Twelve," was probably penned sometime in the last half of the fifth century BC. Biblical scholars have moved it around the map of prophetic chronology, precisely because it contains no other temporal referents than the terrible plague of locusts that shaped its contents. The sweeping devastation of successive waves of locusts devouring the entire crop in Palestine that year caused Joel to hear a higher word of judgment against the nation of Yahweh. Partly because it contains no mention of kings, and also because of some words and language forms that seem more in tune with nuances of later Hebrew and post-exilic times (see, for instance, the note in Joel 3:4–6), many now believe it was written sometime after Malachi.

The exact historical setting for Joel is not essential to understanding its message. In fact, Joel's prophecy is a marvelous summary and distillation of all points of theology scattered throughout the rest of the prophets. After the strident tattoo of approaching judgment, still in rhythm with the grinding march of locust plague, Joel sees a critical and decisive turn of history taking place when Yahweh breathes new life across the face of the earth. Everything turns on the imminent "Day of the Lord" (Joel 2:11).

The "Day of the Lord": The Prophets in Summary

The prophets began to emerge on Israel's scene shortly after its settlement in Canaan. At first, they functioned as lingering echoes of Moses' booming voice, now fading in the historic distance. Although they continued in this role, seeking ways to translate the theology and social lifestyle of the Sinai covenant into new and changing circumstances for Israel, the prophets also became a third national leadership team, standing somewhere between the cultic role of the priests and the political venue of the kings. There is little evidence that they considered themselves as providing new revelations for Israel. Rather, they were interpreters of the Sinai covenant, subservient to Moses and the original Suzerain-Vassal documents.[12] Their authority, while rooted in contemporary visions, was derived from the ancient standards, and never ran ahead of Exodus or Leviticus or Deuteronomy.

What eventually coalesced from their common declarations, however, was the rallying point of the "Day of the Lord." Increasingly the prophets heard Yahweh declaiming that things were getting so bad, both within Israel and among the nations of her world, that only a direct divine intrusion could set things right again. This impending divine visitation became known as the great and terrible "Day of the Lord."[13]

---

12. Meir Weiss, "The Origin of the 'Day of the Lord'—Reconsidered," *Hebrew Union College Annual* 37 (1966) 29–71; Johannes Lindblom, *Prophecy in Ancient Israel* (Philadelphia: Fortress, 1973), 316–355.

13. C. F. Whitley, *The Prophetic Achievement* (London: R. Mowbray & Co., 1963), 199–207; R. E. Clements, Prophecy and Covenant (Norwich, England: SCM Press, 2012), 103–111.

While God's visible actions in this imminent momentous occasion would probably span a lengthy period of time,[14] the outcomes would be so decisive that it could be termed a single event.[15] Three major things would happen when Yahweh arrived on that "day":

- There would be a catastrophic judgment meted upon all the nations of earth, including Israel/Judah. It would fall as a divine judicial assessment that none were living appropriately to the lifestyle of the Sinai covenant, or changing their behaviors toward that direction because of the missional influence of God's people.[16]

- In spite of the conflagration, a remnant of Israel would be spared. This small group would be evidence that not all of the people had forgotten their God, and similarly that God would never forget the divinely created community.[17]

- After the cleansing of judgment and the restoration of the remnant, a new and vibrant messianic age would be ushered in. This would be a time in which all the implications of the Sinai covenant would be lived out with fresh and natural devotion by the renewed people of Yahweh. Furthermore, throughout the world, every nation would actively seek to conform its moral behaviors to that same pattern of life. The creation itself would be reinvigorated with its Edenic glories, and the Creator and all creatures would find themselves enjoying the harmony and unlimited bounty intended by God at the beginning of time.[18]

14. See, e.g., Nicholas R. Werse, "Obadiah's 'Day of the Lord': A Semiotic Reading," *Journal for the Study of the Old Testament* 38 (2013): 109–124; Thorlief Boman, *Hebrew Thought Compared with Greek* (Norwich, England: SCM Press, 1960), 139.

15. For a concise summary and an extended bibliography, see "Day of the Lord" in *Encyclopaedia Judaica*, edited by Michael Berenbaum and Fred Skolnik (Detroit: Macmillan Reference, 2007): 494.

16. Isa 2:11–12; 2:17; 3:18; 7:18; 7:20; 13:6; 13:9; 13:13; 19:16; 22:5; 22:12; 22:25; 24:21; 27:12–13; 34:8; 61:2; Jer 4:9; 7:32; 12:3; 16:9; 19:6; 23:20; 25:33; 25:24; 30:24; 39:16; 46:10; 47:4; 49:26; 50:31; Lam 1:12; 2:22; Ezek 13:5; 30:3; 31:15; 38:18; Joel 1:15; 2:1; 2:11; 3:14; Amos 2:16; 5:18; 5:20; 8:3; Obad 1:8; 1:15; Mic 2:4; 5:10; Zeph 1:7; 1:14; 1:18; 2:2; 2:3; 3:8; Zech 12:4; 14:3; 14:13; Mal 4:1; 4:3; 4:5.

17. Isa 2:2; 4:2; 10:20; 11:11; 27:13; 28:5; 30:26; 49:8; Jer 5:18; 23:5; 30:3; 30:8; 31:6; 31:31; 31:8; 33:14; 50:4; 50:20; Ezek 29:21; Mic 4:1; Zeph 2:3; Hag 2:23; Zech 2:11; 3:9; 8:23; 9:16; 12:4; 12:8; 14:20–21; Mal 3:17; 4:5.

18. Isa 2:2; 2:11; 2:17; 4:2; 4:5; 10:20; 11:11; 19:18; 19:19; 19:21; 27:12–13; 28:5; 30:26; 49:8; 61:2; Jer 16:14; 16:19; 23:5; 23:7;30:3; 30:8; 31:6; 31:31; 31:33; 31:38; 33:14; 48:47;49:39; 50:4; 50:20; 20:5; 29:21; 39:22; Joel 3:18; Mic 4:1; Hag 2:23; Zech 2:11; 3:9; 3:10; 8:23; 9:16; 12:8; 13:2; 14:20–21; Mal 3:17.

The "Day of the Lord," thus, was to be no less than re-creation itself, but patterned after the disruptive intrusion that initially set Israel's identity in motion, in the cumulative event that encompassed the exodus from Egypt, the establishment of the Sinai covenant, and the settlement in the land of Canaan.[19] It might take a direct intervention of God into human history to bring about,[20] yet when it happened, everything would be set right.

On this note the Old Testament closes. The Creator remains on a mission to recover the lost citizens of the kingdom of heaven, as well as renew the painfully twisted elements of nature. In order to make this restoration happen, the family of Abraham was enlisted as a witnessing partner. Unfortunately, the nation of Israel proved to be unequal to the task, and the divine redemptive enterprise limped toward an inglorious demise, even while the prophets were seeing and stating grander visions of the coming age. In the end, a muted but stirring prophetic voice charmed the hearts of all who waited in longing for the imminent "Day of the Lord."

Seemingly against all odds, what everyone in the covenant community anticipated was about to happen, but in a way that none had expected. Yahweh finally did show up, but appeared as a weak child rather than in the guise of a mighty warrior. Moreover, the "Day of the Lord" itself was split in two, so that the beginnings of the messianic age blessings arrived in whispers, long before the warning trumpets of judgment would be sounded.

19. See Isa 19:19; 19:21; 51:9; Jer 16:14; 23:731:31; 31:33.

20. Gerhard von Rad rooted the concept of the "Day of the Lord" in, what he termed, the "holy war" tradition within Israel's religion, see "The Origin of the Concept of the Day of Y," *Journal of Semitic Studies* 4 (1959) 97–108, and *Theology of the Old Testament* (Philadelphia: Westminster John Knox, 2001), 3–34.

3

John versus Jesus

A *"Day of the Lord" Tug-of-War*

To define a theology of the New Testament is a modest enterprise, and a reasonably uncontroversial task. After all, the textual data is limited (twenty-seven manuscripts, most of them very short), and the nuances of interpretation rather narrow in scope. Although among New Testament theologians there are differences of emphasis or arguments about the significance of certain terms and ideas, they rarely find themselves in fundamentally different camps from one another.

Developing a theology of the Old Testament (or Hebrew Bible) is a much more daunting task. Not only is the literature of this collection considerably more extensive, but it varies widely among multiple genres, topics, and provenance. Added to these challenges are questions of dating, inherent worldviews, and the degree of influence from other ancient Near Eastern cultures. Old Testament theologians can square off from very different ideological points of view.

Most intimidating, however, is any attempt at a biblical theology that encompasses both Testaments, seeking to remain faithful to the origins and directions of each, while pursuing the historical, cultural and religious bonds that have brought them together as the Christian Bible. Fundamental to this challenge is the question of the relationship between the two collections. Choices made here are inherently theological, philosophical, and confessional. Five major options are most often posited:[1]

- *The Old Testament is essential Christian scripture, with the New Testament serving primarily as its explanatory footnote.* Because Jesus and the first Christians were Jewish, and the preaching of the apostles

1. See, for instance, David L. Baker, *Two Testaments, One Bible: A Study of the Theological Relationship Between the Old and New Testaments* (Downers Grove, IL: InterVarsity, 1991).

was based upon the Hebrew Bible, there is a sense in which the Old Testament is sufficient when considering what revelation God might have given. The New Testament documents, in this view, do not alter or add to the theology of the Old Testament. Instead, they provide notes about the life and teachings of Jesus, and collect together the interpretive nuances about him that were put forward by the church's first preachers.

- *The Old Testament is prophecy, and the New Testament describes its fulfillment.* This is a significantly New Testament–centered approach. It views the Hebrew Bible and its context as an incomplete religious world in which its leaders invariably pointed to meanings and future happenings that could not be apprehended immediately by their contemporaries. God's designs, accordingly, were focused on Jesus, and for that reason Israel's history and religion were inherently still evolving, forming at best a prelude or prologue to the real event.

- *The Old Testament is historical background, while the New Testament is essential scripture.* In this overtly church-centered analysis, all Christian theology is derived from the New Testament. It, alone, is the complete "Word of God." The Old Testament is, of course, beneficial and convenient, for it gives historical context to the life of Jesus, and helps explain some of the terms and ideas bandied about in New Testament writings which are shaped by certain ancient cultures. Clearly, however, the New Testament is the guidebook for the church, and for that reason it can be published separately from the Hebrew Bible, and studied independently of that other collection which belongs to a different religion.

- *The Old Testament is primarily an expression of Law, while the New Testament is truly Gospel, "good news."* This approach believes that the God of the Judeo-Christian tradition acted in fundamentally different ways when nurturing the lives of these sibling faith communities. The "Law" of Old Testament covenant theology was a somewhat misguided attempt that viewed God as standing like nanny or teacher over a spiritually immature people, until an appropriate time when they would hunger for freedom as believers come of age. The New Testament breathes with grace and spiritual maturity that was not possible during Old Testament times. Jesus is the one who explained the new religious outlook, and took care of the penal code associated with the Old Testament "Law" so that New Testament believers would not have to worry about it.

- *The Old Testament begins God's covenant mission to reclaim the wayward peoples of earth through a centripetal geographic strategy, and the New Testament reaffirms this core design while retooling its missional thrust centrifugally outward to the far reaches of human settlement and expansion.* In this perspective there is a single unifying motif that binds the two Testaments together: the mission of God. This mission is largely channeled through Israel in Old Testament times, with a result that the nation needed to be located at a significant crossroad of international interaction, so that all peoples might eventually have an opportunity to connect with Israel's God. Furthermore, because the missional activities of God were expressed through a specific cultural context, many of the scriptural teachings were designed in and around and through Israelite engagements and history. The New Testament does not alter this divine missional drive, but it renegotiates the parameters, so that it becomes more portable and transferable. The critical event that initiated the Old Testament era of the mission was the exodus of Israel from Egypt, and the formation of its identity through the Sinai covenant. The critical event that initiated the New Testament era of the mission was the incarnation of the divine identity into human form (Jesus) so that the transition could be made quickly, and its redemptive transaction secured once and for all.

So, the New Testament begins with four documents focused on the unique identity, teachings, life, death, and resurrection of Jesus. Although the gospels of the New Testament are among the most widely recognized and read documents in the world, it remains difficult to explain their exact genre. The gospels have no clear parallel in any other religious or literary tradition.

A Unique Form of Writing

Certainly, the gospels are not mere biographies. They do not offer enough data about the life of Jesus to construct a full story of his existence, or to offer a well-developed social portrait of his presence among his contemporaries. While Matthew (1:18–2:23) and Luke (1:5–2:40) each relate a few events surrounding Jesus' birth, their selections differ significantly from one another. Luke briefly tells of a single incident in Jesus' early adolescence (2:41–52), and then jumps quickly to Jesus' baptism by John, indicating that this took place when Jesus "was about thirty years old" (2:23). The bulk of all four gospels proceed from this inaugurating event, bypassing almost entirely Jesus' first three decades of life. Since John includes notes about Jesus participating in three Passover celebrations (2:13–25; 6:4; 13:1), the last of which became the occasion for his crucifixion, it is commonly assumed that Jesus was thirty-three years old when he died. But the gospels are certainly no clear or concise or comprehensive biographies of Jesus' life.

Nor is it true that the gospels are a complete and systematic summary of Jesus' teachings. What has been preserved as the record of Jesus' sayings and speeches is too haphazardly gathered to form a codified compendium that would neatly explain his wisdom or theology. Indeed, while Jesus' parables and sermons and dialogues are essential to the gospels, the activities of Jesus' life also remain important, even though they do not form a detailed biographical life history. One significant example of this is the Passion narrative, found in all four gospels. There is a deliberate and extensive accounting of what happened during Jesus' last week in Jerusalem, to the extent that approximately one-third of each gospel is consumed by this brief and critical event. If the gospels were intended primarily as teachings of the master, they would not likely give so much place to these other dimensions of Jesus' life.

The most fitting designation for the gospels seems to be that of "proclamation." These documents are records of early Christian preaching about Jesus, describing the significance of his coming, the meaning of his personhood, the content of his teachings, the importance of his actions, the character of his death, and the miracle of his resurrection. Moreover, all of this material is communicated as a means to espouse a particular understanding of the divine mind and initiatives among the human race. The gospels are the church's early homilies.

Although the designations that give name to each of the four canonical gospels are extremely familiar ("The Gospel According to Matthew," ". . . Mark," ". . . Luke," ". . . John"), these were added by the early church on the basis of traditions which emerged very early in the transcription process. Apart from the brief introduction in Luke's gospel (1:1–4), and the few words of personal reflection at the end of chapters 20 and 21 of John's gospel, those who originally penned these documents had no desire to claim the contents for themselves, nor call attention to their own part in the activities recounted. The purpose of these writings was to proclaim Jesus, and that they did.

The Arrival of the "Day of the Lord" through Peter's/Mark's Voice

Yet the ascription of authorship tied each of the gospels to a particular provenance and purpose early in its existence, and this is important for those
who try to probe the uniqueness of each document. Although New Testament scholars continue to debate whether these presumed writers actually
penned the proclamations attributed to them, no widely affirmed, viable
alternatives have ever been put forward. So, the Gospel according to Mark
is as well interpreted as any through the eyes of Papias, a second-century
bishop, who declared (according to Eusebius in Book 33 of his *Church History*): "Mark, who was Peter's interpreter, wrote down accurately, though
not in order, all that he remembered of what Christ had said or done."

Who Was Mark?

What do we know of this Mark? Most of our data comes from the book
of Acts in the New Testament, along with snippets from the "greetings"
sections of Paul's and Peter's letters. The man had at least two names (Acts
12:12; 12:25; 15:37), which was not unusual in his world: *John* was probably used mostly in his Palestinian Jewish context, and *Mark* provided a
Hellenized name for interaction with the larger Roman world. From the
twelfth chapter of Acts we glean a few interesting tidbits about Mark's early
life, growing up in Jerusalem. He is called the "son of Mary," probably indicating that there had been no husband/father in the household for some
time. Most likely this meant that Mark's father had died while he was still
relatively young.

Furthermore, it is clear from the same passage that Mary's house was
the meeting place for the early Jerusalem Christian congregation. When Peter was imprisoned, the Christ-believers of the city gathered for an all-night
prayer meeting at this location. Indeed, Peter himself was aware of it, so
that when he came to his senses after his middle-of-the-night miraculous
release, although he was not a Jerusalem native, he quickly found his way to
Mary's home, expecting help.

The description of the house itself also indicates that Mary was a woman who lived in the more well-to-do part of Jerusalem. When Peter arrived at
her home, he knocked on a gate that was separated from the living quarters
by a courtyard. This arrangement only applied for those with some financial
means, and was not common for most people whose domestic space abutted
the street. Evidently John Mark was from the wealthier part of town.

This information supports a strong probable connection between Mark and the priestly ruling class within first-century Palestinian Judaism. Mark's tribal background, after all, was Levite. His cousin Barnabas (Col 4:10), was a wealthy Levite who had a second home on the island of Cyprus (Acts 4:36). It was probably because of this family link that Mark traveled with Barnabas and Paul to become part of the first Christian church planted outside of Palestine, in the old Greek administrative city of Antioch (Acts 11:27–30; 12:25), and then joined the pair on their initial mission journey into Asia Minor (Acts 13:1–5). Something happened during those travels, which caused Mark to return home to Jerusalem (Acts 14:36) before the rest. Different speculations suggest that Mark might have been angered at the changing role between Barnabas and Paul,[2] or that the harsh experiences of the journey proved too much for Mark to endure. In any case, his failure to go the distance later caused a difficult rift between Barnabas and Paul, to the extent that they parted in anger (Acts 15:38–42).

Mark and Paul were eventually reconciled, as made clear when, a decade later, Paul would write that Mark was his faithful fellow worker (Col 4:10; Phlm 24). Near the end of Paul's life, he even called Mark a useful assistant whom Paul wanted to have with him as he faced martyrdom (2 Tim 4:11). Peter also, just a few years earlier, had called Mark "my son" (2 Pet 5:13), indicating the close bond that had developed between Mark and the key leaders of the apostolic church.

Some rather strange and interesting glimpses of Mark have filtered through the pages of scripture and history. First, only in the gospel attributed to Mark does this very unusual note about someone who observed Jesus' arrest appear: "A young man, wearing nothing but a linen garment, was following Jesus. When they seized him he fled naked, leaving his garment behind" (Mark 14:51–52). Since this incident seems to add nothing to the theology of the gospel, it is often thought that here Mark made a single reference to his own experiences, growing up in Jerusalem during the years of controversy swirling about Jesus.

Second, there are several references to a nickname gained by Mark in the early church. Transliterated from Greek, the appellation would be "Kolobodaktulos," a word that meant "stubby finger."[3] One story suggests that Mark gained this name because he was born into the home of a priest's family. At the age of twenty-five he should have become an apprentice priest

---

2. It seemed that Barnabas' younger protégé was actually becoming the leader of the group, since in his reporting of their travels it was always "Barnabas and Paul" until they had finished crossing Cyprus, after which the two were listed as "Paul and Barnabas."

3. cf. Hippolytus, *Philosophumena*, VII, xxx.

in the temple, along with all other unblemished males from priestly families. But by this time Mark had become a follower of Jesus, and no longer believed it would be proper to continue offering animal sacrifices. In order to mar his features physically, so that he would become disqualified from priestly duty, he cut off part of one of his fingers. Although this report cannot be confirmed, it is interesting to note that when Paul and Barnabas take young John Mark with them on their first mission journey, he is called an "assistant," using the same Greek term which also designated the apprentice priests in the temple.

What Was Mark Trying to Communicate?

Papias knew that the church of his day recognized this shortest of the gospels as consisting essentially of the preaching of Peter about Jesus, even though the words themselves were recorded by Mark. There are several internal hints to support this hypothesis: Peter's call to be a follower of Jesus is the first to be recorded (Mark 1:16), even though each of the gospels reports the various callings in different sequences; Peter is identified as "Simon" early in the gospel (Mark 1:16; 29; 36), which fits with the probable way Peter was addressed by his family and friends, before Jesus renamed him (Mark 3:16) "Rocky" (the essential meaning of the Greek name "Peter"); the story of Jesus healing Peter's mother-in-law is told with more personal detail (Mark 1:29–37) than is found in its other gospel recordings (Matt 8:14–15; Luke 4:38–39). Together these clues cement a close connection between Mark's gospel and the preaching of Peter. Like as not, the old apostle declared these remembrances to his congregation in Rome, and his younger assistant took down notes that eventually morphed into this earliest gospel.

The first glimpse of Jesus in the Gospel according to Mark is found immediately in the introductory heading or title of 1:1—"The beginning of the good news (gospel) about Jesus Christ, the Son of God." Several things are important in this short statement. First, the author presumes there is much more to declare about Jesus than that which will be contained in these proclamations; this is only "the beginning." Second, whatever one might think about Jesus, even with the gruesome crucifixion story still ahead, the impact of his life and ministry is "good news." This colors how one should receive the message that follows. Third, Jesus is already understood at the beginning of this story to be the Messiah foretold by the prophets of the Old Testament. The term "Christ," appended to "Jesus," is a title, not a name (although it would come to be used as such). Jesus was "the Christ," meaning the one anointed to be the great deliverer of the Jews. This is why the baptism and divine commissioning of Jesus are told first (Mark 1:9–11), and are clearly expressed as a divine anointing (verse 10). Fourth, an additional designation is given to Jesus; he is called "the Son of God." While Christianity has made this a common theological phrase, it was originally a very specific political term used to honor the Roman emperor. When Caesar Augustus died, the Roman Senate declared him to be divine. All of the rulers who came after him were, in turn, identified as the "Son of God," when they mounted the throne. For Mark to call Jesus the "Son of God" was a deliberate move to identify him as a rival to the Roman emperor of the day.

> Our initial impressions about Jesus, as the narrative unfolds, are those showing him to be a man of action, healing and power. In the first two chapters alone, Jesus is breathlessly busy, flitting all over Galilee, healing and teaching with such abandon that he is constantly followed (Mark 1:45), and always under urgent demand (Mark 3:7–8). While the gospel seems, at the start, to be merely a collection of stories about Jesus' healings and brief teachings, it soon begins to take linear shape. In fact, its literary form will be copied by Matthew and Luke, who depend extensively on Mark's record. This is why these three are together called the Synoptics (those who see similarly). In very broad outline the gospel of Mark looks like this:
>
> **Chapters 1–8** Jesus blasts the powers that harm human life by means of the greater power of the Kingdom of God.
>
> **Chapter 9** *Transitional event*—transfiguration
>
> **Chapters 9–10** Jesus teaches his close companions about the cost and character of discipleship.
>
> **Chapter 11** *Transitional event*—entry into Jerusalem
>
> **Chapters 11–16** Jesus moves to the cross and beyond in a fulfillment of the cost of discipleship upon himself, and a paradoxical expression of the power of the Kingdom of God.

How Does Mark's Message Flow?

Among the many things that can be said about Mark's gospel, there are a number of interesting and critical features that are unique to it. First, no infancy story is recorded (in distinction from Matthew and Luke). This gospel about Jesus begins with his full-grown adult powers in place, and these are immediately confirmed and amplified by the commissioning endowment of the divine Spirit. In other words, according to Peter's preaching and Mark's penning, Jesus jumps out of the starting gate at full throttle, a man on a mission, with energy and purpose.

Second, the prophecy of Isaiah is recalled up front. That Old Testament spokesperson announced the coming of the great Day of the Lord, speaking of a time when Yahweh would break into human history to bring judgment against the nations of the world and the evil in Israel, save a remnant, and begin the new and transforming messianic age. In this way Mark links the coming of Jesus directly to the Old Testament identity of God, and the actions of salvation history contained in it, including the "Day of the Lord" expectations. This connection is further affirmed when Jesus opens his mouth to preach. His very first words are written by Mark as "the good news of God" (1:14), and commence as a staccato summary of the prophetic "Day of the Lord" theology: "The time has come. The kingdom of God is near. Repent and believe the good news!" (1:15).

Third, within the body of Mark's gospel, Jesus' first extended teaching is the parable of the Sower and Seeds (Mark 4:1–20). Its placing and expansive size, in comparison to the snippets of teaching that came earlier, highlight it as distinctive and important. As one reads these pages in continuous narrative, the pace suddenly slows, and Jesus demands that we reflect on what has happened so far. We have been watching the Jesus of power and action through the eyes of Peter and Mark. Now we must respond to the person of Jesus. How will the sower's seed find root in our own lives? What kind of soil are we? Both for Jesus' initial audience and for those who encounter Jesus through this gospel, the multiple-layered metaphor serves as a call to self-assessment and belief. Reaching behind the literary origins of the gospel, it is clear to see that Peter was not preaching merely to communicate information, nor was Mark recording Peter's sermons as a nice collection of spiritual writings. This was a document intended for volitional reaction. One *must* respond to Jesus, and the outcome of that engagement would be seen in direct changes of lifestyle and behavior.

Fourth, the healings (particularly the raising of the dead girl) in chapter 5, appear to trigger public animosity which will eventually lead to Jesus' death. Chapter 6 opens with the first major negative reaction against Jesus; it is predicated on the idea that people like the "magic tricks" of Jesus' miracles, but they don't appreciate having a local boy regarded as messianically special. What is received as "good news" by the crowds becomes bad news for the social and religious leaders. Without credentials, this man is challenging their authority, since the presence and power of God seems to flow much more easily and immediately than it does through them.

Fifth, this divided outlook about Jesus' actions and character may well be the reason for the unique and somewhat odd emphasis in Mark's gospel toward what has come to be known as the "Messianic Secret." On a number of occasions, when Jesus heals someone, he gives orders for the miracle to be kept quiet (Mark 1:34; 1:43–44; 3:12; 5:43; 8:26; 8:30; 9:9). While there are a few instances in which Jesus encourages people to talk about what he has done (e.g., Mark 5:18–20), it seems that most of the time Jesus does not want his mighty works widely publicized. Although it may seem contradictory for Jesus to expend the energy of heaven so dramatically and then wrap it up in a blanket of secrecy, there is probably good reason for the hushing. Crowds, titillated by these unusual events, might quickly develop into mobs which could short-circuit his full messianic task by trying to crown him as king too early, and only in a temporal realm (see Mark 1:45). If that had happened, Jesus could have ended up becoming merely a temporary human teacher, bogged down with the care of an endless stream of clients looking for a quick fix to their perceived problems. For that reason, Mark records Jesus' urgent warnings, early in his career, for people not to tell what has happened. Later, as the crisis of his life and identity heats up, these warnings will no longer be necessary.

Sixth, while all the evangelists report Jesus' entry into Jerusalem at the time of his final Passover in very similar manners, each nuances the details in a way that hints at the larger themes intended through their writings. In the case of Mark, there is an immediate shadow of rejection reported in the events of the day. "Jesus entered Jerusalem and went to the temple," writes Mark in 11:11. But then he adds this peculiar assessment: "He looked around at everything, but since it was already late, he went out to Bethany with the Twelve."

While it is certainly possible to take this statement as a mere reference to the lengthened shadow on the sundial, Mark couples it immediately with the cleansing of the temple and the cursing of the fig tree. Each of these actions is an overt judgment of Jesus imputed on the religious system of the day. The first rails against the leaders, who have allowed the temple ceremonies to become something foreign from their original purposes, while the latter castigates the nation as a whole for not fulfilling its Sinai covenant mission. The image of the fig tree (or similar domesticated flora) was a recognized cipher in the Old Testament and used to refer to Israel as the unique partner with Yahweh for the blessing of the nations (see Ps 80; Isa 5:1–7; Mic 7:1–6; Jer 8:13). Although it may not have been the season of the annual cycle for this particular tree to bear figs, there was never a time when the planting of Yahweh was not to produce fruits as evidence of its unique mission in the divine global recovery plan. So, when Jesus curses the tree, even though it was not the season for it to hang with ripe figs, he is using it as a metaphor or teaching tool for those who hear him.

Mark assures us that this is Jesus' meaning when cursing the tree, for he adds Jesus' teaching that through true belief "this mountain" (i.e., the place where Jerusalem and the temple were built) could be tossed into the sea. In other words, there was a shift in the mission methods of God taking place through Jesus' ministry. This city and nation, which had been the political, temporal, and geographical vehicle for announcing Yahweh's presence to the world, was now relinquishing those ties. In its wake would come a new focus on the person and work of Jesus, portable in its delivery to all nations through the preaching of his followers.

What Is the Impact?

This message is confirmed at the close of the gospel. The last person to make a declaration about Jesus in Mark's version of the gospel proclamation is the centurion at the cross (Mark 15:38–39). As the overwhelming impact of Jesus' crucifixion begins to shudder through the world, this soldier makes a powerful and overtly religious/political testimony. When he entered the ranks of the Roman military, he was obligated to take an oath of loyalty to the emperor, the "son of god." Here at Jesus' cross, however, he begins to understand that there is a ruler above the man in Rome. Although this person is dying in the ignominy of a social reject, there is something about him which announces a grander outlook on life, and calls for a bigger allegiance in order to make sense of his brief existence. The centurion, in a dramatic transferal of his military oath, publicly declares, "Surely *this* man was the Son of God!"

As a message first being preached by Peter in Rome during the days when Nero was coming to power, and then read by the Christians of Rome while official persecutions were mounted against them, the implication of the "good news" about Jesus was incredibly political. Nero demanded obedience through force; yet even his own soldiers recognized that in Jesus was a higher power, a greater power, a more worthy power that alone could overcome all of the other powers which enslaved people through demon possession, dehumanization, disease, or even death.

Taken as a whole, the "good news" about the "Son of God" in Mark's gospel is clear. Jesus is the heaven-sent Christ (Messiah or "anointed one") who arrives as the means by which the "Day of the Lord" will be accomplished in both judgment and blessing. Jesus tears into his world with action and power, overturning the many threats to human existence, and bringing the healing graces of restoration and hope. Because people might misinterpret his miracles, and want to make him their trophy ruler too quickly, Jesus cautions recipients of his transforming power to keep quiet about these things. Finally, when the big confrontation between Jesus and those who seem to hold social authority is unavoidable, Jesus declares a new strategy in the divine redemptive mission that takes the old "promised land" out of the picture, commissions his close followers begin a "good news" blitz to the nations, and changes all the rules of the game by dying in pain and shame in order to be reborn in power and hope.

The Arrival of the "Day of the Lord" through Matthew's Voice

When the gospels according to Mark and Matthew are placed side by side, it is very obvious that there is a strong literary dependence between them. Approximately 90 percent of the material in Mark's gospel shows up in Matthew's gospel. There are many good reasons to believe that Matthew used Mark's material in developing his own homiletic testimony about Jesus—editing a number of forms and expressions to make them come out more polished, altering terms (like the "Kingdom of God" to "Kingdom of Heaven") to fit a different audience, adding teachings and incidents that expand upon Mark's rudimentary offerings, regrouping certain materials to collect them into more memorably themed sections, and providing additional personal details in the conclusion.

A Gospel for the Jews

Whatever the reasons, the result expands the amount of teachings from Jesus that are made available to the church. Also, a second gospel provides a fuller picture of who Jesus was, and what he did, simply because it highlights his activities and teachings from another angle. Most importantly, through Matthew's account, the specific needs of Jewish Christians were addressed. This was critical because the first century AD was a time in which the people of God were moving from the ethnic, geographic, and cultic parameters surrounding the mission of Yahweh through Israel, to becoming the expanding missionary enterprise of the New Testament church. Matthew's gospel ties together both the past of Israel's Sinai covenant identity and the Christian church's Jesus identity. Both express the single divine mission which remains

unchanged from Abraham's first encounters with God. What is now different is the new strategy by which the Creator will re-engage the world.

By way of internal evidence alone, it is clear that the author of this
gospel was Jewish: he was certainly well versed in customs and beliefs that
were the cultural and religious rites of these heirs of Israel. Moreover, the
author had a good education, for his use of the Greek language is more
polished than that of Mark, and he quotes the Old Testament extensively in
both its Septuagint and Hebrew Bible versions.

Early Christian testimony declared that this gospel was written by
the Matthew, one of Jesus' disciples, and that it was produced during his
pastoral work among the Jewish Christians of Syria.[4] One small historical
note, which certainly supports this theory, is that Matthew's gospel was first
quoted by Ignatius of Antioch around the end of the first century.[5] Antioch
was the capital of Syria, and the place where Matthew based his ministry.
It would make sense that that if Matthew wrote this gospel in Antioch, it
would be first noticed and quoted there.

As with John Mark, Matthew was known also by two names: *Levi*,
probably reflecting his tribal background (Mark 2:14; Luke 5:27–28), and
Matthew, a Greek transcription of the Hebrew name meaning "gift of Yahweh." (Matt 9:9). Matthew is identified as a "tax collector" who sat at a booth
in Capernaum (Luke 5:27–28). This seaside town was the regional customs
center for trade passing along the *Via Maris* ("the Way of the Sea"),[6] the
major commercial route from India to Egypt. It is likely that Matthew was
from a family of at least moderate means, particularly since he was able to
host a large crowd for a banquet at his home (Luke 5:29).

While built upon Mark's earlier gospel manuscript, Matthew's expansion includes the birth narratives of chapters 1–2, extensive inserts of Jesus'

4. Eusebius (c. 260–340) reports Papias (c. 60–130) in *Ecclesiastical History* (3.39):
"Matthew put together the oracles [of the Lord] in the Hebrew language, and each one
interpreted them as best he could." In *Against Heresies* (3.1.1), Irenaeus (c. 130–202)
writes: "Matthew also issued a written Gospel among the Hebrews in their own dialect
while Peter and Paul were preaching at Rome and laying the foundations of the church."

5. There are two passages in Ignatius (c. 35–107) that show clear knowledge of
Matt 15:13 (*Letter to the Trallians*, 11:1 and *Letter to the Philadelphians*, 3:1). Other
Ignatius passages containing allusions to Matthew are: *Letter to the Ephesians*, 5:2 (Matt
18:19–20), 6:1 (Matt 10:40; 21:33–41), 10:3 (Matt 13:25), 11:1 (Matt 3:7), 14:2 (Matt
12:33), 15:1 (Matt 23:8), 16:2 (Matt 3:12), 17:1 (Matt 26:6–13), 19 (Matt 2:2, 9); *Letter
to the Magnesians*, 5:2 (Matt 22:19), 8:2 (Matt 5:11–12), 9:1 (Matt 27:52); *Letter to the
Trallians*, 9:1 (Matt 11:19); *Letter to the Romans*, 9:3 (Matt 10:41–42, 18:5); *Letter to
the Philadelphians*, 2:1–2 (Matt 7:15), 6:1 (Matt 23:27), 7:2 (Matt 16:17), *Letter to the
Smyrnians*, (Matt 12:18), 6:1 (Matt 19:12), 6:2 (Matt 6:28); *Letter to Polycarp*, 1:1 (Matt
7:25), 1:2–3 (Matt 8:17).

6. See note 39.

teaching material,[7] and a more fully developed conclusion (chapter 28). Our first glimpse of Jesus through this gospel's lens clearly connects Jesus with the Jewish community (Matt 1:1–17). Jesus is identified as a son of David and a son of Abraham. The link with Abraham ties Jesus to the unique covenantal community of Old Testament Israel, and all of the religious and missional implications that it carries. The filial relationship with David identifies Jesus as royal stock, and forms the basis for the many references in the gospel to consider Jesus as the true king of Israel or the Jews, based upon the eternal promise of Yaweh in 2 Samuel 7. Both of these themes are more fully developed throughout the gospel as a whole.

Although it might seem strange to begin the story of Jesus in a cemetery, reviewing genealogical tables (Matt 1:1–17), Matthew turns this unusual prologue into a fine homiletic art. Since there are no numerals in the Hebrew language, letters stood in for numbers when communicating quantities. The arithmetical values attributed to the characters found in David's name, when added together, equaled fourteen. Matthew uses fourteen as a reference when defining the movement of salvation history. He counts out fourteen generations from Abraham to David, fourteen more from David to the exile, and another fourteen from the exile to Jesus' birth. In so doing, even though he has to elide some generations together, Matthew declares that the very flow of Israel's existence gives evidence that God was about to do something extraordinary, and of great redemptive significance. In other words, Jesus' coming as Messiah was heralded by the very insistence of time itself. Furthermore, whatever God was doing on this anticipated occasion required double-dipping into the resources of heaven, for "Jesus" is actually the *thirteenth* name of the third set of fourteen generations, with the additional name "the Christ" completing the count for this category. Putting it all together, according to Matthew, history itself tells us that God is going to act in powerful ways once again, and the double nature of Jesus-as-the-Christ explains the uniquely potent dimension of this next great revelation. In symbolic communication, Matthew insists that we know Jesus to be both human ("Jesus") and divine ("the Christ").

The Messiah King Who Relives Israel's Existence

Next, Matthew gets into the birth narrative itself. Immediately he brings a further insight, declaring that Jesus, like Isaac, Samson and Samuel, is a

7. "The Sermon on the Mount" in chapters 5–7, missionary teachings in 10, kingdom parables in 13, instructions about the church community in 18, and the eschatological discourses of chapters 24–25.

divinely sent deliverer (Matt 1:18–25). Each of these great figures in Israel's history was miraculously born to mothers who were barren, and all of them provided new hope for their families and also the whole of the people of Yahweh. As with those earlier stories, here an angelic messenger explains the matter to one of the soon-to-be parents (Joseph), and provides a name for the child. Even more significant, in this case, Jesus will be recognized as both a local *and* a global ruler from birth. "He will save his people," says the angel. But then, almost immediately, foreign dignitaries (the Magi of Matt 2:1–12) follow an internationally available heavenly sign, seeking a king who is *of* the Jews, but who also serves as a beacon to the nations.

Matthew then does a quick-step through a variety of incidents in Jesus' early life to reveal even more about the essential character of this unique lad. Jesus, Matthew makes clear, is destined to replay or relive the life of Israel in a host of dimensions:

- Jesus copies Israel's miraculous existence and purpose, born through divine intervention as savior of nations (1:18–25).

- He is spared from the murderous intents of a scheming king (2:3–8) who goes on to slaughter the innocents (2:16–18), just as Moses was delivered in Exodus 2 while many Israelite boys were slaughtered.

- Like the nation as a whole, Jesus is gathered out of Egypt (2:15).

- From his earliest days, he is dedicated to a divine mission (so the play on the words "Nazirite" and "Nazarene" in 2:23).

- His ministry is set in motion by passing through waters (3), right at the same spot where Israel crossed the Jordan River in order to begin its witness to the nations from the promised land.

- Jesus also wanders in the wilderness for forty days (4:1–11) before he can fully assume his adult responsibilities, mirroring Israel's traumatic forty years described in the book of Numbers.

As Matthew brings these quick comparisons to a close, he relates that Jesus goes up on a mountain (Matt 5:1), and from that vantage point restates and reinterprets the Law or covenant as it was previously mediated through Moses (note the content of Matt 5–7, particularly as most major points of the original Sinai covenant are reiterated and renewed and reinterpreted). What has come to be known as the "Sermon on the Mount" is deliberately cast by Matthew in a manner which identifies Jesus as the new Moses for a new age. These things all connect Jesus' life and identity to the first "Day of the Lord," which later becomes the metaphor for the prophetic anticipations of a follow-up "Day of the Lord."

Following Mark's pattern, Matthew's large outline for unfolding the life and teachings of Jesus has three significant parts:

Chapters 1–16 Jesus teaches the crowds about the kingdom.

Chapter 17 *Transitional event*—the Transfiguration

Chapters 17–20 Jesus teaches the disciples about discipleship.

Chapter 21 *Transitional event*—entry into Jerusalem

Chapters 21–28 Jesus moves through the Passion to his coronation.

A New Moses

But superimposed on this basic development is a second and more subtle arrangement of materials. Since Matthew wants us to know that Jesus is the new Moses who delivers the covenant documents for a new age, he presents the narratives and teachings of Jesus in what is sometimes called a "Five Books of the Law" structure:

- **Prologue:** Jesus identified with Israel and the world (1–3)

- Book #1—**Narrative:** *Preaching and healing in Galilee* (4)—Look! Messiah has come!

  - **Discourse:** *Sermon on the Mount* (5–7)—Listen! Messiah speaks a new world order!

- Book #2—**Narrative:** *Mighty works, especially healings* (8–9:34)—Look! This is the one to follow!

  - **Discourse:** *Mission of the Disciples* (9:35–10:42)—Listen! This is the message of hope for all!

- Book #3—**Narrative:** *Rejection of Jesus* (11–12)—Look! People are becoming divided about Jesus!

  - **Discourse:** *Parables about the Kingdom* (13)—Listen! The Kingdom brings division!

- Book #4—**Narrative:** *Founding of the Church* (14–17)—Look! Here is what the church is about!

  - **Discourse:** *Teachings about the Church* (18)—Listen! This is how the church functions!

- Book #5—**Narrative:** *Travels from Galilee to Jerusalem* (19–22)—Look! We are on the way to the end!

    - **Discourse:** *Eschatological Teachings* (23–25)—Listen! This is how we prepare for the end!

- **Epilogue:** Jesus identified as Global Messiah King (26–28)

Each of these "books" concludes with a similar declaration,[8] noting that Jesus has finished teaching in a particular place or about a certain topic. The implication is simple and direct—Jesus has come to carry out the mission of Yahweh, first initiated with Israel, in a new way for a new, messianic age.

The Return of the King

The theme of Jesus' royal identity is consistently emphasized throughout Matthew's gospel, with a slightly different nuance than that found in Mark's gospel. For Mark, who was publishing the preaching of Peter in Rome during the impending crisis of Nero's persecution, Jesus was declared to be the mighty ruler who alone had the resources to defy and deny dehumanizing oppression in whatever form it challenged. In this way, Mark deliberately showed Jesus to be the only real alternative to the brutish power of the Roman Caesar. That is why even a Roman centurion could make the last and greatest testimony in the gospel, declaring Jesus' preferred rule over that of the might of Rome.

For Matthew, however, Jesus' kingship and kingdom are rooted directly in the covenant Yahweh made with David in 2 Samuel 7. In that passage the themes of God's house and David's house came together in powerful symmetry. David wished to build a house for God, since Israel was now settled in the promised land. While God appreciated this appropriate desire on David's part, through the prophet Nathan God communicated that it would be David's son, a man of peace, who would take up that honor and responsibility. But because David's heart and desires were in the right place, God made a return commitment to him. God would build a royal "house" out of David's descendants, and there would always be one of his sons ruling as king over God's people.

This promise began well, with the amazingly successful reign of Solomon. The great temple was built, the borders of the kingdom were expanded from Mesopotamia to Egypt, the economy soared, and people flooded to Jerusalem from all over the world to hear the wisdom of Solomon and

8. 7:28; 11:1; 13:53; 19:1; 26:1.

experience the blessings of Yahweh. Then it all began to falter. Solomon's massive empire was split at his death (922 BC), and the family successors who ruled the truncated kingdom from Jerusalem were a mixed lot with varying degrees of success in both politics and religion. By the end of Matthew's second set of fourteen generations, only a remnant of the people remained to be deported in the cataclysmic Babylonian exile. Fewer still returned to Jerusalem later, under Persian rule, and they were not permitted to reinstall David's descendants to a self-governing throne. Only recently, through the Maccabean revolt, had a measure of Jewish self-determination been regained. But David's family was not on the throne.

Now, however, Matthew makes it clear that this miraculously born deliverer Jesus is, indeed, the one who will fulfill, both at this time and forever, God's commitment to David. Matthew communicated powerfully in the opening chapters of the gospel, when he linked Jesus to David, and in chapter 2 when the Magi questioned King Herod's authority as the "King of the Jews." But the biggest statement of Jesus' kingly status takes place a bit later in the gospel, when Matthew narrates Jesus' entry into Jerusalem (chapter 21).

Upon Jesus' arrival at the capital city of ancient Israel and modern Judea, he is welcomed as king. The crowds immediately and publicly connect Jesus to David's royal family (21:9), and give him a royal salute. Furthermore, when Jesus enters the city, he moves directly to the temple. This, of course, was "God's House," the dwelling of Yahweh on earth. It was the permanent replication of what the tabernacle had been throughout Israel's wilderness wanderings. Just as when that portable structure had been dedicated by Moses, and the glory of God swooshed in as Yahweh took up residence (Exod 40), so the same had happened while Solomon dedicated the first temple (1 Kgs 8). But a vision later recorded by the prophet Ezekiel announced the awful portent that the glory of God was leaving the temple, and that God had gone back to heaven, moving out of Israel's neighborhood (Ezek 9–10).

It was Yahweh leaving "God's House" that precipitated the Babylonian destruction of Jerusalem and the temple, and initiated the years of Jewish exile and captivity. When Cyrus of the Persians issued an edict sending the exiles back to Jerusalem, they rebuilt the temple on a small scale with their modest resources. But the glory of God never returned to the rebuilt temple. During the times of the prophet Malachi, around 400 BC, the people were still pleading with God to return and take up residence with them again (Mal 3–4).

It is this history that Matthew draws upon, as he marks the steps of Jesus entering Jerusalem. Jesus goes directly to the temple, the house of God, and by implication, his own house *as* God. He cleans the place, a task which only the owner of the house can authorize (Matt 21:12–13). There Jesus receives his kingdom citizens who need royal favors—the blind and the lame (Matt 21:14). While Jesus is holding royal court, he is also presented with an impromptu concert from the most trusting stakeholders in his realm: the children (Matt 21:15). When the "chief priests" (i.e., those who have been left in charge of God's house), chide Jesus for inappropriately seeming to take over, Jesus quotes Psalm 8 as if it were his own, to verify the correctness of these happenings (Matt 21:16). Jesus is king. Jesus is the eternal ruler who has a right to sit on the throne of David, fulfilling the covenant Yahweh made with him. Jesus is the obvious resident of Israel's royal palace. The long-anticipated "Day of the Lord" has arrived!

But, just as Mark ominously noted in his narrative, these tenants have no use for Jesus, and do not want him to disturb their hold on power and territory. A few verses later Jesus' authority is directly questioned (Matt 21:23–27), within the very temple courts themselves. In response, Jesus tells two parables (Matt 21:28–46), each of which declares the horrible things that are about to happen because the tenants reject the royal claims of the Creator's family. Jesus is king, but this rule will not be won easily. It will be gotten only through the horrible death that Jesus is about to endure.

Matthew never relents from this central message that Jesus is the last and greatest and eternal son of David. Before the crucifixion Jesus is identified openly as king at least four different times (Matt 27:1–44). When Jesus dies, the curtain of the temple, which marked Yahweh's hidden quarters and separated God from the people, is torn away, so that the place becomes ceremonially dysfunctional (Matt 27:51) and Israel's ruler must move out of this particular residence. Even the earth itself heaves and groans in the seismic religious shift that is taking place between the Old and New forms of the covenant mission of Yahweh (Matt 27:52).

But the "Day of the Lord" Is not Finalized or Completed!

As Matthew brings his preaching about Jesus to a close, emphasizes Jesus' kingship one more time. The last words of Jesus in the gospel are a royal declaration and commission. Jesus the risen king addresses his key leaders, the ones who will take the mission of Yahweh to the world (Matt 28:18–20), and says to them: "All authority in heaven and on earth has been given to me. Therefore go and make disciples of all nations, baptizing them in the name of the Father and of the Son and of the Holy Spirit, and teaching them to obey everything I have commanded you. And surely I am with you always, to the very end of the age."

History itself predicted that Yahweh, the God of Israel, was about to so something really big, said Matthew (1:1–17). As Yahweh had done in the past, now again he raised up a miraculously born and commissioned savior (1:18–25). This time the deliverer was announced as King of God's people with global impact (2:1–23), and his own life circumstances paralleled and replayed Israel's own existence. When he rose up as leader (4), the old covenant was confirmed and updated (5–7). Then, embarking on a deliberate campaign to reclaim his throne (7–21), this Son of David was challenged on all fronts (22–27). By overcoming death itself, Jesus claimed "all authority," and reinvigorated the divine mission begun with Abraham. "Go and make disciples of all nations . . . "

The King has come! Long live the King!

The Arrival of the "Day of the Lord" through Luke's Voice

If the portrait of Jesus in Mark's gospel is that of the Son of God who arrives with great authority to overcome all other powers that demean, demoralize, demonize, dehumanize, and diminish, and the portrait of Jesus in Matthew's gospel is that of the Messiah King who fulfills Old Testament prophecy, relives the life of Israel, teaches the life of discipleship, and rises to rule over all nations, the Gospel of Luke expands these themes for a more specifically Gentile Christian audience. Luke indicates in his introduction (Luke 1:1–4) that he spent time with eyewitnesses of Jesus' life and ministry in order to gain additional knowledge beyond that which was otherwise available through the oral traditions of the apostles and the written proclamations of Mark's gospel.

Who Is Luke?

As with the other gospels, putting Luke's name to it as author is a bit of a detective search, coupled with a reliance on the testimony of early Christian sources. From the gospel itself we become aware that the author is certainly well educated. He uses excellent literary Greek style and vocabulary, he knows history and current affairs, he is aware of geography and distances in travel, and he understands social customs in various places. He is also curious, and pursues investigative research because he believes that knowledge

is a source of wisdom and insight. More than that, the author of this gospel
shows a special interest in the sick and the culturally marginalized. More
than any of the other gospels, this one resonates with moments when Jesus
sees those who have been turned out by polite society, and shows how they
matter greatly to God.

The introductions to both this gospel (Luke 1:1–4) and the Acts of
the Apostles (Acts 1:1–2) affirm their common authorship. Moreover, when
probing who this writer was, and where he came from, there is a revealing
testimony in Acts 16:6–12.

> Paul and *his* companions traveled throughout the region of
> Phrygia and Galatia, having been kept by the Holy Spirit from
> preaching the word in the province of Asia. When *they* came to
> the border of Mysia, *they* tried to enter Bithynia, but the Spirit
> of Jesus would not allow *them* to. So *they* passed by Mysia and
> went down to Troas. During the night Paul had a vision of a
> man of Macedonia standing and begging him, "Come over to
> Macedonia and help us." After Paul had seen the vision, *we* got
> ready at once to leave for Macedonia, concluding that God had
> called *us* to preach the gospel to them. From Troas *we* put out
> to sea and sailed straight for Samothrace, and the next day on
> to Neapolis. From there *we* traveled to Philippi, a Roman colony
> and the leading city of that district of Macedonia. And *we* stayed
> there several days. [Italics added]

From a literary standpoint, what is interesting about this paragraph, beside
the actual details of the travel itinerary, is the change in third-person to
first-person as the narrative moves from beginning to end. It starts with
a description of what Paul and his companions were doing, and how they
got to Troas. But when this missionary troupe leaves that city, suddenly the
narrative becomes personal: "we" traveled on to Macedonia because God
had called "us" to preach there.

This indicates that the author of the book of Acts (and thereby the
Gospel of Luke) was someone living in Troas, who joined Paul's missionary
tour from that city. Other notes from Paul's letters and testimony from the
early church indicate that this "someone" was Luke, a doctor who may well
have been called in to treat Paul for a recurrent malady. In Colossians 4:14,
Paul called Luke "our dear friend . . . the doctor," and in the greetings of
Philemon 24–25, Luke is listed as one of Paul's "fellow workers."

Because many doctors in that world started their professions as slaves
who functioned as assistant apprentices to other doctors, some have specu-
lated that this may also have been Luke's background. It might help explain

his constant attention to the oppressed social outcasts encountered by Jesus. Some legends also tell of Luke's painting skills, but like other tidbits of information we might glean, this is at best speculation.

If we note the first-person testimony as it dips in and out of the narrative of the book of Acts, we find that Luke is with Paul when Paul makes his final visit to Jerusalem (Acts 21:17), around AD mid-54. Then, when Paul finally sets sail from Palestine to Rome, two years later, Luke again identifies himself as a member of the traveling group (Acts 27:1). These years, when Paul is in Palestine under arrest, would likely be the occasion during which Luke was able to interview those who knew Jesus personally.

How Is Luke's Gospel Shaped?

As with Matthew's gospel, Luke's is also clearly built upon Mark's gospel, and has the same broad outline of Jesus' activities and teachings. Luke's use of Mark is much more selective than was Matthew's, however. Only about 55 percent of the Markan text is incorporated into Luke's gospel, and it comes mainly in three sections.[9]

While it would be interesting to know why Luke made these selections as he prepared his own version of the story and teachings of Jesus, such information is not available to us. At the same time, there are considerable portions of text which are unique to Luke's proclamation of Jesus. First, in a personal introductory note, Luke speaks to his specific intended audience, a man called Theophilus. While this is likely the official name of an actual individual, it is also possible that the term was a nickname or pseudonym for a person whom Luke wanted to protect, because he was in a position of government leadership that could be compromised if he was found to be associating with this suspiciously regarded branch of Judaism. "Theophilus" might also be a generic term used to indicate Christians generally, since it means "God's friend." In any case, this person appears to be a recent Gentile convert to Christian beliefs, possibly through Paul's preaching on one of the mission journeys where Luke was a partner. The designation "most excellent" (Luke 1:3) was often used as a formal manner of address for Roman officials, and this may indicate that Theophilus was a local or regional ruler.

---

9. Chapters 3:1—6:1 (John the Baptist, temptations, call of disciples); chapters 8:4—9:50 (teachings, healings, sending disciples out); chapters 18:15—24:11 (teaching, Jerusalem entry, the Passion). Interestingly, there are two sections of Mark's gospel that are not used by Luke: The "Big Omission"—Mark 6:45—8:26 (teachings and healings), and the "Little Omission"—Mark 9:41—10:12 (teaching on causing others to sin, and on divorce).

As does Matthew, Luke also augments Mark's narrative with birth stories (Luke 1-2). Luke not only tells us about Jesus' miraculous appearance, but also shares the earlier events that precipitated his cousin John's divinely initiated conception. Together these things focus on the preparation that took place to ensure Jesus' appropriate arrival and setting. Luke wants us to know that Jesus came into this world with a divine mandate and under heaven's clear planning and purpose. With great drama the stories unfold, accompanied by the marvelous songs of Mary, Zechariah, and Simeon, all of whom speak of the reversal of fortune that will be brought about by this wonderful act of God.

Luke ties the events of Jesus' life directly to historical circumstances in the greater Roman world. He reports that Jesus' birth occurred during the reign of Caesar Augustus and the governorship of Quirinius (Luke 2:1-2). Later he mentions that the beginnings of Jesus' ministry took place in the fifteenth year of Tiberius Caesar's rule (Luke 3:1). The connection with Caesar Augustus is particularly striking, since Augustus was the great ruler who brought about the *Pax Romana*, the peace of Rome. Luke makes evident, particularly through the song of the angels to the shepherds, that even in those times of relative international calm, the greater gift of divine peace was needed by humankind, and could be brought only through Jesus.

Also unique to Luke's presentation is the strong emphasis on worship and song and prayer. The gospel itself begins and ends in the temple, where people are gathered for times of public devotion. At the coming of Jesus, a number of songs are sung (by Mary, Zechariah, the angels, and Simeon). Prayer also forms a key element of Jesus' teachings, with an even greater emphasis brought to it than noted by Mark (see especially Luke 11:1-13).

Perhaps the most striking and clearly Lukan focus in conveying the message about Jesus, is his recognition that God has special care for the poor (noted in Mary's song, identified in the offering brought by Joseph and Mary at Jesus' circumcision, asserted through the record of Jesus' pronouncements of woes on the rich and blessings on the poor, and insinuated in the story of Lazarus and the Rich Man), the sick (notably the number of demon-possessed who are healed by Jesus, and also the lepers who are cleansed and the paralyzed who are restored to mobility), the marginalized (shepherds, children, tax collectors, prostitutes, Samaritans, and the blind), and women (Mary, Elizabeth, widows, the hemorrhaging woman, Mary and Martha, and the crippled woman).

At the close of his gospel, Luke brings one more unique and representative story (Luke 24:13-35). Two people are walking away from Jerusalem after the terrible events of Jesus' crucifixion. Suddenly they are joined by a man who seems familiar and yet remains a stranger. As they review the sad story of recent days, their fellow traveler, whom Luke has told us is actually the resurrected Jesus, begins to call their attention to the promises of the Old Testament, which somehow illumine both the life of their friend and the recent events that have troubled them. Then, when they enter their village of Emmaus, these two travelers urge Jesus to take a meal and hospitality with them. During time together, while Jesus blesses the bread, they suddenly recognize him, and he disappears. The two quickly retrace their steps to Jerusalem, scurrying to tell the news that they have seen the risen Jesus. Their message is heard with joy by the other disciples, of course.

Luke seems to have a particular reason for including this tale at the end of his gospel. How would those who were not privileged to live in Palestine during Jesus' days on earth (like Luke himself, or Luke's friend Theophilus, to whom this gospel was addressed), ever encounter Jesus? Luke could answer that question from his own experiences: he had found himself seeing Jesus in one special location—the church and its ministries. When the congregation met together to reenact the Last Supper of Jesus with his disciples, Jesus himself was present among them in his post-resurrection, spiritual form. If Luke or Theophilus or any other person wished to see Jesus these days, the place to find him was in the church. So, it was important for Luke to conclude his gospel with this memorable story. It was a clear indicator of the great truth needed in this new, messianic age: Jesus could still be found in the church's breaking of the bread.

What Does Luke Want Us to Know About Jesus?

Our first glimpse of Jesus in Luke's gospel is the heaven-heralded Savior, born in a miraculous way to the poor, and announced to the poor (Luke 2). Our first impressions of Jesus reveal the common pedigree he shares with those around him, that make him one of us in the whole human race (Luke 3:23–38; note the different way that Luke and Matthew handle Jesus' genealogies), his unusual gifts as a teacher (Luke 2:41–52), and his miraculous healing abilities (Luke 4–5). As with the other Synoptics, Mark and Matthew, Luke tells the big-picture story of Jesus' life in three major sections:

Chapters 2–9 Jesus heals, as evidence of the Kingdom of God

Chapter 9 *Transitional event*—the Transfiguration

Chapters 9–19 Jesus teaches the meaning of discipleship

Chapter 19 *Transitional event*—entry into Jerusalem

Chapters 20–24 Jesus teaches through self-sacrifice, and heals even death

But just like Matthew overlaid this general movement with a more specific subtle paradigm, so Luke builds a traveling motif into both this volume and the book of Acts. Here Jesus moves toward Jerusalem as the culmination of his ministry. In Acts, Paul makes a very similar journey toward the capital city in Palestine that serves to climax his missionary efforts. Luke's additional emphasis in the gospel looks something like this:

Chapters 2–9 Jesus' northern ministry of healing

Chapters 9:51–62 *Transitional event*—the road to Jerusalem and the cross

Chapters 10–19 Jesus' journey and ministry of teaching

Chapter 19 *Transitional event*—entry into Jerusalem

Chapters 20–24 Teaching and healing come together in Jesus' own experience

If Jesus' entry into Jerusalem was rather sinister in Mark's gospel (Jesus has no place, so he goes out and curses the fig tree as a sign), and a grand, but temporary homecoming of the glory of God in Matthew's gospel, for Luke, Jesus is the humble King who enters his capital city after the successful northern campaigns. This was a common theme in the Roman world, which had seen great generals leading the legions in northern Europe, and then coming home to Rome for a Senate-declared "triumph." In Jesus' case, however, it was the people who initiated the "triumph" of Palm Sunday (Luke 21), while the leaders whipped up opposition behind the scenes until the celebration was tragically overturned on Good Friday. But this gentle Teacher, loving Physician, and benevolent King had the last word on the matter. On Easter Sunday he came back to rule with grace and beauty, and all who knew that began to pray and worship (Luke 21).

The cumulative impact of Luke's recounting of the life and ministry of Jesus is that the "Day of the Lord" theology is prominent, once again. A climactic shift is taking place in world power politics, even though the nature of Jesus' interruption of human affairs scandalously different than one might expect, given the plays on domination in the news of the day. Tuned to Israel's history with Yahweh, it is clear that the traumatic "Day of the Lord" arrives with Jesus; at the same time, the full impact is defused for now, as Jesus initiates all that the Day implies, while leaving his remnant community to spread the word before the Day ends abruptly, somewhere down the road.

The Arrival of the "Day of the Lord" through John's Voice

The Gospel of John is unlike any other biblical or extra-biblical writing. Since it has most literary kinship with the Synoptic Gospels, in that it rehearses elements from the life and teachings of Jesus, it forms part of the "gospel quartet" of the New Testament. But even a quick read will show significant differences from these other uniquely Christian writings. First, the fourth gospel has a global philosophic introduction that places the story of Jesus in a comprehensive cosmological frame of reference.[10] Second, it is often more cryptic in its conversational narratives than are the other gospels, making it harder to understand how or why some of these dialogues could have taken place. Third, while it acknowledges that Jesus did many miracles, the Gospel of John actually reports only seven (during his public ministry), and then elevates the significance of these few by calling them "miraculous signs," and attaching to them deeper and more complex secondary meanings.[11] Fourth, in these pages there are extended monologues by Jesus which are both mystical and doctrinal, and that have no clear parallel to the manner of Jesus' teachings or conversations as recorded by the Synoptics. In short, the fourth gospel is a wild ride in a theme park of its own.

Yet, at the same time, this gospel is also so homey and comfortable that elements of it are like old slacks and shirts worn easily. The Greek language, through which the text is communicated, is basic and simple, so that even beginner students can quickly read it. Many of the teachings recorded here, from the lips of Jesus, have become the inextricable metaphors and motifs by which we know him and ourselves—the *Good*

---

10. John deliberately uses and repeats the word λογος ("Logos"), a highly nuanced term at the time, as he identifies and begins to tell about Jesus. The philosophic meaning of "logos" was first voiced by Heraclitus (c. 535–475 BC). He believed that our normal discourse and actions were somehow part of a larger cosmic meaning and purpose, which he identified as "logos." *Sophists* like Protagoras (c. 490–420 BC.) continued to link "logos" to the meaning behind our daily conversations. Aristotle (384–322 BC) declared "logos" to be reasoned discourse, and worthy of study in its own right within the field of rhetoric. Eventually the *Stoics*, headed by Zino (c. 334–262 BC), explained "logos" as the divine principle that animated the whole of reality. By the first century AD, as John was incorporating the term into the Prologue of his gospel, Roman writers such as Seneca (4 BC–AD 65) and Epictetus (AD 55–135) had popularized "logos" to mean the ultimate divine thought behind the cosmos and the energizing principle that guided things to exist as they were supposed to be and interact as they had been designed. This is the connection John was trying to make.

11. 2:1–11—water into wine; 4:43–54—nobleman's son raised; 5:1–15—man at pool healed; 6:1–15—crowds fed; 6:16–21—waters tamed; 9:1–41—blind man's eyes opened; 11:1–44—Lazarus raised.

Shepherd, the *Light of the World*, the *Resurrection and the Life*, the *Vine*, etc. Some of the conversations Jesus has with others are conveyed in a manner that makes us feel as if we were the only ones they were penned for, and we are always sitting next to Jesus again when we read them. Even our Christian theology and worldview has been so shaped, over the centuries, by themes from this document, that we cannot separate it from us, or imagine Christianity apart from these twenty-one chapters. The gospel according to John is a key element of biblical faith.

Who Was John?

Johannine scholars continue to debate the complex questions about who wrote the Fourth Gospel. From early church sources comes testimony that it was penned by the beloved disciple and closest friend of Jesus (Irenaeus), and that the apostle (Tertullian) who wrote it in Ephesus (Origen, Clement) as the last among the gospels (Irenaeus, Eusebius), under the urging of others, was nearing the end of his life (Clement). From within the text of the gospel other clues confirm these perceptions:

- It was written by a Jew:
  - Someone who had clear knowledge of Jewish customs (e.g., the water ceremonies on the final day of the Feast of Tabernacles in 7:37–38)
  - Someone who thought in the languages and linguistic patterns of Palestinian speech, giving evidence of this in his choice of words and phrases (e.g., the dialogue with the Samaritan woman in chapter 4, particular with reference to different interpretations of ancient Israelite customs and theology)
- It was written by a Jew of Palestine:
  - Someone who knew Palestinian geography firsthand (e.g., the location of the "Sheep Gate" and pool of "Bethesda" with its "five covered colonnades in chapter 5:2)
  - Someone with a knowledge of festival practices in Jerusalem (e.g., the Sabbath laws in chapter 5)
- It was written by an eyewitness:
  - This person knew specific topography and incident details from the travels of Jesus (e.g., the location and geographical features of Aenon in 3:23)

- It was written by a disciple of Jesus:

  - The writer knew intimate and minor details of travels and events that would not likely be reported by someone who had only later researched these matters as an investigative reporter (e.g., the conversations of specific people in 1:35–51; 2:3–10; 3:1–10; 4:7–38; 5:6–8; 6:60–71; 11:1–44)

- It was written by John the Apostle, the beloved disciple:

  - So the text leads us to understand, from both the writer (John 13:23; 18:15–16; 19:25–27; 20:1–9, 30–31) and his own disciples (John 21:24)

At the same time, a good number of scholars do not believe this John wrote the gospel.[12] There seems to be, they say, historical confusion about several different possible Johns (the Apostle, the Evangelist, the Elder), and the variety of different ways in which the obviously edited text reached its final form. While these conversations continue with great energy, it is still widely recognized that there is a very close link between this gospel and Jesus' disciple John, however issues of authorship might one day be resolved.

How Is the Gospel Shaped?

Although its development is markedly different from that of the Synoptic Gospels, there is a very clear pattern to John's portrayal of Jesus' activities and teachings in this gospel. When reading straight through the document, one notices several significant literary points of change. For instance, John 1:1–18 is a kind of philosophic reflection on time and space and the incarnation. Then, suddenly, at 1:19, we are brought directly into the daily life of first-century Palestine, walking among crowds who are dialoguing with John the Baptizer about his identity. Clearly a shift of some kind takes place between 1:18 and 1:19.

The flow of life in real time continues through the next several pages, as John the Baptizer points to Jesus and then steps out of the way (1:19–36), Jesus gains a following through his miracles and teachings (1:37–12:50), and then predicts his impending death (13:1–38). What transpires next seems to move into another kind of literature once again. From chapter 14 through chapter 17, Jesus is almost lost in a last reverie, a kind of mystical intimate moment with his disciples. The monologue weaves back and forth on itself

---

12. For a good overview of this discussion, see Barnabas Lindars, Ruth Edwards, and John M. Court, *The Johannine Literature* (Sheffield, England: A&C Black, 2000).

until it shoots upward toward heaven in a prayer that surrounds Jesus and his disciples in a divine blanket of engulfing holiness (17). Abruptly the light dissolves, and with a kind of staccato journalistic pedantry, the events of Jesus' arrest, trial, death and resurrection are recorded (18–20). Chapter 20 ends with a brief but sufficient conclusion to the book as a whole. Yet suddenly another story appears, and the finality of the wrap-up in chapter 20 is broken and ignored (21). The disciples are listless and almost devoid of the power revealed when they earlier had realized that Jesus was come back to life. They now decide to go fishing, for lack of anything better to do. But then Jesus appears, and their lives are quickly refocused so that they will be his followers to the end of their days. With that said, a second brief conclusion is offered, and the gospel is finished.

Stepping back from the whole of this narrative, and reviewing the obvious literary disjunctures or sudden stylistic shifts in gospel, it becomes apparent that a significant transition happens between chapters 12 and 13 (related to the coming of "the hour" for Jesus; note 2:4; 4:23; 7:6; 12:23; 13:1; 17:1). This pivotal point is further accentuated by the grouping of all of Jesus' "miraculous signs," as John calls them, into chapters 1–12. This is why the first part of John's gospel is often called "The Book of Signs," while the last part wears well the name "The Book of Glory" Because Jesus terms it so (12:23).[13] Bookending everything, a cryptic prologue opens the gospel (1:1–18), and an epilogue, perhaps written by another party and added after the initial gospel was completed (chapter 21), brings it to a close. Each of these four sections deserves a closer look.

The gospel's unique prologue highlights several ideas. First, both Jesus and the message of Christianity are tied to the comprehensive foundational values shaping common philosophic systems of the day. "Logos," in the Greek mind, was the organizing principle giving meaning and identity to everything else. By using this term to describe Jesus, John portrays him as more than just a fine teacher who said a few nice things on a Palestinian spring afternoon. Jesus is, in fact, according to John, the very creator of all things, and the one who gives meaning to life itself. Apart from Jesus, nothing makes sense or has any intrinsic meaning.

Second, "light" and "darkness" explain everything. Right up front, John helps us think through life and values and purpose in a stark dualism that is engaged in a tug-of-war for everything and everybody. Nicodemus will come to Jesus in the darkness of night (chapter 3), only to be serenaded by Jesus' fine teachings about walking in the light. The blind man of chapter

---

13. Cf. Raymond E. Brown, *The Gospel According to John, Volume 1* (Garden City, NY: Doubleday, 1966).

9 is actually the only one who can truly see, according to Jesus, because all of the sighted people have darkened hearts and eyes. Judas will enter the room of the Last Supper basking in the light of the glory that surrounds Jesus (chapter 13), but when he leaves to do his dastardly deed of betrayal, the voice of the narrator ominously intones, "and it was night." Evening falls as Jesus dies (chapter 19), but the floodlights of dawn rise around those who understand the power of his resurrection (chapter 20). Even in the extra story added as chapter 21, the disciples in the nighttime fishing boat are bereft of their netting talents until Jesus shows up at the crack of dawn, tells them where to find a great catch, and is recognized by them in the growing light of day and spiritual insight. Darkness, in the Gospel of John, means sin and evil and blindness and the malady of a world trying to make it on its own apart from its Creator. Light, on the other hand, symbolizes the return of life and faith and goodness and health and salvation and hope and the presence of God.

Third, as a corollary to these ideas, John shows us that salvation itself is a kind of re-creation. Using a deliberate word play to bind the opening of the gospel to the sentences that start Genesis, John communicates that the world once made lively by the Creator has now fallen under the deadly pall of evil, and needs to be delivered. The only way that this renewal can happen is if the Creator re-injects planet Earth with a personal and concentrated dose of the original Light by which all things were made. Although many still wander in blindness or shrink back from the light like cockroaches or rodents who have become accustomed to the inner darkness of a rotting garbage dump, those to whom sight is restored are enabled to live children of God once again.

This leads to a fourth theme of the prologue, namely that the New Testament era is merely the Old Testament mission of God revived in a new form. Jesus, the Logos, comes to earth and "tabernacles" among us (verse 14), just as the Creator had done when covenanting with Israel, and commissioning her to become a witness to the nations. Furthermore, those who truly recognize Jesus for who he is, see in him the "glory" of the Father. This is a direct link to the Shekinah glory light of God that filled the tabernacle and the temple, announcing the divine presence. The mission of God continues, but it will now be experienced through the radiance that glows in all who are close to Jesus. The "tabernacle" that houses the glory of the divine presence is on the move into the world through this "only begotten Son of God" (1:14) and all who become "children of God" (1:12) with and through him.

What Significance Do the "Signs" Have?

On this philosophic foundation, John organizes a very deliberately shaped encounter with Jesus. The seven "miraculous signs" of chapters 2–11 not only provide healing and hope to those who were first the objects of divine grace through Jesus, but they also dig deeper into biblical history to replay major scenes of the Old Testament in a way that reasserts the mission of God, while shifting its agency from Israel to Jesus. For instance, just as sin first disrupted the marriage of Adam and Eve in the Garden of Eden, so Jesus first displays his regenerative powers by restoring the celebration at a wedding (chapter 2). Again, while Adam and Eve mourned the loss of their son through murder brought about by sin, a new nobleman (John deliberately sets this character above national, tribal, or ethnic limitations that are otherwise used to identify all other persons in the gospel) receives back his son from the dead (chapter 4). Next, Jesus encounters a man who has been ailing for thirty-eight years (chapter 5), and who can only otherwise be healed by passing through waters that have been divinely disturbed. Interestingly, Moses, in Deuteronomy 2:14, gives the only other reference to the number thirty-eight in all of the Bible, mentioning it as the amount of time that the Israelites have been wandering in the wilderness, waiting for the shalom that can come to them only if they pass through the waters of the Jordan River, which will be divinely disturbed in order to make the crossing possible.

In this way John continues to portray Jesus as the new agent of divine redemption, functioning in parallel to the manner in which God dealt with Israel of the Old Testament. Jesus, too, feeds the people of God in the wilderness (chapter 6) and tames the raging waters that in the darkness prevent God's people from entering the promised land (chapter 6). Furthermore, as Isaiah was told about the blindness of the people in his day (Isa 6), Jesus contends with similar dysfunctional eyes (chapter 9). And just as Ezekiel had to preach to the dead nation of Israel in order to resurrect it from the grave of exile (Ezek 37), so Jesus brings back to life one of his dear friends who has died (chapter 11), symbolizing the ultimate goal of divine grace.

It is only when the seven signs have been published to the world in this manner, that the "Greeks" (John's notation for the whole world out there, beyond our tiny Jewish enclave) come seeking Jesus (12:21). Then, immediately, Jesus declares that his "hour" has come. Why? Because the salvation of God sent to this world (John 3:16–17) has been recognized through the signs, and has been received by the world. It has begun to make an impact, and the world will never again be merely content with darkness. Dawn is breaking.

What Is the "Book of Glory" About?

Once the transition takes place from the "Book of Signs" to the "Book of Glory," only two major events happen. First, Jesus meets for an extended meal and conversation with his disciples (chapters 13–17). This lengthy monologue seems somewhat meandering and repetitive until it is viewed through the Hebrew communication lens of chiasm.[14] Then the "Farewell Discourse," as it is known, takes on new depth, as it weaves back and forth, and climaxes in the middle. This parting exhortation becomes an obviously deeply moving instruction Jesus' followers to remain connected to him by way of the powerful "Paraclete" (a Greek term meaning "counselor" or "advocate"), in the face of the trouble that will come upon them because of his imminent physical departure, and the rising persecutions targeted toward them by the world that remains in darkness. In chiastic summary, the Farewell Discourse can be portrayed in this manner:[15]

Gathering experience of unity	*13:1–35*
Prediction of disciple's denial	*13:36–38*
Jesus' departure tempered by Father's power	*14:1–14*
Promise of the "Paraclete"	*14:15–24*
Troubling encounter with the world	*14:25–31*
"Abide in Me!" teaching	*15:1–17*
Troubling encounter with the world	*15:18–16:4a*
Promise of the "Paraclete"	*16:4b–15*
Jesus' departure tempered by Father's power	*16:16–28*
Prediction of disciple's denial	*16:29–33*
Departing experience of unity	*17:1–26*

Every element of this "Farewell Discourse" is doubled with a parallel passage except for Jesus' central teaching that his disciples should "abide in me." Furthermore, these parallel passages are arranged in reverse order in the second half to their initial expression in the first half. At the heart of it all comes the unparalleled vine and branches teaching, which functions as the chiastic center and ultimate focus of the discourse as a whole. In effect, John shows us how the transforming power of Jesus as the light of the world

14. See note 37.

15. Wayne Brouwer, *The Literary Development of John 13–17: A Chiastic Reading* (Atlanta: SBL, 2000).

is to take effect. Jesus comes into this darkened world as a brilliant ray of re-creative light and life. But if he goes about his business all by himself, the light will have limited penetrating value, over against the expansive and pervasive darkness that has consumed this world. So a multiplication and amplification has to happen. Jesus himself spoke about this at the end of the "Book of Signs." He said:

> The hour has come for the Son of Man to be glorified. I tell you the truth, unless a kernel of wheat falls to the ground and dies, it remains only a single seed. But if it dies, it produces many seeds. The man who loves his life will lose it, while the man who hates his life in this world will keep it for eternal life. Whoever serves me must follow me . . . (12:26)

In this chiastic "Farewell Discourse," Jesus makes clear the meaning of everything. His disciples have been transformed from darkness to light (and thus from death to life) through Jesus' incorporation of them into fellowship with himself and the Father (chapters 13 and 17). This does not free them immediately from struggles, as seen in Judas' betrayal and the coming denial of them all. But the connection between the Father and the disciples is secure, because it is initiated by the Father, and will last even when Jesus disappears from them very shortly, because the powerful "Paraclete" will arrive to dispense Jesus' ongoing presence with them all, wherever they go and in whatever circumstances they find themselves. Of course, that will only trigger further conflicts and confrontations with "the world." So (and here's the central element of the discourse), "abide in me!" Either you are with the darkness or you are with the light. Either you are dead because of the power of the world, or you are alive in me. And, of course, if you "abide in me," you will glow with my light, and the multiplication of the seed sown will take place. Eventually, through you, the light that comes into the world through Jesus will bring light to everyone. It is a picture of the mission of God, promised to Abraham, enacted geographically through Israel, but now become a global movement through Jesus' disciples who "abide" in him through the power of the "Paraclete."

The second half of this "Book of Glory" shows Jesus as he moves through his Passion into the resurrection. While the details of Jesus' trial and crucifixion are virtually identical with those given in the Synoptic Gospels, there are a number of little incidents reported that could only have been written by an eyewitness—the name of the servant of the high priest who is wounded by Peter's sword (18:10); the reason for Peter's access into the area where Jesus was being tried (18:15); the words of the conversation between Annas and Jesus (18:19–24); the transfer of Mary's care from Jesus to the beloved disciple (19:27). These are reminders again that the fourth gospel was authored by someone who was with Jesus at every turn, and remained Jesus' deep friend right through the end.

When describing the events of resurrection morning, John gives us some wonderful analogies to see its meaning on several levels. For one thing, when Mary looks into the empty tomb (20:10–12), the scene as John describes it immediately calls to mind the Ark of the Covenant that symbolized Yahweh's presence in the tabernacle and later the temple. While the other gospel writers tell of angels being present, John views them through Mary Magdalene's eyes, and sees two such creatures in exactly the same position as the cherubim that stood guard over the Mercy Seat throne. This time, however, the divine presence was missing, indicating the dawning of a new age in which the Creator's power and presence would not be confined to or limited by a particular geographic location. The second strategy in the divine mission had come, and the gospel was now to be preached to the whole world through Jesus' disciples.

Then, when Mary Magdalene weeps because she misses her "Lord" (which is the Greek version of "Yahweh"), a man appears on her periphery, and she assumes that he is "the gardener." Of course, Mary's perception is incorrect, because the man is not a local horticulturalist. But is she really wrong? John never says that she was mistaken; only that Mary Magdalene had assumed Jesus was the gardener. In fact, John appears to want his readers to get the subtle message that Jesus is *indeed* the gardener. After all, at the beginning of time, the Creator placed Adam and Even in a garden and came to walk and talk with them (Gen 2). Now, in the re-creation of all things, it is quite appropriate for new life to begin anew in a garden where the great Gardener is again meandering and sharing intimacy with those who are favored friends. John confirms this symbolic intent when he tells about Jesus speaking Mary's name. Just as Adam and Eve, along with all the animals and all elements of creation, came into being when they were named in the first beginning, so now Mary is restored to life in a new way as her identity is regenerated when Jesus speaks her name. Jesus, however, cannot be held in this garden (20:17) as partner in only one local friendship, for the process of re-creating all things is only just beginning, and he must leave to finish the task. Only when he goes, as he said in the "Farewell Discourse," will he be able to multiply his presence through the gift of the "Paraclete."

This coming of the "Paraclete" is enacted next, when Jesus meets with the rest of his disciples later that day. John tells us that he "breathed on them" (20:21), imparting to them the divine Spirit, and sending them out as his ambassadors, exactly in the manner of which he prayed in chapter 17. Is this, as some have suggested, John's different version of Pentecost (Acts 2)?

No; it is a final expression of the re-creation process. Just as Adam only came alive to his life and livelihood at the beginning of time when God breathed into him the divine breath (Gen 2), so now this tiny gathering of the new humanity cannot function until they are divinely enthused in a similar, very literal manner. The Creator who breathed the breath of life into Adam in the first creation now breathes the same breath of life into his disciples in this re-creation. The dead of the world are coming back to life!

John ends his gospel with the story of Thomas, who demands the proof of physical evidence in order to believe this good news. Although Jesus provides Thomas' requested touch, Jesus commends those others who can become reborn human creatures through faith, which is not dependent upon direct experiential contact with Jesus' physical body. In this, the missionary nature of John's gospel message is confirmed, for John ends by issuing an invitation to the same trust and belief to all who read it (20:30–31), even though they do not have opportunity to touch Jesus' physical features.

What Is the significance of the epilogue?

The epilogue (chapter 21), possibly added later, does several things. First, it reveals the uncertainty that plagues the disciples and the church, wanting to be witnesses of Jesus, but caught up in the cares and demands of the times. Second, it reaffirms the missionary character of the apostolic church, particularly when 153 fish are caught in the disciples' net only at Jesus' instigation.[16] Third, it provides a way for Peter to be fully restored to leadership graces, since he will become the key communicator and witness among the disciples. Fourth, it announces both Peter's early death (by crucifixion under Nero's persecution around AD 65) and John's longevity, each of which contributed in different ways to the formation of the Christian church in the first century.

---

16. The specific number of the total fish caught by the disciples has led to a fascinating history of speculation and interpretation. Some discount its significance as merely the end product of typical fishing habits—fishermen count their fish! Most prominent among speculations is Gematria (the rabbinic fascination with scriptural numerology) manipulation. Since 153 is the triangular sum of integers 1 through 17, and 17 plays a special role as the product of the numeric divinations of the Hebrew names "Gedi" and "Eglaim" (which were springs along the Dead Sea, marking the limits of a miraculous territory of freshening water for fishing in Ezek 47), 153 might symbolize a connection between the gospel witness and the arrival of the end times. More in the realm of interpretation is Jerome's reference to Oppian's second-century didactic poem *Halieutiká*, which identifies 153 different species of fish in the waters of the ancient world. Jerome tied this single last haul of the fishermen of Galilee who became Jesus' "fishers of men," to their next mission of gathering in all nations of the world.

Jerome wrote that when John was a very old and feeble man living in Ephesus, he was brought each Sunday to the front of the congregation's gathering on a pallet carried by others. Invariably John would be asked to speak a word, and just as constantly he would raise himself on one elbow and with great effort whisper out with a hoarse rasp, "Little children, love one another." When asked why he always said the same thing, he would reply that this message was enough; that it was all that was necessary.[17]

It was during those final years of John's life, according to Jerome, that others urged him to write another gospel, in addition to the Synoptics which were by then widely circulated and read. Since John was the last of Jesus' original disciples still living, it would be a final direct link with the One who had changed the world. So it is that we have this amazingly crafted testimony of the light and life of the world.

What is clear in John's reflections about his best friend and Savior is that John saw Jesus as a history-changing divine interruption into the darkened and dead world, no longer responsive to its Creator. In replaying the ministry of Jesus as framed in parallel to Israel's Old Testament missional identity and journey, through the seven signs, John dramatically identifies the redemptive designs of God through Israel as recurring in Jesus. The first "Day of the Lord," inaugurated by the Exodus, shaped by the Sinai covenant, and commenced from the strategic platform of the "promised land," is now repeated in Jesus' own engagements. The Gardener has returned to bring life and beauty to his garden. But the process by which the miracle of rebirth spreads, shifts the focus from land-locked Israel to mobile witnessing bands who extend the light into a darkened world. They do this by remaining connected to Jesus (John 15:1–17), linked to the glorious Logos through the divine Paraclete within them who enables them to glow, and empowers them to spread the original Light that brings life.

The "Day of the Lord" foretold by the prophets has arrived. Yet it is split and lingering. Jesus endured the judgment, gathered a remnant team, and through them spreads the widening circles of messianic kingdom blessing. But what has begun will culminate. The last word Jesus speaks to his disciples, according to John, is his promise to return soon (John 21:20, 23), bookending this world-restoring "Day of the Lord" event.

---

17. Jerome, *Commentary on Galatians*, VI.1.

Personifying the Queries regardin
"Day of the Lord" Split: John the F

More than any other New Testament figure, John the
edge of this disruptive splitting of the "Day of the Lo:
the last of Israel's great prophets,[18] haranguing from th
vine authority,[19] and announcing the imminence of the "Day of the Lord."[20]
It was clear for all who came to John, intrigued by his demeanor and morally
charged preaching, that John believed Jesus' arrival to be the in-breaking of
the "Day of the Lord," complete with its judgment, chastised remnant, and
messianic age of blessing.[21] When John's message to local Jews drove them
to repentance and action, John baptized them as part of what he thought
would be the remnant community which would survive the "Day of the
Lord" conflagration.[22] Jesus arrival, one day, signaled to John that the "Day
of the Lord" had itself arrived.[23] In fact, after wrestling with Jesus about who
should baptize whom,[24] Jesus prevailed upon John to do the honors,[25] and
then, apparently with John's blessing, created his own nucleus of disciples
from among John's close followers![26]

John then drops from the records of the gospels for at least several
months, probably because he was arrested by Herod Antipas,[27] the son of
Herod the Great and his last wife Malthace. John had been the target of
Herod Antipas' ire because John regularly preached that Herod had committed murder and was living in sin. Herod Antipas had killed his brother
Herod II (son of Herod the Great and his second wife Miriamne II) in order
to wed Herod II's wife and their common niece,[28] Herodias. Herod Antipas
was already married at the time, but divorced his wife, the daughter of Nabi-
tean King Aretas IV, in order to make the new union seem more palatable.
In response, John gave voice to Jewish consternation about these immoral

---

18. Matt 3:1–3; Mark 1:2–3; Luke 3:2–26; John 1:6–8, 15–17.

19. Matt 1:3–9; Mark 1:4–6; Luke 3:2–14; John 1: 15–24.

20. Matt 3:10–12; Mark 1:7–8; Luke 3:15–17; John 1:25–31.

21. Matt 3:11–17; Mark 1:7–11; Luke 3:15–22; John 1:25–34.

22. Matt 3:1–17; Mark 1:2–11; Luke 3:15–22; John 1:25–34.

23. Matt 3:13–14; Mark 1:7–9; Luke 3:15–22; John 1:25–34.

24. Matt 3:14–15.

25. Matt 3:13–17; Mark 1:9–11; Luke 3:21–22; John 1:32–34.

26. Matt 4:12–22; Mark 1:14–20; Luke 5:1–11; John 1:35–51.

27. Matt 4:12; Mark 1:14.

28. Herodias was the granddaughter of Herod the Great and his first wife Miriamne I.

of their imposed and despised ruler. So, Herod Antipas incarcerated to curtail his unwelcomed public diatribes and accusations.

While in prison, however, John's deeply held assumptions about Jesus began to collapse. John heard reports of Jesus' ministry, and it did not sound like a divine thunderbolt of cataclysmic judgment.[29] John became confused, sensing that Jesus was failing to follow through on the critical elements of the classic "Day of the Lord" theology. John sent two of his own followers to check things out. They were to demand of Jesus whether he was, in fact, the vehicle of heaven intended to fulfill prophetic judgment day warnings.

Jesus did not debate with John's disciples. Instead, he took them along on a day of blessing, where "the blind receive their sight, the lame walk, the lepers are cleansed, the deaf hear, the dead are raised, and the poor have good news brought to them."[30] He then sent the duo back to John to report. While we are not made aware of John's response, it is clear that Jesus, and eventually the gospel writers and early church with him, understood what was going on. Instead of bringing the full impact of the prophetic "Day of the Lord" as a single act of global divine judgment which would immediately transition into the eternal Messianic age of blessing, Jesus had split the "Day of the Lord" in two. He would absorb the full weight of heaven's retributive justice into his own person on the cross of torment, sparing the rest of the world that trauma for the short term. But he would also pull together a remnant community of witness, beginning with his twelve closest disciples and their followers, and, most importantly, Jesus initiated the blessings of the eternal messianic kingdom through his healings, death-raisings, demon-exorcisms, and general kindnesses. Jesus confirms this interpretation of what is taking place, in fact, by identifying John as the "Elijah" messenger foretold through Malachi to be the forerunner of the "Day of the Lord,"[31] and also by connecting his own miracles to Isaiah's grand testimony about what Messiah would bring on the "Day of the Lord."[32]

John the Baptist personalizes the great struggle of the Jews to believe that Jesus might be their promised Messiah, foretold by the prophets. If the "Day of the Lord" is understood as a single, massively interruptive, world-changing event, Jesus did not bring it, and cannot be considered the great Messiah. But if God chose to unfold the "Day of the Lord" in a manner that no one had ever considered, splitting it in two, so that the judgments would be contained within the person of Jesus at the start, the remnant

29. Matt 11:2–3; Luke 7:17–20.

30. Matt 11:5; see also Luke 7:21–23.

31. Mal 3–4; Matt 11:7–10.

32. Isa 6, 35, 61.

community would serve as a witnessing mission for an unresolved and compromised world, and the blessings of the future age would be inaugurated through miracles and healings and renewed lives over time, Jesus was precisely the harbinger of a new world order. The "Day of the Lord" had indeed arrived in Jesus. It did not, however, culminate in his initial coming. The "Day of the Lord" was, instead, split, and we live now in a world awaiting the second half of its interruption.

And that gives rise to all of New Testament, Christian theology.

4

The Turn No One Saw Coming

Ascension/Pentecost "Day of the Lord" Surprise Split

A NOTED BUSINESSMAN WAS in high demand on the speakers' circuit. He had succeeded well in developing a multi-million-dollar enterprise, and now start-ups and entrepreneurial companies sought his advice at their board meetings and planning sessions. While he still guided his growing corporate empire through black bottom-line quarters and overseas expansions, a good portion of his schedule was now devoted to playing the expert as he hobnobbed from one city and market to the next.

Few realized that his insights and public strengths were built substantially on the planning and preparations, behind the scenes, by his long-term administrative assistant. She was skilled, tactful, adaptive, and a life-long learner. She had managed to understand his goals and perspectives so well that she could put him on the right conference seminar speakers' lists, and keep him off the ones where he would not shine. She also prepared his travel arrangements and even typed out the rudiments of what he should be presenting at each event.

One day he breezed through his office, making enough noise to appear important, but sticking around only long enough on the way to somewhere else where he would be greeted as the honored expert. His administrative assistant handed him travel documents and folders containing all that was necessary for his next venture. He slid these into his satchel quickly, confident that, as always, everything would be in order, and he would not have to worry about anything. Also, in his usual myopic fashion, he received rather than gave, offering no thanks or appreciation for this woman who essentially made his "good life" possible.

Arriving later at his next board meeting, a high-powered affair where he was surrounded by critically acclaimed industry leaders, he felt the glow of his honored position. They looked to him for direction. They saw him as a key influencer. They believed he had the words of life that would sustain them and their companies for the next fiscal cycle.

Basking in their affirmations, he stepped to the podium, opened the folder prepared by his administrative assistant, and launched into another brilliant introduction, reflecting his own good sense, but made better by her engaging words. The first page ended with a promise that heaven itself would open in the next thirty-five minutes, and divine revelation would spew generously out of his mouth: "We will now consider these matters under seven headings."

He turned the page. And froze. In horror. There was only one line on the sheet. It exclaimed, in bold type: "YOU'RE ON YOUR OWN NOW!"

"You're on Your Own Now!"

Jesus' disciples must have felt that way on the day described in Acts 1. Devastated by Jesus' crucifixion, demoralized by Judas' betrayal, and scandalized by their own cowardness and ineptitude, these men had deflated to ghosts until the outlandish reality of Jesus' resurrection made them human and powerful again. Now they were unconquerable. Now the revolution was in sight. Now there was no stopping the Kingdom Train. "Lord, is this the time when you will restore the kingdom to Israel?" they asked Jesus (Acts 1:6). They could see it already—the Romans beaten, those wily Idumean Herodians tossed from Masada's palace into the Dead Sea, foreigners driven from the land, Samaritans put in their place, and Jews taking over their country as the true remnant of Israel. Fires of expectation and vindication danced in their eyes as they huddled around Jesus. "Lord, is this the time when you will restore the kingdom to Israel?"

His response puzzled and terrified them. First, he pricked their inflated pride. "It is not for you to know the times or periods that the Father has set by his own authority," he told them (Acts 1:7). They had not yet graduated, nor were they privy to all things important.

Second, Jesus affirmed them. "You will receive power when the Holy Spirit has come upon you," he promised them (Acts 1:8), linking their lives supernaturally to his own amazing abilities. Having distributed Jesus' multiplied bread and fish, having walked on the waters of Galilee with him, having cast out demons and healed the sick, these men were drooling at the thought of having power over death itself!

Third, Jesus changed the rules of the game. "You will be my witnesses in Jerusalem, in all Judea and Samaria, and to the ends of the earth," Jesus announced (Acts 1:8). But this was a big turn of strategy! The reason for

Canaan to be the homeland of the Israelites was precisely because it was at the center of traffic and commerce in the world. God was creator of all places and nations. God had chosen Israel to be God's special ambassadors of this good news, in an age where peoples had generally forgotten their creator, and played at little allegiances with tiny gods, mirroring their own selfish whims.

Now, suddenly, this spot of real estate, bounded on the east by the Jordan River (along with its Galilee source and Dead Sea drain), on the north by towering Mount Hermon, on the west by the Great Sea (Mediterranean Sea), and on the south by the wilderness wastes, would no longer be the base of operations for Yahweh's take-back-the-world campaign. Instead of creating a community shaped by the Sinai covenant that would intrigue passersby into renewed interaction with their creator, the army of God would now be sent in bands and forays among the nations. The divine mission continued, but centripetal strategy one was replaced by centrifugal strategy two.

Fourth, Jesus left. Just when his disciples thought they could survive the next crisis, the source of their confidence drifted up toward heaven and was gone. "You're on your own now!" How frightening!

And how empowering! Jesus trusted them! Jesus believed in them! Jesus affirmed their place in the next phase of operations of the divine missional enterprise!

There is an ancient legend first told by Christians living in the catacombs under the streets of Rome. It pictured the day when Jesus went back to glory after finishing all his work on earth. The angel Gabriel met Jesus in heaven and welcomed him home. "Lord," Gabriel asked, "who have you left behind to carry on your work?"

Jesus told him about the disciples, the little band of fishermen and farmers and housewives.

"But Lord," said Gabriel, "what if they fail you? What if they lose heart or drop out? What if things get too rough for them and they let you down?"

"Well," replied Jesus, "then all I've done will come to nothing."

"But don't you have a backup plan?" Gabriel asked, nervously. "Isn't there something else to keep it going, to finish your work?"

"No," said Jesus, "there's no backup plan. The church is it. There's nothing else."

"Nothing else?" repeated Gabriel, worried. "But what if they fail?"

And the early Christians knew Jesus' answer. "Gabriel," Jesus explained patiently, "they won't fail."

A New Missional Strategy for a New Age

There is something wonderfully paradoxical about the Christian church. Its origin as a unique social phenomenon clearly dates from the Pentecost events described in Acts 2. Yet, at the same time, Jesus' disciples, who were at the center of the church from its very beginning, would say that this "new" community of faith was simply part of a centuries-old already existing people of God, stretching back all the way to Abraham and his family. The connection between the old and the new is rooted in several theological axioms.

First, it is built upon the confession that there is a God who created this world and uniquely fashioned the human race with attributes that reflected its maker. Second, through human willfulness the world lost its pristine vitality, and is now caught up in a civil war against its Creator. Third, intruding directly into human affairs for the sake of reclaiming and restoring the world, the creator began a mission of redemption and renewal through the nation of Israel. Fourth, Israel's identity as a missional community was shaped by the Suzerain-Vassal covenant formed at Mt. Sinai. Fifth, in order to be most effective in its witness to other nations, Israel was positioned at the crossroads of global societies, and thus received, as its "promised land," the territory known as Canaan. Sixth, the effectiveness of this divine missional strategy through Israel was most evident in the tenth century BC, during the reigns of David and Solomon, when the kingdom grew in size and influence among the peoples of the ancient Near East and beyond. Seventh, this missional witness eroded away, almost to oblivion, through a combination of internal failures and external political threats, until most of the nation of Israel was wiped out by the Assyrians, and only a remnant of the tribe of Judah (along with religious leaders from among the Levites, and a portion of the small tribe of Benjamin) retained its unique identity as the people of Yahweh. Eighth, because of the seeming inadequacy of this method of witness, as the human race expanded rapidly, the creator revised the divine missional strategy, and interrupted human history in a very visible manner again in the person of Jesus. Ninth, Jesus embodied the divine essence, taught the divine will, and went through death and resurrection to establish a new understanding of eschatological hope, which he passed along to his followers as the message to be communicated to the nations. Tenth, Jesus' teachings about this arriving messianic age were rooted in what the prophets of Israel called the "Day of the Lord," a time when divine judgment for sins would fall on all nations (including Israel), a remnant from Israel would be spared to become the restored seed community of a new global divine initiative, and the world would be transformed as God had intended for it to be, so that people could again live out their intended purposes and destinies. Eleventh, instead of applying all aspects of this "Day of the Lord" in a single cataclysmic event, Jesus split it in two, bringing the beginnings of eternal blessings while withholding the full impact of divine judgment for a time. Twelfth, the Christian church is God's new agent for global missional recovery and restoration for the human race, superseding the territorially bound witness through Israel with a portable and expanding testimony influencing all nations and cultures. Thirteenth, since the "Day of the Lord" is begun but not finished, Jesus will return again to bring its culmination. Fourteenth, the church of Jesus exists in this time between Jesus' comings as the great divine missional witness.

Each of these themes is implied or explicit in the first two chapters of the book of the Acts of the Apostles. God and sin and the divine mission are all part of the fabric of the narrative, while Israel's role in the divine mission, along with the changing strategies, is declared openly. Jesus is at the center of all these things, but the unique divine intrusion he brought into the human race is now being withdrawn, as he ascends back to heaven. Now the church must become the ongoing embodiment of Jesus' life and teachings, so that it may live out the divine mission until the remainder of the "Day of the Lord" arrives when Jesus returns.

The Structure of Acts

The book of Acts is the second of Luke's two volumes on the life and work of Jesus, presented first through his immediate person in the gospel, and now through his extended "body," the church. There are several guiding forces that shape the way in which Luke tells this second part of Jesus' story. One of them is clearly stated by Jesus in Acts 1:8—"You will receive power when the Holy Spirit comes on you; and you will be my witnesses in Jerusalem, and in all Judea and Samaria, and to the ends of the earth." With that in mind, Luke describes the way in which this witness emerged first in Jerusalem (chapters 2–7), then swept through Samaria (chapters 8–12), and finally began its push toward the ends of the earth (chapters 13–28). Jesus' declaration provides the big outline of Acts.

But there are other themes that group these materials as well. For instance, because the witness of the church in Palestine was first guided by Peter, and that beyond Palestine gained its momentum from Paul, these two figures are central to the contents in each major section of Acts, in succession:

- Peter and the Jewish/Palestinian witness (Acts 1–12)
- Paul and the Gentile/Mediterranean witness (Acts 13–28)

This pair is often joined by other leading figures who play dominant roles in fits and spurts. We see, in Luke's unfolding narrative, a succession of key "witnesses:" Peter (1–5), Stephen (6–7), Philip (8), Saul (9), Peter (10–12), Paul and Barnabas (13–14), James (15), Paul and Silas (16–17), Paul and his companions (18–20), and Paul (21–28).

The initial organizing structure of Jesus' missional command in Acts 1:8 seems to be further developed by Luke in a clear series of church expansions that are tracked throughout the work. Each successive wave of missional outreach is built upon the previous field of witness, but pushes the engagement one step further:

- The witness to Jerusalem (2:1–6:7)
- The witness to Judea and Samaria (6:8–9:31)
- The witness to the Gentiles (9:32–12:24)
- The witness to Asia Minor (12:25–16:5)
- The witness to Europe (16:6–19:20)
- The witness to the ends of the earth by way of Rome (19:21–28:31)

All but the last of these regional (or, in the case of the move to a Gentile audience in 9:32–12:24, ethnic) expansions is brought to a similar conclusion of the type: "And the word of God grew and multiplied . . ." It appears that Luke perceived of the missional witness of the church in each of these sections as having pervaded those regions sufficiently enough that all persons within them had access to the message about Jesus. In the last section, however, the gospel is again briefly stated to both the Jews (Acts 22) and the Gentiles (Acts 26), but there is no concluding progress report of completion. Some believe this indicates that Luke was planning a third volume, intending to track Paul's next series of journeys once he was released from Rome after his appeal to Caesar had been adjudicated. A more likely theological hypothesis, however, is that Luke deliberately leaves the story of the expanding witness open-ended. The mission work begun at Pentecost has reached worldwide levels of impact by the close of Acts. But it has not yet succeeded in reaching "the ends of the earth," or bringing all of the world's citizens back into relationship with their creator. So, the testimony put forward in the book of Acts is never complete, but continues on in the life of the church. Viewed in this way, the church is always writing chapter

Pentecost = Mission catalyst for Church

29 to the book of Acts, so that any attempt at a final "progress report" is only partial and interim.

The Symbols of Pentecost and the Mission of God

The momentum of the stories told in the book of Acts is derived from a single critical incident that took place in Jerusalem during the Jewish religious festival known as Pentecost. Jesus' instruction for his disciples to stay in Jerusalem and wait for a special gift (Acts 1:4), must have seemed vague at the time, but the arrival of the explosive power of the Holy Spirit during the Pentecost feast made sense. This celebration was both a harvest festival[1] and a time for recalling the gift of the original covenant documents to Moses at Mount Sinai.[2] These two themes intersected marvelously with what was taking place. First, there was the dawning of a new age of revelation and divine mission, paralleling the first covenant declaration in the book of Exodus. Second, during the Pentecost harvest festival, the first sheaves of grain were presented at the temple, anticipating that God would then bring in the full harvest. This expression of faith served as a clear analogy to the greater missional harvest of the church, which was begun through a miraculous "first fruits" in Jerusalem that day.

Those in Jerusalem that day would have had their senses charged to understand these things. For instance, a single word, both in the Hebrew[3]

1. In the Old Testament it is called the "Feast of Harvest" (Exod 23:16), the "Feast of Weeks" (Exod 34:22; Deut 16:10; 2 Chron 8:13), and sometimes the "Day of the First-Fruits" (Num 28:26). In Palestine, grain harvest lasted around two months, beginning with barley, usually during the Passover, and ending with wheat about the time of Pentecost. This is why Pentecost was considered the culmination of harvest, or the "Harvest Festival." Instructions regarding this "Feast of Weeks" are first given in Exod 23:10–17 and 34:18–26. Israelites were to bring to the Tabernacle (and later, the Temple) "the first-fruits of wheat harvest," not as a prescribed offering, but rather as a freely given token of thanks and appreciation for divine favor, shown through the harvest season and its abundance. The offering itself was to be shared with family, friends, Levites, the needy, and strangers, as a reflection of God's care for the whole community (Deut 16:9–12). At one point, according to Lev 23:15–22, some of the first threshed grains of the wheat harvest were to be pounded into flour and baked as two loaves, which were then to be waved before Yahweh at the Altar of Burnt Offering, and then incinerated on that altar, so that God could share in the festivities and community meals associated with the festival.

2. This aspect of Pentecostal celebrations was a much later addition to the themes of the day. See "Pentecost," in Kaufmann Kohler, J. L. Magnus, and Judah David Eisenstein, editors, *The Jewish Encyclopedia* (New York: Funk & Wagnalls, 1906) 592–595.

3. רוּחַ, *ruach*.

and Greek[4] languages, serves to designate "wind," "breath," and "spirit." Thus, the sound of a rushing wind captured the attention of all who were about to breathe in the Spirit of God. Second, this fresh, divine breath was confirmed visually by the single blaze of fire from heaven that became multiple flames burning from each head. Jesus' cousin John had said that he baptized with water, but that Jesus would baptize with the Holy Spirit and with fire (Luke 1:16). Now, in full view of all, the single divine Spirit baptized everyone at the same time.   *baptism by fire*

One more image had to come to mind among the Jewish faithful, steeped in scriptural history. Although not explicitly stated, there seems to be a conscious undoing of the troubles that started at Babel through the miracle of multiple-language communications at Pentecost. In Genesis 11, the human race was becoming unified against its creator, and the divine solution to dissipate this rebellion was to multiply the languages spoken, forcing the community to become segmented into competing groups. At Pentecost this action was reversed, and the many people who communicated in their diverse local languages suddenly all heard the same message of grace at once, and were knit together into a new common humanity of the church. Babel was undone by Pentecost!

Peter capitalized on these themes when he preached a sermon explaining Joel's prophecy of the "Day of the Lord." Peter tied together God's extensive mission, the history of Israel, the coming of Jesus, and the splitting of the Day of the Lord so that the blessings of the messianic age could begin before the final divine judgment fell. The pattern for entering the new community of faith was clearly outlined: repent and be baptized. The former indicated a transforming presence of the Holy Spirit in individual hearts, while the latter became the initiation rite by which the ranks of this missional society were identified.[5]   *symbol, not salvation*

Reaction to the rapidly developing Christian fellowship was swift and sharp. Within Jerusalem's dominant religious community there was consternation about the apostles' identification of Jesus as the Jewish Messiah (Acts 4), creating tensions and divisions. Inside the newly organizing church itself, there were ethical issues that needed to be addressed (Acts 5–6). Soon the followers of Jesus needed to expand their leadership team (the deacons of Acts 6), and found themselves the targets of increasingly organized persecutions (Acts 8:1–3). Although this disrupted the close fellowship of the Jerusalem congregation, those who moved elsewhere to

---

4. Πνευμα, *pneuma*.

5. Replacing the badge of circumcision in its unique application to the nation of Israel—see Col 2:11–12.

find safety brought the message of Jesus' teachings, death and resurrection with them (Acts 8:4).

An amazing turn happened, however, when the leading persecutor, a zealous Pharisee named Saul, suddenly went through a miraculous conversion (Acts 9), and began to preach that Jesus was indeed the Messiah. When Peter's exploits with the Roman centurion Cornelius at Caesarea nurtured the new Gentile mission of the church (Acts 10–11), Diaspora-born Paul (Saul by his other name) became the perfect candidate to partner with Barnabas in establishing an international congregation in the eastern Roman capital city of Antioch (Acts 12). Soon this congregation served as the launching pad for the great mission journeys of Paul and his companions (Acts 13–19) that would forever relocate the expansion of the Christian church outside of Jerusalem and Palestine.

What had been a centripetal energizing motion during the first phase of God's recovery mission on planet Earth (that is, drawing all nations toward a re-engagement with their creator through the strategically placed people of Israel), was now shifted into a centrifugal motion of divine sending out these blessings of testimony to the world, in ever-widening circles of witness. The Christian church, born as a Jewish messianic sect, became a global religion.

The "Day of the Lord" Split

At the center of all this energy, in the establishment and momentum of the Christian church, was the ancient theology of the "Day of the Lord." In the book of Acts, this core concept is expressed both overtly and covertly.

Overtly, it is the heart of Peter's declaration about the significance of the Pentecost events in Acts 2. Responding to the Jerusalem crowd's uncertainty and derision, as it sought for a public explanation of the seemingly bizarre behaviors of Jesus' friends when boldly empowered by the Holy Spirit, Peter begins by quoting the prophet Joel. The prophecy of Joel, although traditionally assigned a position early in the collection of "the Twelve," was probably penned after the rest of them, sometime in the last half of the fifth century BC. Biblical scholars have moved it all over the map of prophetic chronology, precisely because it contains no temporal referents, other than the terrible plague of locusts that shaped its contents. The sweeping devastation of successive waves of locusts, devouring the entire crop in Palestine that year, caused Joel to hear a higher word of judgment against the nation of Yahweh. Partly because Joel's prophecy contains no mention of kings, and also because of some words and language forms that seem more in tune with nuances of later Jewish post-exilic times,[6] most now believe it was written after Malachi's oracles.

In reality, it is not very important to place Joel in a particular historical setting. In fact, Joel's prophecy is a marvelous summary and distillation of all points of theology scattered throughout the rest of the prophets. After the strident tattoo of approaching judgment, still in rhythm with the grinding march of the locust plague, Joel sees a critical and decisive turn of history taking place when Yahweh breathes new life across the face of the earth. Everything turns on the imminent "Day of the Lord" (Joel 2:11).

In dramatic images, Joel paints the three dimensions of the "Day of the Lord:"

- The judgment of Yahweh will fall (1:1–2:17): "Alas for the day! For the day of the Lord is near, and as destruction from the Almighty it comes" (1:15).

- A remnant will be spared (2:18–27): "Then the Lord became jealous for his land, and had pity on his people . . . I will no more make you a mockery among the nations" (2:18–19).

- The Messianic age of renewal, restoration and shalom will begin (2:20–3:21): "In that day the mountains shall drip sweet wine, the hills shall flow with milk, and all the stream beds of Judah shall flow with water; a fountain shall come forth from the house of the Lord . . . (3:18).

Although Joel uses many descriptive analogies and figures of speech, there is no mistaking that all of these are related to the dominant image of the "Day of the Lord." The "Day of the Lord" is the reason for the wrathful, cleansing judgments of Yahweh:

> Alas for the day!
> For the day of the Lord is near,
>> and as destruction from the Almighty it comes. (Joel 1:15)

> Blow the trumpet in Zion;
>> sound the alarm on my holy mountain!
> Let all the inhabitants of the land tremble,
>> for the day of the Lord is coming, it is near—

6. See, for instance, the note in Joel 3:4–6, where Yahweh accuses the seacoast peoples of Palestine with selling "the people of Judah and Jerusalem to the Greeks." Rather than talking about the people of God as "Israel," the community is now limited to "Judah and Jerusalem." And rather than mentioning the might of Assyria, or the onslaught of the Babylonians, or the domination of the Persians, the key enemy is "the Greeks."

a day of darkness and gloom,
>a day of clouds and thick darkness! (Joel 2:1–2)

Truly the day of the Lord is great;
>terrible indeed—who can endure it? (Joel 2:11)

Similarly, when God acts to spare a remnant of God's people, it happens on this same "Day of the Lord:"

You shall know that I am in the midst of Israel,
>and that I, the Lord, am your God and there is no other.
And my people shall never again be put to shame. (Joel 2:27)

For then, in those days and at that time, when I restore the fortunes of Judah and Jerusalem . . . (Joel 3:1)

The Lord roars from Zion,
>and utters his voice from Jerusalem,
>and the heavens and the earth shake.
But the Lord is a refuge for his people,
>a stronghold for the people of Israel. (Joel 3:16)

And, finally, this "Day of the Lord" will bring a decisive new age of blessing upon all earth:

I will show portents in the heavens and on the earth, blood and fire and columns of smoke. The sun shall be turned to darkness, and the moon to blood, before the great and terrible day of the Lord comes. Then everyone who calls on the name of the Lord shall be saved; for in Mount Zion and in Jerusalem there shall be those who escape, as the Lord has said, and among the survivors shall be those whom the Lord calls. (Joel 2:30–32)

In that day
the mountains shall drip sweet wine,
>the hills shall flow with milk,
and all the stream beds of Judah
>shall flow with water;
a fountain shall come forth from the house of the Lord
>and water the Wadi Shittim . . .

Judah shall be inhabited forever,
>and Jerusalem to all generations. (Joel 3:18–20)

Peter is well aware of these dimensions of the theology, captured in the prophetic code phrase the "Day of the Lord," as he addresses the crowds in Jerusalem on Pentecost. He clearly announces that the portents expected on the "Day of the Lord" are happening,[7] and that the impact of the "Day of the Lord" is causing the uproar in Jerusalem (Acts 2:17–21). And, in the same breath, he identifies the arrival of this "Day of the Lord" as coinciding with, and resulting from, the coming of Jesus into Jewish society personally and physically (Acts 2:22–36), even drawing on the messianic Psalms of David[8] to prove his point.

At the same time, Peter and the other disciples of Jesus are still reeling from what has come to be known as the ascension, where, ten days prior, Jesus left this world. Again, the surprising move taken by Jesus, precisely at the hour of triumph and victory, was coupled with a promise, announced by the messengers of heaven (Acts 1:10) who pastored Jesus' disciples in their moment of confusion, that Jesus was neither abandoning them nor giving up on the mission of the Kingdom. Instead, through a game play that no one saw coming, Jesus split the "Day of the Lord" in two, and would return to finalize its ultimate fulfillment.[9]

This central message regarding the splitting of the "Day of the Lord" is confirmed covertly by a number of accompanying events that draw attention to the parallels between the aftermath of the first "Day of the Lord" interruption and things happening now. For instance:

- The number of the disciples who will become the Apostolic shepherds of the new community is restored to twelve,[10] reflecting the twelve sons of Jacob whose names became identified with the tribes of Israel.

- The blessing of the nations through the descendants of Abraham shifts from the Palestinian presence of Israel to the mobile witness of the church.[11]

---

7. See also Peter's message in Acts 3:12–26, which reiterates these same ideas.

8. Pss 110, 16, and 2.

9. "Men of Galilee, why do you stand looking up toward heaven? This Jesus, who has been taken up from you into heaven, will come in the same way as you saw him go into heaven." (Acts 1:11)

10. Acts 1:12–26. Interestingly, Matthias, chosen to replace Judas, is never mentioned again in the New Testament or the writings of the early church. Yet the act of restoring the number 12 for the Apostolic leadership team is significant enough that it is the only event among all of the actions of Jesus' disciples between the Ascension and Pentecost that gets recorded. Later in Acts, it becomes apparent that Paul is uniquely called and commissioned to fulfill this role of twelfth disciple, as Jesus specifically appoints him to that station (Acts 9).

11. Gen 12:1-3; Acts 1:8; Acts 2:5-12.

- The circumcision identification badge of those belonging to the new community is superseded by the similar mark of baptism.[12]

- The "exodus" from confinement is repeated.[13]

- The lowliness of the faith community is recognized by those around in both instances, confirming that this is not an act of humans initiating their own affairs, but a truly divine interruption and occurrence.[14]

- Miracles are performed by the leaders of the community in both settings.

- A single family within the community of faith is punished on each occasion, marking the seriousness of these times and events.[15]

- The challenges which mounted against the Israelites during the initial phase of the first "Day of the Lord" event are paralleled against the followers of Jesus in this second "Day of the Lord" manifestation.[16]

The net effect is unmistakable. Peter, as the voice of the disciples of Jesus and the clear testimony of the early Christian church, announces publicly that everything anticipated by the prophets in their "Day of the Lord" had arrived in the person and work of Jesus. At the same time, this great divine shaking and renewal of creation, is not a punctiliar action, accomplished

---

12. Acts 2:37–42.

13. Exod 13-15; Acts 12. There strangeness stories of Acts 12 seem symbolically connected to the Exodus of Israel from Egypt. Luke tells us:

"This happened during the Feast of Unleavened Bread" (3)—the time of the Passover (release from Egypt)

Peter is released from prison and goes "home" (Mary and John Mark's home)

People praise Herod as a god because he provides food

Herod is struck down by disease and "eaten by worms" and dies!

"But the word of God continued to increase and spread" (24)

There is a kind of mirror reflection in the Christian church's dispersion from Jerusalem and the release of ancient Israel from Egypt. Each event takes place under the totalitarian control of a ruler who provides food and enslaves God's people. Each results in the death of that tyrant by divine judgment. Each involves the celebration of the Passover meal. In each case, the released folks go "home," and the purposes of God grow and multiply, in spite of challenges and opposition.

14. Deut 7:7–11; Acts 4:13.

15. Achan and his family were sentenced to death when they violated the command to destroy all of the material substance of Jericho (Joshua 7); similarly, Ananias and Sapphira died when they violated the sacred openness, truthfulness, a generosity of the new Christian church community (Acts 5:1–11).

16. Num 20:14–21, 22:1–25:18; Acts 3–7.

in a moment, but rather has been split, so that the blessings of the messianic age are being spread, even as the full impact of its horrific judgment is temporarily stayed.

Jesus has come. And Jesus will come again. The "Day of the Lord" has been split in two.

5

Interpreting the Obvious

Apostolic "Day of the Lord" Testimony

A DOZEN TIMES IN the minimal literature of the New Testament epistles, the apostles announce the looming "Day of the Lord," tying it specifically to the return of Jesus. Paul refers to the "Day of the Lord" as the end of time,[1] the moment of final judgment,[2] the time of Jesus' return as ruler of all,[3] the unknown hour that brings an end to this world order,[4] the promise of the fullness of salvation,[5] and the occasion on which the delayed fulfillments of divine promises will arrive.[6] Peter clearly connects the return of Jesus and the cataclysmic cosmic judgment that the prophets had forecast as essential to the "Day of the Lord,"[7] echoing the dark images of Joel's prophecy,[8] and also the bright collages of the renewed world initiated by this event.[9] The writer of Hebrews builds his split "Day of the Lord" concepts on the utterances of Jeremiah regarding the "new covenant."[10]

1. 1 Cor 1:8.
2. 1 Cor 5:5.
3. 2 Cor 1:14.
4. 1 Thess 5:2.
5. 2 Thess 2:2.
6. 2 Tim 4:8.
7. 2 Pet 2:9.
8. 2 Pet 3:10.
9. 2 Pet 3:18.
10. Jer 31:31–34; Hebrews 8, especially verses 8–10.

Eschatological Ethics

There are only a few references to dates and rulers in the New Testament, and one of them occurs in the story of Paul meeting Aquila and Priscilla. This couple had recently resettled from Rome to Corinth "because Claudius had ordered all the Jews to leave Rome."[11] In his *Lives of the Caesars*, Roman historian Suetonius wrote that Emperor Claudius expelled the Jews because they were constantly causing disturbances in their arguments over a man named *Chrestus*.[12] The edict occurred in AD 49,[13] which allows us to pin Paul's arrival in Corinth to late AD 49 or early 50.

Although Paul would spend the next year and a half in Corinth, at the outset his heart remained back in Thessalonica. Already when he was traveling through Athens, Paul worried about how the fledgling Thessalonian congregation was faring,[14] and sent Timothy back to find out more and make a report.[15] Paul had already continued on to Corinth by the time Timothy caught up with him, and was elated at the good word his younger associate brought.[16] With emotions running high, Paul dashed off a letter of appreciation and encouragement to his new friends.[17]

Paul's First Letter to the Thessalonians

Most of this short letter is given to expressions of praise for the great testimony already being spoken about from those who observed the grace and spiritual energy of this newborn congregation. Paul rehearsed briefly[18]

11. Acts 18:2.

12. "He banished from Rome all the Jews, who were continually making disturbances at the instigation of one Chrestus" (295.25). Most believe this is a misunderstanding of *Christus*, and the arguments in Jewish communities over whether Jesus was the Christ.

13. According to Paulus Orosius, quoting Josephus.

14. 1 Thess 2:17–20.

15. 1 Thess 3:1–5.

16. 1 Thess 3:6–10.

17. 1 Thess. Paul's first letter to the Thessalonian congregation might be summarized in this manner:

The marvelous witness of this young church even through oppressive circumstances (1–3)

Living faithfully because Jesus is coming soon (4:1–12)

What about those who have recently died? (4:13–18)

Jesus is coming soon! (5)

18. 1 Thess 1–3.

the recent history that had deeply connected them, and told of his aching heart now that they were so quickly "torn away" from one another.[19] Only after these passionate confessions does Paul spill some ink on a few notes of instruction.[20] While most of what Paul has to say are typical exhortations toward quiet and godly living, a surprising topic suddenly jumps out as prelude to a new and unique trajectory in Christian doctrinal development. Paul wrote:

> Brothers, we do not want you to be ignorant about those who fall asleep, or to grieve like the rest of men, who have no hope. We believe that Jesus died and rose again and so we believe that God will bring with Jesus those who have fallen asleep in him. According to the Lord's own word, we tell you that we who are still alive, who are left till the coming of the Lord, will certainly not precede those who have fallen asleep. For the Lord himself will come down from heaven, with a loud command, with the voice of the archangel and with the trumpet call of God, and the dead in Christ will rise first. After that, we who are still alive and are left will be caught up together with them in the clouds to meet the Lord in the air. And so we will be with the Lord forever. Therefore encourage each other with these words. (1 Thess 4:13–17)

The central message of Paul's missionary preaching focused on the resurrection of Jesus. This was, for Paul, the astounding confirmation of Jesus' divine character. It was the undeniable proof that Jesus was the Messiah, and that his words and teachings had ushered in the new age of God's final revelation and redemptive activity.

Paul understood that Jesus was the great "Day of the Lord" event foretold by the Old Testament prophets,[21] and that out of gracious forbearance, Jesus had split this cataclysmic occurrence in two, so that the beginning of eternal blessings could be experienced before the final judgment fell.[22] This meant that Jesus had gone back to heaven only briefly, and would be returning to earth very soon—probably next week, but maybe next month. It was the generous grace of God which had provided this brief window of opportunity, allowing Jesus' disciples a chance quickly to tell others the good news, so that those who believed would also reap the benefits of the looming

---

19. 1 Thess 2:17.

20. 1 Thess 4–5.

21. 1 Thess 5:1.

22. 1 Thess 5:2–11.

messianic age. Neither Paul nor God wanted anyone to be destroyed in the judgments that were still ahead.

Paul's Second Letter to the Thessalonians

The response of the Thessalonian church to this insistent focus on Jesus' imminent return apparently echoed back to Paul through Timothy's report in a way he had not expected. Rather than energizing the new believers in Thessalonica, with anticipations of divine vindication after the painful struggles they had recently endured, some had instead become deeply discouraged. In the few intervening weeks or months since they had come to faith in Jesus under Paul's passionate preaching, several members of the congregation had died. The grief of those who survived was heightened, because they supposed that their lost loved ones had come so close to sharing in the powers and perfections of the new age, only to succumb to death virtually on its threshold. They assumed that the dead were excluded forever from the messianic kingdom.

Paul corrects this mistaken notion with a brief eschatological teaching. Jesus will return soon, to be sure, and those of us who are alive when that happens will enjoy renewed direct interaction with him. But those who have already died will not be left behind. Their bodies will be raised and restored, just as happened with Jesus himself on resurrection morning. Assurance of this comes from "the Lord's own word,"[23] according to Paul. Although none of the gospels records this exact teaching from Jesus, evidently it had become part of the oral tradition already being passed along from one believer to another.

Paul then went on to reaffirm the central imminent-return-of-Jesus proclamation that had precipitated these reflections in the first place.[24] Jesus will come back very soon, most likely in the foreseeable future. Paul fully expected that he himself, and most of his readers there in Thessalonica, would experience this event firsthand, and probably nearer on the calendar than more distant.

The letter closes with a quick litany of moral and ethical exhortations, urging faithful living regardless of circumstances.[25] It was probably sent in early AD 50, just as Paul was getting started with his work in Corinth.

A month or two later Paul received a follow-up report on the Thessalonian congregation. It may have been written as a result of another visit

23. 1 Thess 4:14.
24. 1 Thess 5:1–11.
25. 1 Thess 5:12–28.

by Timothy, but we do not know for sure. What is certain is that Paul's letter had increased the climate of expectation for Jesus' return very dramatically, to the point where a significant number of the Thessalonian Christians had either stopped working their careers, believing that these were no longer necessary because Jesus was coming so soon,[26] or came to the conclusion that the messianic age had already arrived, and they were free to carry on with no normal social restraints or obligations.[27] Paul's second letter to the Thessalonians addresses both issues. After a rousing note of appreciation for their growing faith,[28] Paul tempers his imminent-return-of-Christ teachings by injecting a likely waiting period during which a "man of lawlessness" will appear.[29] Who this person will be or when it will happen remains unclear. For a moment, Paul's writing verges on apocalyptic speculations,[30] but then it settles quickly back into exhortations of moral behaviors consistent with the "sanctifying work of the Spirit."[31]

In his final instructions,[32] Paul urged the Thessalonian Christians to live lifestyles of faithful service toward others, not getting caught up in the disease of idleness which seems to have sprung among some from overzealous expectations of Jesus' imminent return. A closing line, apparently in Paul's own handwriting, indicates that once again he has used an amanuensis for creating this document.[33]

Paul's letters to the Thessalonian congregation occurred early in his ministry, with both epistles most likely penned in AD 50. These writings are very short, and do not spell out a fully explored eschatology. But in their brief exhortations they contain some of Paul's most direct and explicit eschatological teachings.

First, it is clear that the emphasis in Paul's preaching was on the resurrection of Jesus. This was the confirmation that Jesus was the Messiah foretold by the prophets. It was also the most profound sign that the new messianic age had arrived. Since the messianic age was part of the promised "Day of the Lord," a time of divine judgment was sure to arrive soon.

Second, Jesus' first coming brought the beginnings of the blessings of the messianic age, but it delayed the judgments of God for a time, so that

26. 2 Thess 3:6–12.

27. 2 Thess 2:1–3.

28. 2 Thess 1.

29. 2 Thess 2:3–4.

30. 2 Thess 2:5–12.

31. 2 Thess 2:13–17.

32. 2 Thess 3.

33. 2 Thess 3:17.

the followers of Jesus could spread the news of salvation far and wide. Splitting the "Day of the Lord" in two was an act of kindness on God's part, providing more opportunity for people to respond in faith. It also placed upon the church a missionary urgency. The reason Jesus left his followers behind during the gap between his ascension and return was to send them as ambassadors of hope to the nations.

Third, the return of Jesus was imminent, and likely to take place within weeks or months. This was the expectation that made any trials, persecutions or difficulties endurable. Knowing that one can outlast an opponent, no matter how nasty or strong, gives great resilience to hang on and survive with dignity.

Fourth, all who trusted in Jesus when he returned would share in his glory and power. But so too would those who had believed in Jesus and then died before Jesus had made his return. This teaching profoundly changed the burial habits of Christians, and altered expectations at dying. Rather than closing doors to human existence, death instead opened them to eternal life. Many early Christians welcomed death by martyrdom, knowing that through this act they were immediately secure in resurrection hope.

Fifth, the yawning gap of time that had been widening since Jesus' ascension required meaningful explanations for the delay of his return. Answers came in three major varieties. Some saw this lengthening "in-between" age as evidence of divine grace: God was not going to bring final judgment until more people could respond to the gospel message in faith. Others declared that the delay was a tool for testing the faithfulness of those who said they believed in Jesus. A final group called to mind Jesus' words about signs that would appear before the final days, and tried more closely to define the number of specific events must still take place prior to his return.

Intertwined together, these three dimensions of eschatological expectations became hardwired into the church, and infused it, for Paul, with a missionary urgency and an uncompromising ethic. The church must speak to everyone with loving passion about Jesus. At the same time, Christians were responsible to live in a profound moral simplicity that assessed every behavior by the question, "What should we be doing when Jesus returns?"

Paul's Big Metaphor

This question becomes the focus of one of Paul's biggest theological metaphors, appearing especially in his Prison Epistles. Four of Paul's letters mention that he is a prisoner at the time of their writing: Ephesians,[34] Philippians,[35] Colossians,[36] and Philemon.[37] According to the book of Acts,[38] Paul was imprisoned a number of times. On most of these occasions, however, his incarceration was very brief.[39] Two imprisonments, though, were of significant duration: Paul's two-year stint in Caesarean confinement[40] and the doublet of years he spent in Rome while waiting for Caesar to hear his appeal.[41] Paul's prison letters could have been written from either of these, though there are good reasons to opt for Roman origins.

For one thing, it is clear that Paul's letters to the Colossians, Ephesians, and Philemon were written at the same time. They are sent by way of the same human carriers, Tychicus[42] and Onesimus.[43] They refer to the same people surrounding Paul in prison.[44] And they deal with identical theological and pastoral issues in almost verbatim repetition of words.[45] Such hints not only confirm the connections among these letters, but they also contain clues as to where Paul was when he wrote them. It is highly unlikely that Philemon's slave Onesimus would run away from the Lycus and Maeander river valleys in Phrygia (southwest Asia Minor) toward Palestine. Conversely, with trade and communications moving between that region and the capital of the empire, it is very likely that Onesimus would end up in Rome. So, it is very reasonable to believe that Paul wrote his letters to the Colossians, Ephesians, and Philemon from Rome.

Similar arguments can be made about Philippians. Paul's reference to the "whole palace" in 1:13 could possibly indicate that he was in Caesarea, among the court officials who created a small replica of Roman governance in that provincial town. But it is highly unlikely, especially when Paul goes on to talk about fellow Christians "who belong to Caesar's household."[46] This can hardly be taken as anything other than a mention of the royal courts in

34. Eph 3:1; 4:1; 6:20.
35. Phil 1:13–17.
36. Col 4:10; 4:18.
37. Phlm 1; 23.
38. Acts 16:23–40; 21:32–33; 23:10; 23:35; 24:23; 28:30. See also 2 Cor 12:23.
39. E.g., in Philippi; Acts 16:16–40.
40. Acts 24.
41. Acts 28:30.
42. Eph 6:21; Col 4:7.
43. Col 4:9; Phlm 8–19.
44. Timothy, Aristarchus, Mark and Epaphras.
45. Cf. Ep 5:21—6:9 and Col 3:18—4:1; Col 1:3–6, Phlm 4–6, and Eph 3:14–19.
46. Phil 4:22.

Rome. Because of these clues, it seems obvious that all of Paul's prison letters were written while he was in Rome, between AD 57 and 59.

When looking at the contents of the letters themselves, it appears that Philippians was written earlier in Paul's Roman stay, while the other three were likely penned near the end of it. Paul seems to be somewhat settled into prison life when he writes to the Philippians; but in Paul's note to Philemon, he makes it clear that he expects to be released soon, and free again to travel. This would date Colossians, Ephesians, and Philemon to sometime in AD 59, while Philippians probably was sent in late 57 or early 58.

Paul's Letter to the Philippians

Despite its brevity, Paul's letter to the Philippians contains many notes about Paul's changing situation and the people who are in and out of his social circle. Paul is "in chains,"[47] and around him are a number of preachers who testify about Jesus,[48] some for more noble reasons than others. Paul may have been depressed about his circumstances,[49] and maybe even thought at one time that he was about to die,[50] but he believes there is still a future ministry ahead of him in this life.[51] Recently the Philippians had sent their pastor or key leader, Epaphroditus,[52] to bring a gift of food and clothes to Paul,[53] along with their warm wishes. Now Paul is sending this letter of thanks, and will soon commission his trusted associate Timothy to bring Epaphroditus home to Philippi.[54]

Pulling together these bits of information, a reasonable chronology surrounding the writing of Paul's letter to the Philippians might look like this:

- Sometime in the spring of AD 57 Paul arrived in Rome. While he was clearly a prisoner awaiting adjudication before Caesar himself, Paul was also a Roman citizen with rights and freedoms. And since the charges against him were sectarian (related to Jewish religious practices) rather than capital crimes, Paul was able to establish his own

47. Phil 1:13.
48. Phil 1:14–18.
49. Phil 1:22–24.
50. Phil 2:16–17.
51. Phil 1:25–26.
52. Phil 2:25–30.
53. Phil 4:18.
54. Phil 2:19–30.

living circumstances within the larger palace precincts, while remaining under a type of house arrest.

- Probably late in AD 57 or early in 58, Epaphroditus, who had been serving as pastor or congregational leader in Philippi, brought Paul a rather significant gift from that church (Phil 2:25; 4:10). It may have included both money and supplies; in any case, it greatly enhanced Paul's comfort in his limited circumstances.

- Epaphroditus stayed on with Paul for some time, assisting him as a servant. Unfortunately, Epaphroditus became ill and nearly died (Phil 2:25–30), and only very recently had returned to full health.

- Paul believed that homesickness for Philippi and the congregation there might have contributed to Epaphroditus' grave malady, and vowed to send him back home as soon as he was able to travel. Of course, a letter of appreciation and encouragement was a necessary part of all these things, so Paul penned Philippians, probably sometime in early AD 58.

Paul's letter to the Philippians is the most joyful and uplifting note of the entire New Testament. Even in Paul's confinement, he is filled with delight in his relationships, and amazed at what God is doing.[55] Almost without needing to do so, Paul reminds the congregation of the great example of Jesus, who gave up everything in order to express the love of God to us.[56] Another example of this selfless care is found in both Timothy and Epaphroditus, each of whom had sacrificed much in order to serve others, especially the faith community in Philippi.[57] More encouragement to serve follows, with Paul reflecting on his own changes of behavior and value systems once he was gripped by the love of God in Jesus.[58] A few personal instructions and notes of appreciation round out the letter.[59]

---

55. Phil 1.

56. Phil 2:1–18.

57. Phil 2:19–30.

58. Phil 3.

59. Phil 4. Paul's letter to the Philippian congregation might be summarized in this manner:

Praise and thanksgiving from prison (1)

Great hymn of Jesus' humility and witness, plus the ministry of Timothy and Epaphroditus (2)

Paul's old testimony and his new one (3)

Much joy and much appreciation (4)

Although other letters of Paul are more intentionally "theological," this small epistle has a particularly wonderful poetic reflection encapsulating the entire ministry of Christ in a few lines.[60] Because of its condensed and hymnic character, some think Paul brought these verses into his letter from an early popular Christian song or creedal statement. Perhaps so. Nevertheless, the whole of this short book is lyrical, and reaches for the superlatives in life through lines that are both economical and majestic:

> Finally, brothers, whatever is true, whatever is noble, whatever is right, whatever is pure, whatever is lovely, whatever is admirable—if anything is excellent or praiseworthy—think about such things (Phil 4:8).

Paul's Letters Known as Philemon, Colossians, and "Ephesians"

Sometime after the letter to the Philippians was sent, and Epaphroditus had made the journey home, accompanied by Timothy (probably near the end of AD 58), another visitor arrived. His coming would eventually elicit a whole new spate of letters from Paul. Onesimus, a runaway slave from Paul's friend Philemon, came to Rome and found Paul. Perhaps Onesimus was overwhelmed by the alien environment of the big city, and heard that Paul, someone he had met a few years earlier, was in town. Or maybe Onesimus came to Rome specifically because he knew Paul was there, remembering how kindly Paul had treated him while the itinerant evangelist was staying at Philemon's home. In any case, Onesimus and Paul had a joyful reunion, and for a time Onesimus lived with Paul, acting out the true meaning of his name: "useful."

After a while, however, Paul began to have qualms about ignoring the property rights that bound Onesimus to Philemon. Paul was sure that sometime soon he would run into his old friend again, and this secret of Onesimus spending time with him would not come to light without great damage to their relationship. In fact, Paul was beginning to make plans for his next travels, since he expected to be released from prison very shortly. Evidently Paul had received word that his case was soon to be on Caesar's docket, and knew from Herod Agrippa's testimony (Acts 26:32) that royal judgment would clearly be in his favor. When freedom did come, Paul wanted to spend time with Philemon, as one stop on the next journey.

60. Phil 2:6–11.

So, probably in early AD 59, Paul made plans to send Onesimus back to Philemon, accompanied by a trusted friend named Tychicus. Paul penned a short note to Philemon, explaining Onesimus' circumstances of both frustration and faith, and pleading with his friend to treat the young man well.

About the same time, news came to Paul regarding a doctrinal controversy that was threatening the church in Colossae. This congregation had been established under the ministry of Epaphras,[61] a local believer who had originally come to faith through Paul's ministry in nearby Ephesus,[62] just down the Lycus and Maeander river valleys.

Since Colossae was very close to Philemon's home, Paul decided to send a letter to that congregation, addressing these threats to the church's faithfulness and stability. Tychicus was asked to deliver this letter at the same time as he brought Paul's personal note to Philemon.[63]

While he was in the writing mood, Paul also dictated a third letter, to be sent in the same direction at the same time. It was less personal and more general in the themes that it expressed than either of the others, and may well have been intended as a more generic epistle of encouragement to be circulated around the area churches. This letter seems to have arrived first in Laodicea,[64] and began a circuit around the regional congregations. Because Ephesus had been the launching pad for mission efforts throughout the region, the Christian congregation in Ephesus soon became recognized as the "mother church" of the rest, and probably came to be the official caretaker and repository of important documents. For that reason, this circular letter from Paul eventually ended up in Ephesus, became known as Paul's letter to the "Ephesians."

Paul's short letter to Philemon consisted mostly of kind greetings and personal good wishes. At its core, however, was a brief note about Onesimus' recent situation, and Paul's hopes for the slave's future honorable and brotherly treatment. This note from Paul precipitated centuries of lively debate and ultimately strong tensions and divisions in the Christian church. Since Paul affirms Philemon's right to own Onesimus as a slave, some have argued that slavery as a social institution is not intrinsically wrong, so long as the slaves are well cared for. Others, of course, have argued that the logical implication of Paul's letter is a mandate for Philemon to release Onesimus from slavery, and make him a paid employee, while treating him as a social

61. Col 1:7–8.

62. Col 4:12–13.

63. Col 4:7–9.

64. Col 4:16.

equal. If so, Paul's letter to Philemon is actually diametrically opposed to slavery, and Paul is only making polite requests in a spirit of friendship and according to established social conventions.

The irreconcilability of these views eventually split Christian denominations in the United States into "northern" and "southern" factions over slavery. What seems to be a short, kind innocuous letter, has, unfortunately, produced a maelstrom of whirling controversy that continues to engender debate. Fortunately, Paul and Philemon did not seem to come to blows about the matter. At the close of that letter Paul told Philemon to get the guest room ready, for Paul was sure he would be traveling soon to visit both Philemon and Onesimus.

Paul's letter to the Colossians is quite short, but it packs a big punch of theology and perspective. First, Paul celebrates the faithfulness of these disciples of Jesus, and also the great majesty and power of the one they serve.[65] After a short declaration of Paul's immense care for the Colossian congregation,[66] he addresses the problem that was beginning to divide the congregation.[67] Although it is difficult for us to know exactly what were the specific elements of the false teaching that some were embracing, it appears to have included the worship of angels, certain forms of asceticism, and possibly a unique version of how the commands given through Moses were to be kept. These slim details suggest, to some, that an early form of Gnosticism was taking root. Others find a Jewish connection, with certain leaders pushing for a Palestinian ritualistic legalism of the kind that Paul had reacted against so strongly in his letter to the Galatians. Whatever the case, Paul's response was to urge the congregation to focus on the superlative transformation brought by Jesus, which did not need to be supported with secondary rules and regulations.

In an almost counter-intuitive move, Paul then goes on to give what might be termed "rules" for Christian living. But these commands about marriage, family, and work relationships are more a projection of the social outcomes that should emerge when everyone's focus remains on Jesus,[68] rather than a new set of legalistic instructions. It is interesting that after brief statements about the responsibilities of wives,[69] husbands,[70] children,[71]

---

65. Col 1:1–23.
66. Col 1:24–2:5.
67. Col 2:6–23.
68. Col 3:1–4:1.
69. Col 3:18.
70. Col 3:19.
71. Col 3:20.

and fathers,[72] Paul's advice to "slaves" is rather extended.[73] Philemon's slave Onesimus might well be carrying this packet of letters, and would certainly know many of the slaves who were part of this nearby congregation! Paul does include a brief challenge to "masters" as well,[74] exactly in line with the contents of his letter to Onesimus' master, Philemon. A few personal notes and many personnel reports bring Paul's letter to a conclusion.[75]

Paul's third letter in the same dispatch is shaped in nearly the same as his letter to the Colossians. "Jesus is Lord of all," Paul fairly shouts at the beginning, and this produces wonderful new life in all who are part of the church.[76] In place of Paul's instructions about the false teaching at Colossae comes a brief reminder that Jews and Gentiles are together on the same footing before God because of the powerful redemptive work of Jesus.[77] As he begins to celebrate this amazing grace of God through prayer,[78] Paul interrupts himself, reminding his readers of the specific calling he has received to know and communicate this divine revelation.[79] Then Paul resumes his powerful and profound prayer of praise,[80] and launches into an extended metaphor on what it means for the living body of Christ to function in a dark world.[81] Very similar to his instructions in Colossians 3, Paul outlines specific behaviors that are expected in Christian households.[82]

---

72. Col 3:21.

73. Col 3:22–25.

74. Col 4:1.

75. Col 4:2–18. Paul's message in Colossians might be summarized in this manner:

You are great and Jesus rules! (1)

Some of you are putting too much emphasis on rituals and disciplines; trust Christ! (2)

Get the view from above in order to set your values and practices in order (3:1–17)

Treat one another with respect. (3:18–4:6)

Final greetings (4:7–18)

76. Eph 1.

77. Eph 2.

78. Eph 3:1.

79. Eph 3:2–13.

80. Eph 3:14–21.

81. Eph 4:1–5:20.

82. Eph 5:21–6:9. Paul's message in Ephesians might be summarized in this manner:

Jesus is Lord of All! (1)

Jesus has broken down the barrier between God and us (2:1–10) and between Jews and Gentiles (2:11–22), uniting all by grace

Paul's Gentile ministry explained (3:1–13)

In a brief but scintillatingly clear analogy, Paul dresses up the Christian warrior in full battle gear.[83] Only one final note, telling of Tychicus' mission on Paul's behalf,[84] and a short word of blessing,[85] bring this letter to a close.

Paul's letters from prison addressed a couple of specific social issues—the nature of a relationship between master and slave, for instance, when both were Christians, and a proper response to the false teaching that was being promulgated at Colossae. But mostly these writings paint, in vibrant colors, the character of moral choices in a world that is compromised and broken. Darkness and light are the key metaphors. Evil has wrapped a blanket of pain and harm around all that takes place in the human arena. Jesus is the brilliant light of God, penetrating earth's atmosphere with grace and reconciliation. Because of Jesus' physical departure at the ascension, his followers now must step in and become thousand million points of light, restoring relationships and renewing meaning. Jesus is great, and because of our connection with him, we can be great too. Not for our own sakes, of course, but as witnesses of the eschatological hope that tomorrow's amazing future of God is something we already participate today. That is why Christianity is the religion of the dawn, existing as God's missional community of testimony in a world where the "Day of the Lord" has arrived, but is not yet culminated.

Peter's Dark Notes

About the time that Paul was engaged in his final communications with Timothy and Titus, Peter made his own last swing through churches of northern and eastern Asia Minor. This was quite a trip for an older man to take,[86] since Peter was based in Rome at the time. He calls Rome "Babylon,"[87] a code term already circulating throughout the Christian

---

Paul's magnificent prayer (3:14–21)

Building up Christ's body (4:1–16) and living as witnesses of God's goodness (4:17–5:20)

Respecting one another in social relationships (5:21–6:9)

Putting on the "Armor of God" (6:10–20)

Final greetings (6:21–24)

83. Eph 6:10–20.

84. Eph 6:21–22.

85. Eph 6:23–24.

86. Traveling from Rome to the places listed in 1 Peter would require walking further than all of Paul's journeys recorded in Acts!

87. 1 Pet 5:13.

church, hinting at the persecutions looming from the ruling center of the world in a way similar to the Babylonian pressures mounted against Judah centuries before. It may well have been that Peter was invited to officiate at a number of large baptism ceremonies in the congregations to which these letters are written, since Peter's tone is that of instruction for new believers, and baptism is a central concern.[88]

Peter reminds his readers that he was an eyewitness of Jesus' life and sufferings,[89] and directly echoes a number of Jesus' teachings in his words.[90] Peter writes in powerful terms of the great salvation recently brought to humankind by Jesus.[91] This new life is irreversibly guaranteed by way of both Jesus' resurrection and ascension for those who believe.[92] Peter next provides an extended exhortation to holy living, because these believers in Jesus are God's special people,[93] who follow in the footsteps of Jesus[94] and must face, with their master, the sufferings that will fall on all his disciples in challenging times.[95] Peter gives a special word of encouragement to the elders who lead the various congregations,[96] and then expands these same ideas for the broader community[97] before closing with brief personal greetings.[98]

The tone of Peter's letter is far darker than any of Paul's writings. There is an ominous pall of suffering that clouds every perspective. Jesus suffered. You will suffer, if you are faithful. You must follow Jesus in and through suffering. New trials and greater suffering are coming. Whether by way

88. 1 Pet 3:13–22.

89. 1 Pet 5:1; see also 2:23.

90. Compare 1 Pet 2:12 with Matt 5:16; 1 Pet 2:21 with Matt 10:38; 1 Pet 3:14 and 4:13–14 with Matt 5:10–12.

91. Some scholars believe this letter could not have been written by Peter, since its use of the Greek language is too educated, too well crafted. But the double pairs of brothers from the fishing trade in Capernaum that Jesus called to follow him (Peter and Andrew, James and John), probably came from middle class families where education was important. Moreover, just as Paul had amanuenses writing out his letters, so in 1 Pet 5:12 the letter-writing skills of Silvanus (a variant of Silas) are recognized. Peter may well have been accomplished in his use of the Greek language, and certainly Peter's letter-writing scribe was.

92. 1 Pet 1:3–12.

93. 1 Pet 1:13—2:10.

94. 1 Pet 2:11–3:12.

95. 1 Pet 3:12–4:19.

96. 1 Pet 5:1–4.

97. 1 Pet 5:5–11.

98. 1 Pet 5:12–14.

of external hints or from the inner promptings of the Spirit, Peter seems to have been anticipating the sharp clout of Nero's official pogroms, just ahead.[99]

Yet through the murky shrieks and sinister valleys, Peter never loses confidence in God's sovereignty or care. God is judge over evil, the ever-faithful Creator, and the Chief Shepherd who will soon bring untarnishing crowns of glory for those who remain true.

The second letter attributed to Peter has been dogged by some controversy throughout the years. Its language and style seem different from 1 Peter, and it focuses on the second coming of Jesus[100] in a way that is not done anywhere else in the New Testament.[101] Yet the majority of the church accepted it as Peter's letter from the very beginning. Once again, stylistic and vocabulary differences can be attributed to the secretarial assistance Peter used, and the particular false teaching that Peter wanted to address.

After all, the author identifies himself as Jesus' disciple, Simon Peter,[102] seems to be an old man looking back over a long career,[103] speaks of being with Jesus during his earthy ministry,[104] and uses these connections to confirm his teachings and authority.[105] All of this does not prove the letter is from Peter, of course, but, together with the affirmation of the early church, these things support its a ring of authenticity.

---

99. Peter's first letter might be summarized in this manner:

Great salvation has recently been brought by Jesus (1:3–12)

So live holy lives because you are God's special people (1:13–2:10)

Follow the pattern of Jesus to live in humility and service (2:11–3:12)

And follow Jesus through the suffering of discipleship, especially because the end is near (3:12–4:19)

A word of encouragement to the elders (5:1–4)

Final general encouragements and greetings (5:5–14)

100. 2 Pet 3.

101. Peter's second letter might be summarized in this manner:

I want to tell you one last time about Jesus and the transforming power of the gospel (1)

Watch out for the growing problem of false teachers who are compromising the message of Jesus for their own personal gain (2)

Live under the urgent expectation that Jesus is about to return (3)

102. 2 Pet 1:1.

103. 2 Pet 1:12–15.

104. 2 Pet 1:16–18.

105. 2 Pet 1:19–21.

It seems that the letter was written because a number of pseudo-Christian teachers were compromising the core message of Jesus for their own personal gain.[106] It is not clear whether they were seeking money for their teaching ministries, or if they just wanted fame and a high standing in their communities. In light of these developments, Peter presses the same apocalyptic ethic that Paul touted so often: Jesus is coming soon, so be ready, and live appropriately.[107] What is particularly striking about Peter's version is that he clearly identifies the times in which he is living, coupled with the imminent return of Jesus, as the "Day of the Lord."[108] In this, Peter affirms the truth of Old Testament prophecy, links its anticipations of God's impending interruption of human affairs to Jesus, and recognizes the splitting of the "Day of the Lord" into two events, bounded by Jesus' first and second comings.

Peter anticipates his nearing death,[109] and certainly believes difficult times are ahead for all believers. It is likely, therefore, that Peter wrote this letter sometime in late AD 63 or early 64, probably a year or so after his first letter, and shortly before his arrest and crucifixion under Nero's persecution.

The New Testament on the Split "Day of the Lord"

The incarnation was a curve ball no one saw coming. As the great story of God's work in ancient Israel (particularly expansive during the reigns of David and Solomon) ignominiously tapered off into oblivion, with the demise of the Northern Kingdom (also called Israel) under the Assyrian onslaught in 722 BC, and the limping into exile of the Southern Kingdom (also called Judah) initiated by the Babylonian captivity finalized in 586 BC, the prophets logged in with an increasingly shrill message: "Here comes the 'Day of the Lord'!"[110]

106. 2 Pet 2.

107. 2 Pet 3.

108. 2 Pet 3:3, 8, 10, 12.

109. 2 Pet 1:12–15.

110. Isa 2:2, 11, 12, 17; 3:18; 4:2, 5; 7:18, 20; 11:11; 13:6, 9, 13; 19:16, 18, 19, 21; 22:5, 12, 25; 24:21; 27:12, 13; 28:5; 30:26; 34:8; 49:8; 51:9; 61:2; Jer 4:9; 5:18; 7:32; 12:3; 16:14, 19; 19:6; 23:5, 7, 20; 25:24, 33; 30:8, 24; 31:6, 27, 31, 33, 38; 33:14; 39:16; 46:10; 47:4; 48:47; 49:26, 39; 50:4, 20, 31; Lam 1:12; 2:1, 22; Ezek 12:23; 13:5; 20:5; 29:21; 30:3; 31:15; 38:18; 39:8, 13, 22; Joel 1:15; 2:1, 11, 31; 3:14, 18; Amos 2:16; 5:18, 20; 8:3; Obad 1:8, 15; Mic 2:4; 4:1; 5:10; Zeph 1:7, 8, 14, 18; 2:2, 3; 3:8; Hag 2:23; Zech 2:11; 3:9, 10; 8:23; 9:16; 12:4, 8; 13:2; 14:3, 13, 20, 21; Mal 3:17; 4:1, 3, 5.

This "Day of the Lord" talk was a reflection based first on the divine in-breaking into human history that initiated God's redemptive plan. In its earliest stages, the biblical salvation story was a dialogue between God and the key figures of Abram's[111] family, particularly the great patriarch himself[112] and his notorious grandson Jacob.[113] The real fireworks erupted some 500 years later, however, when the family had grown very large, but was debilitated through enslavement in Egypt.[114] God forcibly stepped into the days of our lives, fighting against the Pharaoh of Egypt for the right to own and lead Israel to her destiny.[115] Out of this traumatic divine engagement, Israel was born as a nation, shaped at Mount Sinai through a Suzerain-Vassal covenant, and planted as a witness to the nations in the narrow strip of territory called Canaan, bridging three continents and serving as a trade and conquest route for virtually every nation on earth at the time.[116]

As the dark days of Assyrian destructions and Babylonian limitations dominated, Israel's prophets gained regular visions of a coming time when God would again break into human history, this time righting all wrongs, judging nations, cleansing the world, and inaugurating an eternal kingdom of peace and well-being.[117] The Old Testament ends with these fearful, hopeful, almost wistful expectations,[118] and the Jewish world holds its breath for the big day to arrive.

Then Jesus comes. John the Baptist ties Jesus' arrival to prophetic fulfillment of the "Day of the Lord" prophecies.[119] Jesus himself makes the same connection when he speaks in his hometown synagogue and engages in the healings of the messianic age.[120] Peter clearly affirms exactly this when he preaches to the Pentecost crowds about Jesus using Joel 2 as his text.[121]

Yet it was all a bit of a conundrum. Jesus was supposed to be the central element of this new "Day of the Lord," but his arrival was a lot tamer

---

111. Known throughout scripture as "Abraham" after Yahweh changed his name in the covenant making ceremony of Gen 17.

112. Gen 12–22.

113. Gen 26–34.

114. Exod 1.

115. Exod 4–15.

116. Notice Isaiah's keen sense of this missional purpose for Israel, and the unique role of its geographical location in Isa 2:1–4.

117. Note especially Isa 11–12, 54–64; Jer 31, 33; Ezek 34–48; Zech 9–14; Joel 2.

118. Note the language of Mal 3–4.

119. Matt 3; Luke 1, 3.

120. Luke 4.

121. Acts 2.

than the prophets seemed to foretell. Even John the Baptist began to wonder whether he had gotten the message about Jesus wrong.[122]

What nobody had seen coming was that God split the "Day of the Lord," bringing the beginnings of all that was promised in the person of Jesus himself, while delaying the worst of its effects on our world until more might participate in its best. Jesus endured the horrific pains of judgment and punishment on the cross. Jesus called out a remnant community of witness. Jesus displayed the hopeful signs of the coming age through his miracles of healing and life-renewal, and empowered his followers to bring the same touch of eternity into time.

122. Matt 11.

6

Looking Forward

Anticipating the "Day of the Lord" Culmination

WHEN I WAS A radio announcer during my college days, our station began a late-night contemporary Christian music program, one of the first in the nation. We talked about the format for a while, and discussed the content. And, of course, we debated what to call the show.

An early suggestion was "The Solid Rock Hour." Though the double entendre in that title was cute, the name itself didn't ring with any contemporary feel. Our final choice was "Illumination," and both the name and the program became a major hit.

"Illumination" speaks of darkness and shadows, while at the same time pointing to the growing clarity produced by light and insight. There is a lot of spirituality contained in thoughts of illumination.

It certainly expresses well the God-talk of the Bible: darkness and chaos lurk, until God speaks Light and Life; the Psalmist wanders through the Valley of the Shadow of Death, but with the testimony "The Lord is my Light and my Salvation" on his lips; Jesus appears as the Light of God entering a dark world; when he hangs on the cross, darkness steals the light away, and the Shades of Hades appear to take over for a time; yet on Easter morning, resurrection comes with the dawn. For these reasons and more, the Apostle John says that "God is Light,"[1] and Paul tells us to live as "Children of the Light."[2]

---

1. 1 John 1:5.
2. Eph 5:8; see also 1 Thess 5:5.

Cosmic Tensions

C. S. Lewis captured the tension of Light and Darkness in spiritual combat, in his space trilogy about Venus.[3] The planet Mars, in his tale, is populated by an ancient race of God's creatures who never gave in to the lure of evil, and remain holy and just. Earth, as we know, has fallen under the domain of the dark shadows, and the Great Creator has posted warning signs around it in space. It is off limits to other races, quarantined until the end of time.

Venus, though, is a freshly birthed planet with a more recent "Paradise" story of creaturely development. A newly formed pair, similar to Earth's Adam and Eve, dance about in innocent delight.

The evil power in the universe will not allow a divine masterpiece to go long unmarred, however, and he sends a vicious Earth scientist named Weston to introduce sin on Venus by corrupting its Lord and Lady. In a countermove, the Great Creator sends an ambassador of his own to Venus. The universe holds its breath as the future of this bright world hangs in the balance.

In these novels, Lewis pictured the tension in every human heart. Like Adam and Eve at Earth's creation, and like the Lord and Lady of Venus, we are surrounded by dark powers, yet long for the light of redemption and love. Most of our lives we struggle to see more clearly.

Still, life gets lost for us, often, in the shadows. But grace breaks through, now and again, in moments of insight and illumination, and those are the moments we have to hang onto. That is why John 3:16[4] has become one of the most widely known verses of the Bible; it summarizes the scriptural message as that of God looking for us in love.

Like a mother who brings a child into this world, God is protective of the lives birthed on planet Earth. When sin stains and decadence destroys, God's first thought is to rescue and redeem and recover the children God so dearly loves.

This is a theme repeated throughout the Bible, and shouted from its final pages, in the book of Revelation. If we are able to hear God communicating anything in the Bible, at least this much is clear: it is the whisper of divine love. And it is the true source of our deepest illumination.

---

3. C. S. Lewis, *Space Trilogy* (*Out of the Silent Planet, Perlandra,* and *That Hideous Strength*), (New York: Simon and Schuster, 2011).

4. "For God so loved the world that he gave his only Son, so that everyone who believes in him may not perish but may have eternal life."

The Apocalyptic "Day of the Lord"

The name of the final book of the Bible is associated with an entire genre of literature. Its first word, in the original Greek text, is transliterated into English as "apocalypse," and its meaning is most often translated as "revelation." This word means to uncover something, or to take a thing out of hiding. It explains the primary feature of what has become known as "apocalyptic literature."[5] Scenes, ideas, and information that have been hidden from human view for long ages are now brought out into the open.

But this does not mean that the details of such "revelation" are easily understood. The "revealing" process itself is often arduous, and produces at least as many questions as it suggests to answer. In Revelation, as well as in other apocalyptic literature, the process of revealing usually happens through a special communication link which pairs a heavenly messenger, who knows or understands the significance of the dream-like scenes, with a divinely selected human correspondent, who is particularly attuned to spiritual realities, or who has passed through refining trials that make him specially prepared for the sensory overload involved.[6]

The Revelation of Jesus Christ brought to John at Patmos is both mysterious and majestic. It contains one of the most powerful scenes of worship recorded anywhere (Rev 4–5), and yet remains complex and mysteriously cryptic to the general reader. Because of this, four major strategies of interpretation have developed:

- **Preterist**: Revelation is a coded document designed to give comfort and encouragement to those in John's day, but its specifics largely escape us today. Both John and his readers understood all of the symbolism in

5. Characteristics of "Apocalyptic Literature" often include:

Temporal dualism: strong distinction between current and coming ages

Pessimism about current age, optimism about future age

History is to be understood as occurring in eons or segments (4, 7, 12) reflecting a divine plan

Imminent arrival of God's reign which will destroy current temporal powers

Cosmic vantage points explaining the global impact of unfolding events

Vindication of "the righteous" and restoration of natural perfections and harmonies

Involvement of supernatural beings in current conflicts, as well as future gories and glories

Clear messianic figure who is at the center of all things and events

6. See, for instance, the manner in which Ezekiel (Ezek 2–5, 8–12), Daniel (Dan 7–12), and Zechariah (Zech 9–14) were guided through their growing awareness of transcendent things.

the words he was writing, since it was aimed at people, places, and events in their own experiences. The encoding was necessary to keep Roman officials from understanding, and thus minimize the possibilities of reprisals and more martyrdoms.

- **Historicist**: Revelation outlines the history of the church through the centuries, and close analysis of its contents can actually pinpoint events taking place at any given time since Jesus ascended to heaven. Because Jesus has not yet returned, there are mysterious incidents still to come, and these are symbolized in the strange tellings of Revelation's last pages. We must try to decipher the meaning of these cryptic scenes if we wish to read the signs of the times more clearly.

- **Futurist**: Revelation mostly foretells the specific events which will lead to the end of the world Jesus' second coming. Beyond the first three chapters, which were notes of encouragement given to the church in John's day and remain beneficial as promises and warning for churches everywhere, the rest of the book is probably talking about a single generation of people who will live shortly before the return of Jesus. Many believe that the reestablishment of the modern state of Israel is linked to an imminent fulfillment of these things, and that the crises portrayed graphically in Revelation are rapidly unfolding around us.

- **Idealist**: The book of Revelation is non-historical, in that it does not, for the most part, try to identify specific, recordable experiences of persons or cultures either past, present, or future. Instead, it is a type of allegory which powerfully pictures the perennial and ongoing combat between God and the Devil, between the church and the world, and between good and evil generally. Instead of trying to find contemporary or past events linked to certain scenes in the book, we should interpret every situation of human history in light of the overarching themes of the book:

  - Jesus is the powerful resurrected and ascended Savior.

  - Evil is constantly trying to usurp God's authority and destroy God's creation and God's people.

  - We are living on a battlefield in which all people are affected by the scars and wounds of war, and few signs of victory are ever seen.

  - All human beings must choose to confess Jesus as Lord and Savior, and stand firm to that testimony no matter what the cost, or they will slip into an alliance with evil that will eventually destroy them.

- Jesus is returning to make all things new, but before that happens, this world will undergo even more powerful and threatening advances of evil.

- One day the faith of the faithful will be rewarded, and the dead and living together will enjoy the perfections of the new creation in which all evidence of parasitic evil will have been removed.

While each of these approaches to the book of Revelation has merit, the last (Idealist) is most directly connected to the literary development of the text itself. Although the paragraphs and scenes may seem convoluted and unrelentingly dense in many parts, there is also an obvious momentum to the flow of its passages. Driven by sevens, the images and happenings are grouped into clearly defined sections. When these collections of sevens are marked out from one another, it becomes apparent that they are triggered by exactly three critical scenes in which Jesus is shown to play a pivotal role. Here is how the text of Revelation unfolds:

- **Jesus addresses the church living in the city of humanity** (1–3)

  - *Vision of Jesus as Risen Lord* (1)

  - *Letters of Jesus to seven representative churches* (2–3)

- **Jesus delivers the church out of the destruction of the city of humanity** (4–18)

  - *Vision of Jesus as lion/lamb redeemer* (4–5)

  - *Three series of sevens:*

        Seven seals anticipate divine judgment (6–7)

        Seven trumpets announce divine judgment (8–11)

          Interlude: Clarifying the combatants (12–14)

        Seven bowls of plagues accomplish divine judgment (15–18)

- **Jesus restores the Holy City** (19–22)

  - *Vision of Jesus as bridegroom/conquering king* (19:1–10)

  - *Seven actions of restoration* (19:11–22:5)

- **Epilogue** (22:6–21)[7]

When observed in this manner, carefully responding to the literary movements of the text itself, greater clarity emerges. John has three major visions

7. For a fuller treatment of this literary development, see M. Eugene Boring, *Revelation* (Philadelphia: John Knox, 1989), 28–33.

of Jesus,[8] and each is followed by one or more series of sevens. Overall the progression moves from local congregations that are experiencing persecution, heresy and compromise (chapters 2–3), to a global battlefield in which all citizens of planet Earth are caught up in the horrible conflict between evil and good (chapters 6–18), and finally on to a transcendent victory brought about by the return of Jesus and the divine renewal of creation itself (chapters 19–22).

Jesus Addresses the Church Living in the City of Humanity

John writes that he is on the island of Patmos,[9] as he receives these visions. Patmos is about fifty miles to the southwest of Ephesus, where John had been pastor and church leader for the previous three decades.[10] Although the book of Revelation does not mention the Roman Emperor Domitian by name, early church sources indicate that an empire-wide persecution of Christians took place during his reign (AD 81–96). Tertullian adds a note about this in chapter XXXVI of his *On the Prescription of Heretics*, stating that in Rome, "the Apostle John was first plunged, unhurt, into boiling oil, and thence remitted to his island-exile."

There is evidence on Patmos today that the island had been a quarry for building stones during Roman times, and that slave labor was used in this arduous work. However, it came to be that John was on Patmos, he remained vitally connected to both his resurrected friend Jesus, and to the congregations back on the mainland of Asia Minor who were praying for him.

---

8. In Rev 1 (as the resurrected savior), 4–5 (as the lion/lamb who alone can break the seals on the scroll of human history and its ending events), and 19 (as the bridegroom of the church who returns to earth as conquering king).

9. Rev 1:9.

10. Papias (c. 60–130), Bishop of Hierapolis, about 120 miles east of Ephesus, was a younger contemporary of John, and wrote about meeting him and his successor Polycarp (c. 69–155), talking with them, and hearing them preach. Papias authored five volumes called *Exposition of the Sayings of the Lord*. Only fragments of these books remain, transmitted through the writings of Irenaeus (Polycarp's disciple), who noted the friendship between Polycarp and Papias (*Against Heresies* 5.33), and Eusebius, who included a number of Papias' declarations about the origins of the gospels in his *Ecclesiastical History* (3.36–39). According to Pliny (*Natural History* 4.69–70) and Tacitus (*Annals* 4.30), Roman officials had created penal colonies on three islands, including Patmos, in the Sporades, for banishing political prisoners.

In the opening vision, Jesus is identified as the Creator and Consummator,[11] and is shown symbolically in the temple,[12] bringing the glory of God into the human arena. While Jesus is clearly human in his physical features, these have been translated by his resurrection[13] so that they pummel the observer with transcendent power and glory.[14]

Each of the seven letters[15] that follows begins with a self-description by Jesus, in which some aspect of his revealed glory in chapter 1 is reiterated. The letters are a mixture of warning and encouragement, clearly articulating the experiences of actual congregations living in the first century. They appear to be representative messages, so that even as they speak directly to these seven churches, they communicate Jesus' ongoing relationship to all congregations generally.

The location of these churches and the order in which the letters are dictated is very interesting.[16] Ephesus is first on the list, for good reason. John has been the key pastor and leader at the church in Ephesus for at least three decades by this time, so his congregation comes first into view. The next church is directly north of Ephesus, about fifty miles directly overland, but much further by sea, also on the coast of the Aegean. Today "Smyrna" is the large Turkish port of Izmir. "Pergamum" ("Bergama" today) lies another seventy-five miles directly north of Smyrna, a little inland up a broad agricultural valley. Fifty miles east-southeast is Thyatira ("Ahkisar" today), on the ancient trade route from the Hellespont to Ephesus. Sardis ("Salihli" today), the ancient capital of Persian in its western province, is another thirty-five miles almost due south of Thyatira. Its commanding perch on the mountainside above a broad and fertile farming valley made it a key military site. Only twenty-five miles up the valley to the southeast stood Philadelphia ("Alesehir" today), with Laodicea ("Denizli" today) another seventy miles in the same direction. From Laodicea, by way of the Meander River[17] valley, Ephesus was just a hundred miles directly to the west.

11. "I am the Alpha and the Omega" (1:8); "I am the first and the last" (1:17).

12. Walking among the lamp stands.

13. Rev 1:18.

14. Rev 1:13–16.

15. Rev 2–3.

16. Why these seven churches? Ephesus stands at the head of the list among these congregations to whom John is instructed to send letters from Jesus. This was John's home congregation, so it makes sense that the series would begin there. Furthermore, Ephesus was the regional center of commerce and distribution, placing all of the other cities in direct trade connection with it. The order of the letters is like a normal distribution pattern fanning out from a base of operations in Ephesus.

17. The whimsically slow and wandering river that has given us the term

So the loop formed by the roads connecting these seven churches followed three significant trade routes. Ephesus was the cultural and commercial pivot, while directly opposite on the circle, Sardis was the political and military bastion of the region. Paul, Timothy, and John had probably traveled this "ring road" a good number of times while each was stationed in Ephesus.

The letters to each church are also quite telling:

- **Ephesus** had the first church in the district, and enjoyed a place of ecclesiastical prominence, but seems to have grown sophistically indifferent to Jesus over time.

- **Smyrna** was a wealthy city, but its first Christians were among the poor and the slaves; Jesus notes their oppressed condition.

- **Pergamum** was a wealthy city with a medical school, and was renowned for its famed Altar of Zeus, which Jesus seems to refer to in his letter.

- **Thyatira** was a thriving commercial center, whose citizens cannily played the markets, in bed with whichever prophetess would predict the next windfall (note Jesus' warnings!).

- **Sardis** was the mountaintop political and military command post. Although impregnable by reputation, Persian troops had scaled its unguarded cliff and surprised the sleeping inhabitants, just as Jesus now threatened to do in the church there.

- **Philadelphia** had experienced devastating earthquakes, which caused doors and gates to seize up. Jesus uses that imagery to declare a future stability based upon the unshakable foundation of his temple.

- **Laodicea** had both hot and cold running water, brought in by aqueducts from cold mountain rivers and nearby mineral springs. The fertile valley at its feet was known for its sheep industry, and the production of short black wool jackets. Jesus plays on the water theme, and offers white tunics to cover spiritual nakedness.

Jesus Delivers the Church out of the Destruction of the City of Humanity

In John's second major vision of Jesus, the scene shifts from earth to heaven.[18] God is not represented by creatures or beings or shapes or symbols,

---

"meander"!

18. Rev 4–5.

but only as the shimmering of pure light itself, in pulsating and changing hues covering the whole spectrum. The throne from which God rules is not backed against the wall of some palace room, but is at the center of everything, so that all created reality flows out from it, surrounds it with worship, and receives its light and life from God. Everything everywhere participates in synchronized waves that emanate out from this point of origin, and the pulsating undulations send back to the throne of God choruses of praise and songs of reverence.

Occupying the key places of honor closest to the divine throne are the twenty-four elders, representing the combined leadership of the people of God through biblical history—twelve patriarchs in the Old Testament, twelve apostles in the New.[19] As the rhythms of worship resound, and catch all things in heaven and on earth and in the seas into their vibrations and beats, a new element is suddenly introduced: a scroll is extended out from the indescribable light of the One on the throne. This parchment is covered

---

19. There are a variety of symbolic numbers in the book of Revelation, all of which are used in consistent manners:

One-Third (τρίτος): describes a massive but not total destruction or catastrophe on earth (Rev 8:7, 9, 10, 11, 12; 9:15, 18; 12:4).

Three and One-Half (τρεῖς καὶ ἥμισις): half of human history, also expressed as forty months or 1,260 days (Rev 11:9, 11; 12:14).

Four (τέσσαρες): the dimensions of created reality and those who control it (Rev 4:6, 8; 5:6, 8, 14; 6:1, 6; 7:1, 2, 11; 9:13, 14, 15; 14:3; 15:7; 19:4; 20:8; 21:16).

Seven (ἑπτά): the expression of completeness (Rev 1:4, 11, 12, 16, 20; 2:1; 3:1; 4:5; 5:1, 5, 6; 6:1; 8:2, 6; 10:3, 4; 12:3; 13:1; 15:1, 6, 7, 8; 16:1; 17:1, 3, 7, 9, 11; 21:9).

Twelve (δώδεκα): connected to the actions of God with Israel and the church (Rev 12:1; 21:12, 14, 21; 22:2).

Twenty-Four (εἴκοσι τέσσαρες): combined symbolic leadership of Israel and the church (Rev 4:4, 10; 5:8; 11:16; 19:4).

Forty-Two (τεσσεράκοντα καὶ δύο): always with months; thus = three-and-a-half years (Rev 11:2; 13:5).

666 (ἑξακόσιοι ἑξήκοντα ἕξ): the number of evil, promising completeness (777), but always missing the mark (Rev 13:18).

1000 (χιλίας): Symbolic of long complete period of time (Rev 20:2, 3, 4, 5, 6, 7)

1,260 (χιλίας διακοσίας ἑξήκοντα - 1,260 days = 3½ lunar years): parallel to three-and-a-half years and forty-two months (Rev 11:3; 12:6).

10,000 (μυριάδες): a "myriad" or host of those beyond number (Rev 5:11; 9:16).

12,000 (δώδεκα χιλιάδες): similar to "myriad," but now applied specifically to the people of God (Rev 7:5, 6, 7, 8), and multiplied to create the overwhelming, uncountable number 144,000 (τεσσεράκοντα τέσσαρες χιλιάδες): Rev 7:4; 14:1, 3.

with writing, and appears to be of critical importance for whatever has to happen next. Yet no one seems to have access to it, so John weeps.

Quickly, however, John is told that the "Lion of the tribe of Judah, the Root of David," is approaching, and that he will unfasten the seals that bind the scroll. Expecting a roaring and powerful beast, John is amazed to see instead a "lamb, looking as if it had been slain." It was "standing in the center of the throne." Subsequent lines make it clear that this one is Jesus. In these quick descriptors John tells us several things. First of all, Jesus is human, a king in the line of David. Meanwhile, he is also the "root" of that whole royal family, giving the rest of its members their royal authority. At the same time, he is the one who died as the true Passover lamb, fulfilling the meaning of that ritual right which gave identity to the nation of Israel. But he also came alive again in the resurrection of Easter Sunday, and rules over all things with supreme and unequaled authority. He is, in fact, truly God.[20]

Jesus slowly, but deliberately, opens the seven seals in succession.[21] As they are cracked, scenes of partial devastation wreaked upon earth and human societies provide anticipation of the coming comprehensive judgment of God. Before the full impact of these things annihilates humanity, however, a group symbolically numbering 144,000, but visually identified as "a multitude that no one could count," is ceremonially protected from the combined destructive power of evil and the awful judgment of God.[22] It is *remnant* important to pay close attention to the manner in which John records his vision here, because the symbolic 144,000 and the innumerable host are identified as one and the same group. Since John brings this number back again in Revelation 14:1, it is critical to understand 144,000 as a descriptive collective, rather than an itemized tally.

The opening of the seventh seal[23] triggers the beginning of the blowing of seven trumpets which announce the near arrival of holocaustic divine judgment. New visions accompany these blasts, and with each, the seismic tremors on earth increase in intensity, as more profound destruction ensues. Just prior to the blowing of the seventh trumpet, John is given a scroll to eat,[24] clearly marking him as a prophet like Ezekiel,[25] whose

---

20. Notice that he stands at the center of the throne, which is a position that can solely be claimed by the creator deity of the universe.

21. Rev 6–8.

22. Rev 7.

23. Rev 8:1.

24. Rev 10.

25. See Ezek 3:1–13.

earlier visions provide many of the themes and expressions that are part of the revelation to John.[26]

Before the bowls of plagues are poured out,[27] accomplishing the final judgments of God and the time of transformation into the eternal age of renewal, there is what appears to be a kind of face-off between the super-powers who are behind the scenes, and who shape the battlefield skirmishes of this conflict. In Revelation 12 and 13, evil in personified form is shown to mirror the identity and activities of the Holy Trinity. As the Father is creator and sustainer of all things, so the dragon tears at these material wonders, skewing and destroying them in a wild rage to harm God's people and God's plans.[28] Defeated in a bid to kill the divine Messiah born of the woman (symbolically drawing together the representation of the great mother Eve of Gen 3:15, the nation of Israel that was God's bride and gave birth to the Messiah, and the Church of the New Testament age which is under attack, all combined into a single descriptive package), the dragon conjures up helpers from the human arena. The beast from the sea[29] is an unholy counterpart to Jesus, receiving power and authority from its wicked master, and displaying a "fatal wound" that had been healed, mimicking Jesus' own death and resurrection. Because it takes up residence in the human realm, this beast begins to receive worship from all of humankind. Its authority is enhanced when the beast from the earth emerges,[30] eliciting fire from heaven and miraculous signs at its appearance, just as happened when the Holy Spirit of God came to earth on Pentecost.[31] And like that third person of the holy Trinity, this unholy entity turns the attention of the human race to the one who came before, which is in this case the beast that had the fatal wound that healed.

In striking images John portrays the nasty game of imitation that evil tries to play, in a bid to win humanity away from its true relationship of

26. Virtually all the images in Revelation draw upon similar visualizations in several Old Testament books:

Exodus: The plagues

Ezekiel: The scroll of prophecy/judgment
The war with Gog and Magog
The restored temple and new creation

Daniel: The use of terms ("Son of Man," "seven")
Tour of spiritual visions by way of angelic guide

27. Rev 15–18.

28. Rev 12.

29. Rev 13:1–10.

30. Rev 13:11-18.

31. See Acts 2.

worship with the creator. In fact, Revelation 13 ends with the great and mysterious marking ceremony, in which all of humanity is branded with 666. While many interpretations swirl about, in reality John makes it clear that this is a devilish counterpart to baptism, since the only ones who escape the trauma of this identification are those who wear instead the names of God.[32] The 777 mark of belonging to Father, Son, and Spirit is the only antidote to the mesmerizing and dehumanizing promises issued by the great enemy of God and of God's people. While they glow with tantalizing power, they end up short (only a 666) and are destined for the ultimate trash bin, where everything imperfect is consumed or purified by fire.

Despite the power and wily maneuvering of the dragon and his helpers, they are no match for the true God. Revelation 14 concludes with a harsh indictment upon the unholy trinity and all who fall under its sway, and a great promise that soon the final judgment will begin. Indeed, in chapters 15–18, the stored-up wrath of God upon evil and sin is poured out from seven bowls which replay the majority of the devastations brought on Egypt during the days of Moses.[33] In the end, the personification of evil as it coalesces in the human community is destroyed, doomed just as ancient Babylon was ruined because of its part in attacking the people of God.[34]

Jesus Restores the Holy City

Then comes the third vision of Jesus, who now appears both as conquering king and ravishing bridegroom (Rev 19:1–10). Before the victory and wedding celebrations can begin, however, a mopping-up operation takes place in which seven aspects of judgment and restoration are sorted out (mostly introduced by John with "then I saw"):

- The King appears to fulfill his destiny (Rev 19:11–16).

- The last battle is fought, in which all the evil in the human arena is focused and repelled (Rev 19:17–21).

- Satan is bound for a certain period of time (Rev 20:1–3).[35]

32. Rev 14:1–5.

33. See Exod 7–11.

34. Rev 17–18.

35. The "one thousand years" of Rev 20:2–7 has been a theological puzzle since John wrote it. From the early seventeenth century on, the term "millennium," a Latin compound word, has been used to describe this cryptic time period which occurs nowhere else in the Bible or in other contemporary sources. Three major interpretive positions have emerged, each attempting to connect the thousand years to human

- The dead are raised to life for good or for ill (Rev 20:4–6).

- Evil is destroyed (Rev 20:7–10).

- The final judgment, determining the eternal destiny of all humankind (Rev 10:11–15).

- Earth is re-created and restored in its relationship with the creator (Rev 21:1–22:5).

Revelation ends where it began, with a call to faithfulness in the face of mounting opposition. While its details provide endless fodder for teachers, preachers and theological speculators, a consistent core message emerges: during times of crisis, when evil seems to dominate the human scene, don't lose heart, because God is still in control of all things, and Jesus is returning

---

history in some meaningful manner. **Amillennialists** understand the millennium as a code term for the complete period of time between Jesus' first and second comings. For that reason, they do not interpret the thousand years as a literal period of time (hence the designation a-*millennial*, indicating no specific thousand-year boundaries). **Postmillennialists** believe the thousand years period is a specific portion of human history extending through exactly one thousand earth orbits around the sun. This era has already begun, and is experienced as a period of great gains for the Christian church, as well as all of human society generally. Our modern times give evidence of great strides in human endeavors, according to this approach, so the thousand-year period must be in progress, although there is no certainty about the specific point at which Jesus chose to begin it. Likely markers put forward are the Reformation, or the Enlightenment, or the social and scientific revolutions of the nineteenth century. Whenever it might have begun, this period of great acceleration of human and gospel progress will last for exactly one thousand years, and then the way will be prepared for Jesus to rather naturally re-enter human society as ultimate ruler, declaring that the fullness of the messianic age has arrived. **Premillennialists** declare that the thousand-year period is still in the future, and will be a time of transition between the struggles of this age and the perfections of eternity. Just before the thousand years begins, according to this theory, there will be a seven-year period (called the "Tribulation") of tremendous global social upheaval and enormous persecution directed at Christian. Somewhere during this seven-year time, the Christian church will be "raptured" out of the world, setting the stage for a complete breakdown of society which can only be remedied by divine intervention. So, for one thousand years, Jesus will re-appear on earth to restore the Israelite/Jewish kingdom in Jerusalem, establishing peace and order. Most Jews will understand that Jesus is the foretold messiah, and will become Christians. Yet many others, around the world, will despise this religious imposition on human society, causing a revolt that will lead to a cataclysmic battle at the end of the thousand years. Although a huge portion of earth's population will be destroyed, Jesus and his Jewish-Christian armies will gain the victory, Judgment Day will address the wrongs of the nations, and the eternal messianic age will begin. For a more extended treatment, see Robert G. Clouse, George Eldon Ladd, Herman A. Hoyt, Loraine Boettner, Anthony A. Hoekema, *The Meaning of the Millennium: Four Views* (Downers Grove, IL: IVP Academic, 2010).

soon to annihilate evil and transform creation into all that God intended for it to be.[36]

Obviously, this was a necessary message late in the first century, when first Nero's and then Domitian's persecutions of the church killed many and caused thousands of others to huddle in fear. Since the language and cosmological perspectives in the book are very similar to those in the Gospel of John and the Letters of John, there is every reason to suppose that they, along with this book, were written by the disciple of Jesus who pastored the congregation in Ephesus late in the first century. This John was exiled to Patmos by Domitian as a way of undermining the courage of the Christian church which he despised. Since Domitian ruled from September of AD 81 through September of 96, the Revelation of Jesus to John was probably penned and sent sometime in the mid- to late-80s.

Its message is timeless:

- To be a Christian is to be in conflict in this world.

- If one tries to opt out of this conflict, one automatically joins the other side, and has been trapped by the powers of evil.

- Faithfulness to Jesus almost invariably leads to martyrdom, because this conflict is all or nothing.

- But those who trust in God will find the strength to remain faithful through suffering, die in hope, and have their confidence rewarded by Jesus' ultimate victory and the renewal of creation which includes the resurrection and glorification of all God's people.

Revelation as the Other Bookend to the "Day of the Lord"

It is obvious that the entire message and substance of the book of Revelation is established on the Old Testament prophetic concept of the "Day of the Lord." First, the book of Revelation reiterates and emphasizes the three major ideas that form the substance of the "Day of the Lord" theology:

- Divine judgment on the world due to the wickedness of the nations and their refusal to connect or re-connect with the creator.

---

36. For a fuller investigation of biblical statements and expressions regarding end times, see Anthony A. Hoekema, *The Bible and the Future* (Grand Rapids: Eerdmans, 1994).

- The sparing of a remnant community, chastened through times of persecution but faithful to the testimony of God's existence, care and ultimate redemptive designs.

- The ushering in of the eternal messianic age in which all wrong will be righted, all evil will be eradicated, all suffering will end, and all glory will break loose.

Clearly, the book of Revelation rides the key themes of prophetic "Day of the Lord" pronouncements, and pulls them together in a singular package of both dread and anticipation. In this respect, it is as punchy and powerful as the short, but very descriptive, prophecy of Joel.

Second, the language, visual images, development of events, and expressions of both tragedy and bliss come from the prophets and apocalypticists of the Old Testament. The "sevens" of Daniel form a framework for the key movements of Revelation. John, on Patmos, receives a divinely imprinted scroll to eat, as part of his prophetic task, just as Ezekiel had experienced at the beginning of his prophetic ministry. Seven of the ten plagues upon Egypt, which are part of the substance for the antecedent upon which all of the "Day of the Lord" articulations are built, reappear in Revelation as the method by which God deploys judgment on humankind, this time in a global arena. The angelic beings which guide John through his experiences of discovery and illumination are described in similar manner to those which served Ezekiel, Daniel, and Zechariah in their journeys into the transcendent realms. The assessments of wickedness provided to John, as the world is being weighed for judgment, resonate with similar analyses in Ezekiel's and Zechariah's prophecies. The tumult of nations mounting for unified battle against God's kingdom and its remaining human expressions, is clearly mirrored to the descriptions of warfare involving Gog and Magog in Ezekiel's prophecy. The call for God's people to remain faithful through trying times echoes the messages of Jeremiah, Ezekiel, Daniel, Zechariah, and Malachi. The restoration of Jerusalem and the temple, as symbols of the messianic age, match descriptions provided earlier in Ezekiel's visions. The renewal of all of creation is explained, in the latter part of Revelation, using identical images to those given to Ezekiel at the end of his prophecy.

Third, the initiation and culmination of the visions John sees are connected to the coming of Jesus as the Messiah of both Israel and the nations. Jesus is the Passover lamb, the Lion of the tribe of Judah, the Bridegroom married to the people of God, the conquering King, the resurrected Savior, the One who is on the throne of Heaven, the Judge of the nations, the catalyst who transitions this age into the next, the restorer of creation, and the essence of God dwelling among the people of God. In other words, everything that was anticipated in the distant visions of the prophets as they saw the "Day of the Lord" on the horizon, will be brought in completion through the impending activities of Jesus as he returns to earth.

The New Testament is consistent in is exploration of the "Day of the Lord" as a split entity. Everything anticipated by the prophets as an expression of the "Day of the Lord" is initiated in Jesus' first arrival as the culmination of Old Testament promises: miracles, formation of a small community of witness, divine judgment. But these are limited in impact to Jesus' own life and social influence. Splitting the "Day of the Lord" in two provided for a future fulfillment of the same dimensions of the "Day of the Lord" on a global scale.

This bifurcation of the anticipated "Day of the Lord" established the unique perspectives of Christian theology. It remains rooted in the monotheism of Israelite religion, but it expresses a unique turn of events that were never clearly understood by the Hebrew prophets who forecast the "Day of the Lord."

7

Conclusion

Christianity's "Day of the Lord"
Theological Cornerstone

WE SAT DOWN TO EAT. My graduate school supervisor had invited me to join his family for a meal so that we could get acquainted. Conversation ranged from simple family matters (addressing a young son, "Eat your beans!"), to biographical notes ("How did you get from Nigeria to here?"), to theological ("What got you particularly interested in the Gospel of John?").

But the question that lingered, long after the hospitality had ended, was a simple query: "Do you think the Synoptic Gospels were written before or after AD 70?"

I fumbled at an answer, trying to play both sides of the divide, since the commentaries on the gospels were similarly split. My mentor smiled and nodded, and we finished the meal with other interesting repartee.

What Does It Matter?

I did not realize, until much later, that this simple question was about much more than scholarly banter. It touched perspective, worldview, faith, confession, and a host of other heart matters. You see, the early church leaders all believed that the gospels were either written by Jesus' disciples (Matthew and John) or by those who were trustworthy reporters of Jesus' disciples (Mark taking down the teachings and preachings of Peter about his Lord; Luke seeking out Jesus' disciples and family in order to accurately summarize the testimony of eyewitnesses). Moreover, they understood that the Synoptic Gospels (Mark, Matthew, and Luke), which show a great literary connection with one another,[1] were written sometime between AD 40 and 60, based upon a series of elementary deductions:

- Luke wrote both the Gospel of Luke and the Acts of the Apostles.

- The Gospel of Luke was written before the Acts of the Apostles.

- The Acts of the Apostles ends with the presumption that Paul was under house arrest in Rome, awaiting his appearance before the emperor to seek resolution against the charges issued against him in Jerusalem.

- Paul's two-year wait in Rome happened from roughly AD 56–58.

- Therefore, the Acts of the Apostles was written around the mid-fifties.

- Therefore, the Gospel of Luke was written around the early- to mid-fifties.

- Since the Luke used the Gospel of Mark in his writing of his own gospel, the Gospel of Mark must have been written around AD 50.

- Since Matthew used the Gospel of Mark even more extensively than did Luke, when preparing his own gospel, the Gospel of Matthew must have been written in the early fifties.

All of this fits with the early church's testimony about the origins of the Synoptic Gospels. But modern scholars, with their perceived greater wisdom, have often declared that the Synoptic Gospels were all written in the seventies or eighties. What evidence do they have for this? Only a combination of three verses, one found in each of the Synoptic Gospels, each literarily related to the others.

Mark, Matthew, and Luke each report, at some length and with generally greater detail than is found in the earlier stages of Jesus' ministry, the events that happened in Jesus' final week of life in Jerusalem, before his crucifixion. One incident, in particular, captured their attention. Jesus and his disciples were wandering through the temple expanses, and his disciples, all from the more rural environs of Galilee, were quite taken by the size and magnificence of the buildings that Herod the Great had renovated to match the grandeur of Solomon's temple.[2] They made comments about the overwhelming strength and beauty of these structures to Jesus, who

---

1. There are a number of ways in which this literary dependence has been perceived (see Stanley E. Porter and Bryan R. Dyer, editors, *The Synoptic Problem: Four Views* (Grand Rapids: Baker Academic, 2016)), but most often Mark is understood as being written first, with both Matthew and Luke using Mark's outline and contents as the platform upon which to build their more extensive and nuanced recollections about Jesus.

2. See Josephus, *Antiquities of the Jews*, 15.11.

immediately responded that someday even these grand building would be torn down:

- "Do you see these great buildings? Not one stone will be left here upon another; all will be thrown down" (Mark 13:2).

- "You see all these, do you not? Truly I tell you, not one stone will be left here upon another; all will be thrown down" (Matt 24:2).

- "As for these things that you see, the days will come when not one stone will be left upon another; all will be thrown down" (Luke 21:6).

Jesus' words are not predictively precise. He does not tell the disciples when or under what conditions these things will happen. Yet, since there is a very specific occasion on which Jerusalem and the temple were, in fact, destroyed in late August of AD 70, after about six months of siege,[3] some New Testament scholars suggest that these references are indications that the Synoptic Gospels must have been written later than AD 70. After all, any hint at Jerusalem's destruction can only come from those who are looking at the great catastrophe of AD 70 in retrospect. Never mind the testimonies of the early church about the writing of these documents. Never mind the assumption of falsity this brings to perceptions about the truthfulness of the gospels. Since no one can predict the future, not even Jesus, any reference to the impermanence of Jerusalem and the temple structures must have emerged after Jerusalem's destruction.

Larger Issues of Interpretation

For some, this unsupported presupposition,[4] repeated often by otherwise respected New Testament scholars, becomes the rationale for dismissing the testimony of early church leaders and centuries of biblical interpretation. Replacing the obvious (that Jesus knew Jerusalem would eventually be destroyed) with the improbable (that all early references to the origin and authorship of the Synoptic Gospels is false, and that these works are anonymous, and fraught with creative fiction rather than eyewitness testimony) has sent a significant portion of New Testament scholarship in a direction of looking for mythological sources, editorial traditions, and historical fabrications that hide, rather than reveal, Jesus and his words and activities.

---

3. Josephus, *The Fall of Jerusalem* (Penguin, 2006).

4. That the Synoptic Gospels must have been written after the destruction of Jerusalem and the temple in AD 70.

In a similar manner, biblical theology as a Christian discipline, becomes fractured when debating whether the Old Testament had its origins

- in an actual exodus of the Israelites and a covenant-making ceremony at Mount Sinai that led these people to settlement in Canaan[5]
- or in a nameless Hebrew writer who created a politically supportive backstory for the Davidic regime that came to powerful prominence during the reign of Solomon[6]
- or in an unknown, disgruntled Levite, who fled the demise of Israel during the Assyrian scorched-earth military campaigns, settling in Jerusalem to rewrite history in praise of the priests of Jerusalem[7]
- or in a revivalist conspiracy that sought to affirm the religious reforms of King Josiah[8]
- or in a somber reflection of Jewish elites who survived Babylonian destructions, and determined to give their people hope and meaning which would carry them through exile[9]

The central assumption in the last four among these possibilities is that all stories of Israelite origins found in Genesis through Judges are mythical

---

5. The internal story of the Old Testament.

6. Walter Dietrich, *The Early Monarchy in Israel: The Tenth Century B.C.E.* (Leiden, the Netherlands: Brill, 2007); Cf. Barry Bandstra, *Reading the Old Testament: Introduction to the Hebrew Bible*, 4th edition (Belmont, CA: Wadsworth Publishing, 2008), 22–23: "The Yahwist composed his story sometime during the reign of Solomon (961–922 BCE), though some scholars would date it as much as a century or more later . . . The Yahwist source was written out of love for the royal house, providing a sense of history and destiny for the grand new kingdom of David. The Solomonic era was most conducive to such a historical project. This golden age had the resources and provided the opportunity to write a national epic. Royally sponsored scribal schools provided the training, royal income supported the work, and the increased international contact afforded by the new status of Israel stimulated historical reflection and perhaps even prompted the need for a national story. The Yahwist was especially interested in those traditions that supported the legitimacy of Davidic rule and the centrality of the tribe of Judah."

7. Israel Finkelstein and Neil Asher Silberman, *The Bible Unearthed* (New York: Free Press, 2001); Israel Finkelstein, *The Forgotten Kingdom: Archaeology and the History of Northern Israel* (Atlanta: SBL, 2013).

8. Alexander Rofé, *Deuteronomy: Issues and Interpretations* (London: T. & T. Clark, 2001); K. Lawson Younger, Jr., "Early Israel in Recent Biblical Scholarship" in David W. Baker and Bill T. Arnold, editors. *The Face of Old Testament Studies: A Survey of Contemporary Approaches* (Grand Rapids: Baker Academic, 2004).

9. Walter Brueggemann, *Theology of the Old Testament: Testimony, Dispute, Advocacy* (Philadelphia: Fortress Press, 2012).

fabrications created by anonymous influential writers who were fortunate to live in or after late pre-exilic Jewish times when tremendous social turmoil made their ancestor fictions brilliantly supportive of dominant political regimes. Tales without historical basis became the foundations of an entire religious edifice which would change the world.

But what if the diverse writings found in the Bible are held together by a double redemptive interruption of human history that lies at the heart of both the testimonies and the interpretations found in the Jewish and Christian scriptures? What if the "Day of the Lord" theological motif, prolific among Israel's prophets, foundational to Jesus' identity, and central to the apostolic teachings, is rooted in the Torah witness to the Creator's attention-getting revision of human history-writing, and is split by that loving divinity's engagements initiated by the incarnation which established the Christian church and its missional witness?

Reunifying both Biblical Scholarship and Christian Theology

Viewed through this lens, provided by the documents of the Bible themselves, the diverse writings of the Christian scriptures gather around two significant and miraculous events which reveal both the nature of reality from within the human experience and also the divine intention transcending and superseding unguided or uninterpreted historical meanderings. The "Day of the Lord" carries with it three dominant themes:

- Because of the evil in this world, particularly that perpetuated by nations and individuals who seek to establish their dominance at the expense and hurt of others, the Creator must interrupt human history with judgment, destroying the power of wickedness and restoring righteousness as the foundation of society.

- Since humans are uniquely created and endowed with the ability to share aspects of divine identity and purpose, the Creator seeks to spare humanity generally from self-destruction, without imposing divine direction in a coercive manner, and thus uses witnessing communities of the faith-filled faithful to provide an ongoing voice of hope, and a call to repentance.

- The goal of this divine interruption into human history is to renew humanity, earth and the cosmos, and set them fully free to live out and express the best of themselves in an age that has the divine intentions for humankind fully restored.

This "Day of the Lord" theological motif, in the Bible, is built upon the redemptively disruptive divine intervention that established the nation of Israel as a covenantally shaped witnessing community in the uniquely positioned land known as Canaan. When Israel's national history unravels and declines in both covenantal character and influential significance, Hebrew prophets use the interruptive character of the exodus/Sinai covenant/Canaan settlement redemptive event to predict a coming, similar happening. This anticipated "Day of the Lord" arrives in the next unique divine redemptive interruptive event when Jesus, God's incarnation, appears in human history. But rather than causing a catastrophic eschatological destruction and rebirth of humanity and the creation generally in a single act of judgment, Jesus reteaches the missional message of the Creator, and then absorbs into himself the initial rumblings of doom, while raising up a new community of witness which carries elements of God's ultimate blessings. Having inaugurated the second, massive, global "Day of the Lord," Jesus delays its final purifying judgments until the church is able to bring a broader community of humankind into its redemptive hopes. Eventually, though, there will be a fuller reckoning, when the havoc wreaked upon Egypt in the first expression of the "Day of the Lord," will be reasserted cosmically, until, purged and restored, life, as the Creator intended, will flourish forever.

Appendix

"Day of the Lord" References

Exodus 8:22—But on that day I will set apart the land of Goshen, where my people live, so that no swarms of flies shall be there, that you may know that I the Lord am in this land.

Exodus 12:14—This day shall be a day of remembrance for you. You shall celebrate it as a festival to the Lord; throughout your generations you shall observe it as a perpetual ordinance.

Exodus 12:41—At the end of four hundred thirty years, on that very day, all the companies of the Lord went out from the land of Egypt.

Exodus 12:51—That very day the Lord brought the Israelites out of the land of Egypt, company by company.

Exodus 13:3—Moses said to the people, "Remember this day on which you came out of Egypt, out of the house of slavery, because the Lord brought you out from there by strength of hand; no leavened bread shall be eaten.

Exodus 13:8—You shall tell your child on that day, 'It is because of what the Lord did for me when I came out of Egypt.'

Deuteronomy 5:15—Remember that you were a slave in the land of Egypt, and the Lord your God brought you out from there with a mighty hand and an outstretched arm; therefore the Lord your God commanded you to keep the Sabbath day.

Joshua 5:9—The Lord said to Joshua, "Today I have rolled away from you the disgrace of Egypt." And so that place is called Gilgal to this day.

Psalm 20:1—The Lord answer you in the day of trouble! The name of the God of Jacob protect you!

Psalm 41:1—Happy are those who consider the poor; the Lord delivers them in the day of trouble.

Psalm 137:7—Remember, O Lord, against the Edomites the day of Jerusalem's fall, how they said, "Tear it down! Tear it down! Down to its foundations!"

Psalm 140:7—O Lord, my Lord, my strong deliverer, you have covered my head in the day of battle.

Isaiah 2:2—In days to come the mountain of the Lord's house shall be established as the highest of the mountains, and shall be raised above the hills; all the nations shall stream to it.

Isaiah 2:11—The haughty eyes of people shall be brought low, and the pride of everyone shall be humbled; and the Lord alone will be exalted on that day.

Isaiah 2:12—For the Lord of hosts has a day against all that is proud and lofty, against all that is lifted up and high;

Isaiah 2:17—The haughtiness of people shall be humbled, and the pride of everyone shall be brought low; and the Lord alone will be exalted on that day.

Isaiah 3:18—In that day the Lord will take away the finery of the anklets, the headbands, and the crescents;

Isaiah 4:2—On that day the branch of the Lord shall be beautiful and glorious, and the fruit of the land shall be the pride and glory of the survivors of Israel.

Isaiah 4:5—Then the Lord will create over the whole site of Mount Zion and over its places of assembly a cloud by day and smoke and the shining of a flaming fire by night. Indeed over all the glory there will be a canopy.

Isaiah 7:18—On that day the Lord will whistle for the fly that is at the sources of the streams of Egypt, and for the bee that is in the land of Assyria.

Isaiah 7:20—On that day the Lord will shave with a razor hired beyond the River—with the king of Assyria—the head and the hair of the feet, and it will take off the beard as well.

Isaiah 10:20—On that day the remnant of Israel and the survivors of the house of Jacob will no more lean on the one who struck them, but will lean on the Lord, the Holy One of Israel, in truth.

Isaiah 11:11—On that day the Lord will extend his hand yet a second time to recover the remnant that is left of his people, from Assyria, from Egypt, from Pathros, from Ethiopia, from Elam, from Shinar, from Hamath, and from the coastlands of the sea.

Isaiah 13:6—Wail, for the day of the Lord is near; it will come like destruction from the Almighty!

Isaiah 13:9—See, the day of the Lord comes, cruel, with wrath and fierce anger, to make the earth a desolation, and to destroy its sinners from it.

Isaiah 13:13—Therefore I will make the heavens tremble, and the earth will be shaken out of its place, at the wrath of the Lord of hosts in the day of his fierce anger.

Isaiah 19:16—On that day the Egyptians will be like women, and tremble with fear before the hand that the Lord of hosts raises against them.

Isaiah 19:18—On that day there will be five cities in the land of Egypt that speak the language of Canaan and swear allegiance to the Lord of hosts. One of these will be called the City of the Sun.

Isaiah 19:19—On that day there will be an altar to the Lord in the center of the land of Egypt, and a pillar to the Lord at its border.

Isaiah 19:21—The Lord will make himself known to the Egyptians; and the Egyptians will know the Lord on that day, and will worship with sacrifice and burnt offering, and they will make vows to the Lord and perform them.

Isaiah 22:5—For the Lord God of hosts has a day of tumult and trampling and confusion in the valley of vision, a battering down of walls and a cry for help to the mountains.

Isaiah 22:12—In that day the Lord God of hosts called to weeping and mourning, to baldness and putting on sackcloth;

Isaiah 22:25—On that day, says the Lord of hosts, the peg that was fastened in a secure place will give way; it will be cut down and fall, and the load that was on it will perish, for the Lord has spoken.

Isaiah 24:21—On that day the Lord will punish the host of heaven in heaven, and on earth the kings of the earth.

Isaiah 27:12—On that day the Lord will thresh from the channel of the Euphrates to the Wadi of Egypt, and you will be gathered one by one, O people of Israel.

Isaiah 27:13—And on that day a great trumpet will be blown, and those who were lost in the land of Assyria and those who were driven out to the land of Egypt will come and worship the Lord on the holy mountain at Jerusalem.

Isaiah 28:5—In that day the Lord of hosts will be a garland of glory, and a diadem of beauty, to the remnant of his people;

Isaiah 30:26—Moreover the light of the moon will be like the light of the sun, and the light of the sun will be sevenfold, like the light of seven days, on the day when the Lord binds up the injuries of his people, and heals the wounds inflicted by his blow.

Isaiah 34:8—For the Lord has a day of vengeance, a year of vindication by Zion's cause.

Isaiah 49:8—Thus says the Lord: In a time of favor I have answered you, on a day of salvation I have helped you; I have kept you and given you as a covenant to the people, to establish the land, to apportion the desolate heritages;

Isaiah 51:9—Awake, awake, put on strength, O arm of the Lord! Awake, as in days of old, the generations of long ago! Was it not you who cut Rahab in pieces, who pierced the dragon?

Isaiah 61:2—to proclaim the year of the Lord's favor, and the day of vengeance of our God; to comfort all who mourn;

Jeremiah 4:9—On that day, says the Lord, courage shall fail the king and the officials; the priests shall be appalled and the prophets astounded.

Jeremiah 5:18—But even in those days, says the Lord, I will not make a full end of you.

Jeremiah 7:32—Therefore, the days are surely coming, says the Lord, when it will no more be called Topheth, or the valley of the son of Hinnom, but the valley of Slaughter: for they will bury in Topheth until there is no more room.

Jeremiah 12:3—But you, O Lord, know me; You see me and test me—my heart is with you. Pull them out like sheep for the slaughter, and set them apart for the day of slaughter.

Jeremiah 16:14—Therefore, the days are surely coming, says the Lord, when it shall no longer be said, "As the Lord lives who brought the people of Israel up out of the land of Egypt,"

Jeremiah 16:19—O Lord, my strength and my stronghold, my refuge in the day of trouble, to you shall the nations come from the ends of the earth and say: Our ancestors have inherited nothing but lies, worthless things in which there is no profit.

Jeremiah 19:6—therefore the days are surely coming, says the Lord, when this place shall no more be called Topheth, or the valley of the son of Hinnom, but the valley of Slaughter.

Jeremiah 23:5—The days are surely coming, says the Lord, when I will raise up for David a righteous Branch, and he shall reign as king and deal wisely, and shall execute justice and righteousness in the land.

Jeremiah 23:7—Therefore, the days are surely coming, says the Lord, when it shall no longer be said, "As the Lord lives who brought the people of Israel up out of the land of Egypt,"

Jeremiah 23:20—The anger of the Lord will not turn back until he has executed and accomplished the intents of his mind. In the latter days you will understand it clearly.

Jeremiah 25:33—Those slain by the Lord on that day shall extend from one end of the earth to the other. They shall not be lamented, or gathered, or buried; they shall become dung on the surface of the ground.

Jeremiah 25:24—Wail, you shepherds, and cry out; roll in ashes, you lords of the flock, for the days of your slaughter have come—and your dispersions, and you shall fall like a choice vessel.

Jeremiah 30:3—For the days are surely coming, says the Lord, when I will restore the fortunes of my people, Israel and Judah, says the Lord, and I will bring them back to the land that I gave to their ancestors and they shall take possession of it.

Jeremiah 30:8—On that day, says the Lord of hosts, I will break the yoke from off his neck, and I will burst his bonds, and strangers shall no more make a servant of him.

Jeremiah 30:24—The fierce anger of the Lord will not turn back until he has executed and accomplished the intents of his mind. In the latter days you will understand this.

Jeremiah 31:6—For there shall be a day when sentinels will call in the hill country of Ephraim: "Come, let us go up to Zion, to the Lord our God."

Jeremiah 31:27—The days are surely coming, says the Lord, when I will sow the house of Israel and the house of Judah with the seed of humans and the seed of animals.

Jeremiah 31:31—The days are surely coming, says the Lord, when I will make a new covenant with the house of Israel and the house of Judah.

Jeremiah 31:33—But this is the covenant that I will make with the house of Israel after those days, says the Lord: I will put my law within them, and I will write it on their hearts; and I will be their God, and they shall be my people.

Jeremiah 31:38—The days are surely coming, says the Lord, when the city shall be rebuilt for the Lord from the tower of Hananel to the Corner Gate.

Jeremiah 33:14—The days are surely coming, says the Lord, when I will fulfill the promise I made to the house of Israel and the house of Judah.

Jeremiah 39:16—Go and say to Ebed-melech the Ethiopian: Thus says the Lord of hosts, the God of Israel: I am going to fulfill my words against this city for evil and not for good, and they shall be accomplished in your presence on that day.

Jeremiah 46:10—That day is the day of the Lord God of hosts, a day of retribution, to gain vindication from his foes. The sword shall devour and be sated, and drink its fill of their blood. For the Lord God of hosts holds a sacrifice in the land of the north by the river Euphrates.

Jeremiah 47:4—because of the day that is coming to destroy all the Philistines, to cut off from Tyre and Sidon every helper that remains. For the Lord is destroying the Philistines, the remnant of the coastland of Caphtor.

Jeremiah 48:47—Yet I will restore the fortunes of Moab in the latter days, says the Lord. Thus far is the judgment on Moab.

Jeremiah 49:26—Therefore her young men shall fall in her squares, and all her soldiers shall be destroyed in that day, says the Lord of hosts.

Jeremiah 49:39—But in the latter days I will restore the fortunes of Elam, says the Lord.

Jeremiah 50:4—In those days and in that time, says the Lord, the people of Israel shall come, they and the people of Judah together; they shall come weeping as they seek the Lord their God.

Jeremiah 50:20—In those days and at that time, says the Lord, the iniquity of Israel shall be sought, and there shall be none; and the sins of Judah, and none shall be found; for I will pardon the remnant that I have spared.

Jeremiah 50:31—I am against you, O arrogant one, says the Lord God of hosts; for your day has come, the time when I will punish you.

Lamentations 1:12—Is it nothing to you, all you who pass by? Look and see if there is any sorrow like my sorrow, which was brought upon me, which the Lord inflicted on the day of his fierce anger.

Lamentations 2:1—How the Lord in his anger has humiliated daughter Zion! He has thrown down from heaven to earth the splendor of Israel; he has not remembered his footstool in the day of his anger.

Lamentations 2:22—You invited my enemies from all around as if for a day of festival; and on the day of the anger of the Lord no one escaped or survived; those whom I bore and reared my enemy has destroyed.

Ezekiel 12:23—Tell them therefore, "Thus says the Lord God: I will put an end to this proverb, and they shall use it no more as a proverb in Israel." But say to them, The days are near, and the fulfillment of every vision.

Ezekiel 13:5—You have not gone up into the breaches, or repaired a wall for the house of Israel, so that it might stand in battle on the day of the Lord.

Ezekiel 20:5—and say to them: Thus says the Lord God: On the day when I chose Israel, I swore to the offspring of the house of Jacob—making myself known to them in the land of Egypt—I swore to them, saying, I am the Lord your God.

Ezekiel 29:21—On that day I will cause a horn to sprout up for the house of Israel, and I will open your lips among them. Then they shall know that I am the Lord.

Ezekiel 30:3—For a day is near, the day of the Lord is near; it will be a day of clouds, a time of doom for the nations.

Ezekiel 31:15—Thus says the Lord God: On the day it went down to Sheol I closed the deep over it and covered it; I restrained its rivers, and its mighty waters were checked. I clothed Lebanon in gloom for it, and all the trees of the field fainted because of it.

Ezekiel 38:18—On that day, when Gog comes against the land of Israel, says the Lord God, my wrath shall be aroused.

Ezekiel 39:8—It has come! It has happened, says the Lord God. This is the day of which I have spoken.

Ezekiel 39:13—All the people of the land shall bury them; and it will bring them honor on the day that I show my glory, says the Lord God.

Ezekiel 39:22—The house of Israel shall know that I am the Lord their God, from that day forward.

Joel 1:15—Alas for the day! For the day of the Lord is near, and as destruction from the Almighty it comes.

Joel 2:1—Blow the trumpet in Zion; sound the alarm on my holy mountain! Let all the inhabitants of the land tremble, for the day of the Lord is coming, it is near—

Joel 2:11—The Lord utters his voice at the head of his army; how vast is his host! Numberless are those who obey his command. Truly the day of the Lord is great; terrible indeed—who can endure it?

Joel 2:31—The sun shall be turned to darkness, and the moon to blood, before the great and terrible day of the Lord comes.

Joel 3:14—Multitudes, multitudes, in the valley of decision! For the day of the Lord is near in the valley of decision.

Joel 3:18—In that day the mountains shall drip sweet wine, the hills shall flow with milk, and all the stream beds of Judah shall flow with water; a fountain shall come forth from the house of the Lord and water the Wadi Shittim.

Amos 2:16—and those who are stout of heart among the mighty shall flee away naked in that day, says the Lord.

Amos 5:18—Alas for you who desire the day of the Lord! Why do you want the day of the Lord? It is darkness, not light;

Amos 5:20—Is not the day of the Lord darkness, not light, and gloom with no brightness in it?

Amos 8:3—The songs of the temple shall become wailings in that day," says the Lord God; "the dead bodies shall be many, cast out in every place. Be silent!"

Obadiah 1:8—On that day, says the Lord, I will destroy the wise out of Edom, and understanding out of Mount Esau.

Obadiah 1:15—For the day of the Lord is near against all the nations. As you have done, it shall be done to you; your deeds shall return on your own head.

Micah 2:4—On that day they shall take up a taunt song against you, and wail with bitter lamentation, and say, "We are utterly ruined; the Lord alters the inheritance of my people; how he removes it from me! Among our captors he parcels out our fields."

Micah 4:1—In days to come the mountain of the Lord's house shall be established as the highest of the mountains, and shall be raised up above the hills. Peoples shall stream to it,

Micah 5:10—In that day, says the Lord, I will cut off your horses from among you and will destroy your chariots;

Zephaniah 1:7—Be silent before the Lord God! For the day of the Lord is at hand; the Lord has prepared a sacrifice, he has consecrated his guests.

Zephaniah 1:8—And on the day of the Lord's sacrifice I will punish the officials and the king's sons and all who dress themselves in foreign attire.

Zephaniah 1:14—The great day of the Lord is near, near and hastening fast; the sound of the day of the Lord is bitter, the warrior cries aloud there.

Zephaniah 1:18—Neither their silver nor their gold will be able to save them on the day of the Lord's wrath; in the fire of his passion the whole earth shall be consumed; for a full, a terrible end he will make of all the inhabitants of the earth.

Zephaniah 2:2—before you are driven away like the drifting chaff, before there comes upon you the fierce anger of the Lord, before there comes upon you the day of the Lord's wrath.

Zephaniah 2:3—Seek the Lord, all you humble of the land, who do his commands; seek righteousness, seek humility; perhaps you may be hidden on the day of the Lord's wrath.

Zephaniah 3:8—Therefore wait for me, says the Lord, for the day when I arise as a witness. For my decision is to gather nations, to assemble kingdoms, to pour out upon them my indignation, all the heat of my anger; for in the fire of my passion all the earth shall be consumed.

Haggai 2:23—On that day, says the Lord of hosts, I will take you, O Zerubbabel my servant, son of Shealtiel, says the Lord, and make you like a signet ring; for I have chosen you, says the Lord of hosts.

Zechariah 2:11—Many nations shall join themselves to the Lord on that day, and shall be my people; and I will dwell in your midst. And you shall know that the Lord of hosts has sent me to you.

Zechariah 3:9—For on the stone that I have set before Joshua, on a single stone with seven facets, I will engrave its inscription, says the Lord of hosts, and I will remove the guilt of this land in a single day.

Zechariah 3:10—On that day, says the Lord of hosts, you shall invite each other to come under your vine and fig tree."

Zechariah 8:23—Thus says the Lord of hosts: In those days ten men from nations of every language shall take hold of a Jew, grasping his garment and saying, "Let us go with you, for we have heard that God is with you."

Zechariah 9:16—On that day the Lord their God will save them for they are the flock of his people; for like the jewels of a crown they shall shine on his land.

Zechariah 12:4—On that day, says the Lord, I will strike every horse with panic, and its rider with madness. But on the house of Judah I will keep a watchful eye, when I strike every horse of the peoples with blindness.

Zechariah 12:8—On that day the Lord will shield the inhabitants of Jerusalem so that the feeblest among them on that day shall be like David, and the house of David shall be like God, like the angel of the Lord, at their head.

Zechariah 13:2—On that day, says the Lord of hosts, I will cut off the names of the idols from the land, so that they shall be remembered no more; and also I will remove from the land the prophets and the unclean spirit.

Zechariah 14:3—Then the Lord will go forth and fight against those nations as when he fights on a day of battle.

Zechariah 14:13—On that day a great panic from the Lord shall fall on them, so that each will seize the hand of a neighbor, and the hand of the one will be raised against the hand of the other;

Zechariah 14:20—On that day there shall be inscribed on the bells of the horses, "Holy to the Lord." And the cooking pots in the house of the Lord shall be as holy as the bowls in front of the altar;

Zechariah 14:21—and every cooking pot in Jerusalem and Judah shall be sacred to the Lord of hosts, so that all who sacrifice may come and use them to boil the flesh of the sacrifice. And there shall no longer be traders in the house of the Lord of hosts on that day.

Malachi 3:17—They shall be mine, says the Lord of hosts, my special possession on the day when I act, and I will spare them as parents spare their children who serve them.

Malachi 4:1—See, the day is coming, burning like an oven, when all the arrogant and all evildoers will be stubble; the day that comes shall burn them up, says the Lord of hosts, so that it will leave them neither root nor branch.

Malachi 4:3—And you shall tread down the wicked, for they will be ashes under the soles of your feet, on the day when I act, says the Lord of hosts.

Malachi 4:5—Lo, I will send you the prophet Elijah before the great and terrible day of the Lord comes.

Acts 2:20—The sun shall be turned to darkness and the moon to blood, before the coming of the Lord's great and glorious day.

1 Corinthians 1:8—He will also strengthen you to the end, so that you may be blameless on the day of our Lord Jesus Christ.

1 Corinthians 5:5—you are to hand this man over to Satan for the destruction of the flesh, so that his spirit may be saved in the day of the Lord.

2 Corinthians 1:14—as you have already understood us in part—that on the day of the Lord Jesus we are your boast even as you are our boast.

1 Thessalonians 5:2—For you yourselves know very well that the day of the Lord will come like a thief in the night.

2 Thessalonians 2:2—not to be quickly shaken in mind or alarmed, either by spirit or by word or by letter, as though from us, to the effect that the day of the Lord is already here.

2 Timothy 4:8—From now on there is reserved for me the crown of righteousness, which the Lord, the righteous judge, will give me on that day, and not only to me but also to all who have longed for his appearing.

Hebrews 8:8—God finds fault with them when he says: "The days are surely coming, says the Lord, when I will establish a new covenant with the house of Israel and with the house of Judah;

Hebrews 8:9—not like the covenant that I made with their ancestors, on the day when I took them by the hand to lead them out of the land of Egypt; for they did not continue in my covenant, and so I had no concern for them, says the Lord.

Hebrews 8:10—This is the covenant that I will make with the house of Israel after those days, says the Lord: I will put my laws in their minds, and write them on their hearts, and I will be their God, and they shall be my people.

2 Peter 2:9—then the Lord knows how to rescue the godly from trial, and to keep the unrighteous under punishment until the day of judgment

2 Peter 3:10—But the day of the Lord will come like a thief, and then the heavens will pass away with a loud noise, and the elements will be dissolved with fire, and the earth and everything that is done on it will be disclosed.

2 Peter 3:18—But grow in the grace and knowledge of our Lord and Savior Jesus Christ. To him be the glory both now and to the day of eternity. Amen.